HELL NO, YOU CAN'T!

The Roots of Political Extremism

What, Why, and How to Combat

HERB ALTMAN

ISBN: 1470087294
ISBN 13: 9781470087296
Library of Congress Control Number: 2012903243
Printed by CreateSpace, North Charleston, SC

Dedication

Thanks are insufficient but necessary to give to all those teachers who have helped to shape this mind. To them I give a bow of my head, and heart.

To those yet closer, I give a bit more—to my wife, Lora, who, with the patience of what she is—a Mother of Mothers, gave me the freedom to think and to write. But the most special thanks go to someone else…

This book could not have been written were it not for a young man—mentally retarded, non-verbal, incapable of deceit, with all those handicaps which require around-the-clock care, but who, with a smile and a look that out-shone the brightest sun, could fill a heart to bursting. To you, Andrew, do I give each word, each dot, each moment of effort that went into this book. To you, my son, I give more than thanks.

CONTENTS

PREFACE

What is "extremism"? There must be a **benchmark** upon which to base the term.

Our benchmark is us, we as a species. But not enough. This species, us, must be defined as to characteristics, drives, intent, and basic nature. This leads us into individual behavior, behaviors in which each of us engage, as species members, for common goals. Each one of us is both limited in capabilities yet expansive in intent. We speak, and by each word and thought have one goal in mind—the acquisition, protection, and maintenance of our individual ID's, our identities, accumulated over the lives of known time into what we think we are. So call me Sue, Jeff, or Mr. Clean. It matters not. I am what I am, as you are unto you…each a species member, no different in need from any other member, anywhere. So…

Part 1 attempts to establish this standard from which degrees of extremism may be assessed. The normal standard presented herein addresses that same standard referred to throughout this book—the nature of this human species, individually as well as via group, clan, tribe, nation, or ethnic derivation and the vehicle used by species members to inter-relate.

No matter the form, all languages consist of relations within… this to that, that to this, inclusions, separations, disjunctions, conjoint groupings, etc. The "operational relations" discussed lay evidence to those operations of the brain (mind) which we all share in common. We also focus heavily on the human ID—that aware, conscious now-in-time ID which each of us possesses to the exclusion of all else in this universe which we "think we know." Simply, I know me, not you nor anyone or anything else, so that if I die, the entire universe dies with me since I "know" only what is in my mind—that which constitutes my ID and the entire data-bank which so supports. Further, it is a "given" that each of us is not only physically constructed of elements which abound within this universe but that the mental/behavioral processes we each practice are directly derivative of physical and mathematical laws to which everything in this universe is subject, including us. We are not as "unique" as we would like to think. We are a species, which, as "rational," are woefully ignorant as to our nature. Indeed, we ask…

Why do extremist voices incorporate and espouse "ideas" which separate, distinguish, and promote group dissidence rather than species consort? Why is the manner of telling a group (or anyone within it) that it *can't* perform a species-specific act of which it is capable, more powerful than enlisting an invading army? How can we identify a politician in the public arena whose primary need is to justify and validate his ID using any and all means available, any thought of dispassionate governance removed from consideration?

Here, we would explain the underlying *why's* and *how's* of propriety relative to application, for words are really not "words" but simply indicators of nexi of operational relations, an understanding of which is absolutely essential for an understanding of man. Why? To prevent wars, suicide bombings, Columbines, Virginia Tech's, terrorism, genocide, a divisive dysfunctional government, and to promote educational programs which work.

We must tackle, head-on, those stumbling blocs which separate superficial man from an understanding of his operative nature. Language is an example. Linguists have tried to open doors (Chomsky, *et alia*) but, instead of cracking them open, they helped bind them shut. There is a difference between linguists who work in oral media—translating this to that with reasoned discourse, and the linguists who look at disembodied script and attempt resolutions in a darkened closet. We must strip away the layers of conceit, the layers of blinding wish which anchor disparate clusters of men to pools of toxic identity-food—each a mirage in the middle of which is posted a flag claiming ownership…of a mirage.

There is no structural difference between the reticular formations, cerebella, or cortical sulci of a Pope Benedict, a Rush Limbaugh, a Syrian Assad, or between a suicide bomber and a Trappist monk. There are no structural differences but what our lack of understanding of the operational capacities of man and our ignorance of those same capacities as evidenced within the shields of vaporous language would so make. To understand those most basic underpinnings of language—any language, is to understand those most basic constituencies of man and his most false dependencies upon manufactured ephemera so constructed in the absence of self-understanding, created solely to afford ID food for "rational" groups and attendant supplicants. We, each isolated unto death, encumber ourselves within makeshift houses of straw and therein build fires to warm our senses of who-we-think-we-are.

Finally, we desperately require a primer on the universal principles of political-group behaviors as well as a requisite vocabulary to allow productive defense leading to the absence of war and peace among men. Therefore…

Because men are deficient in an understanding of the nature of operational cognition and behavior, we discuss the nature of **A and A'** (A prime).

Because man is certainly deficient in his understanding of the maturational levels of operational behavior, we describe the components of such under the heading **operational relations.**

Because man is woefully unaware of the dependence he has upon physics and universal laws, we discuss **linearity** in depth—the interaction (or lack of) between two-dimensional reality (2D) and 4D STEM reality (Space, Time, ElectroMagnetism, plasma, etc.).

Because all interchange between this species' members consists of language, we discuss the nature of **language** and its total dependence upon man's operational (cognitive) capacities.

Because man, particularly political man, fails to understand the effect of **words** upon the operational nature of man, we discuss why communicative interchange can either succeed or fail.

Because man knows *only* his identity (ID) and its contents at any moment, the **human ID** is discussed in depth as the lynchpin for all behavior.

Because behaviors can often be reduced to formulas or **rules**, we present such, with explanations.

Because every man acquires his identity (ID) *only* through group membership (a man is only what the group "tells" him he is), we discuss the nature of **groups** in depth.

Because most men make decisions based upon **belief** of some sort, we discuss the nature, causes, and results of belief and belief-based act.

Because too large a segment of men make decisions based upon adherence to religious-based tenets, discussed are the nature, causes, and results of **religion** and religious-based act.

Because all actions of politicians are instigated through behavioral need, we discuss the causes and results of **political behaviors.**

Because **terrorists** have particular goals, as do each of us, we discuss what those goals *must be* and how to thwart.

Because **genocide** is caused by fear and deficiencies in ID, we discuss its root causes and steps required for hoped-for intervention, and...

Because political man has the capacity to change behaviors but doesn't understand how, we present a number of **effective techniques** which can be used to disrupt extremist behaviors and to coerce the adoption of new behaviors, constructive unto species welfare (Part III).

To achieve these ends, we must understand ourselves—how we operate, how we think, how we behave, and in each instance, *why*. If we can accomplish these tasks, we can understand how any one of our species operates given particular circumstances and how to extinguish those patterns of extremist behaviors deleterious to our species.

GLOSSARY

STEM   Space-Time-Electro-Magnetism...gravity, plasma, speedy neutrinos, etc, known and unknown, which constitute this Einsteinian universe in which we live.

g/e thread That Genetic/Evolutionary constituent in which we all take part; that "thread" which determined the hairs on our arms, the shape of our ear lobes; the drive to pro-create, to expand, to grow, to produce more of what we have even if numbers on a convertible bond

i/e   Inclusive/Exclusive. Relational operations. There cannot be an inclusive relation without an exclusive counterpart, and vice versa.

d/c or c/d Disjunctive/Conjunctive. Relational operations. Discussed fully in Chapter 2.

A and A' Written A-A' or A and A prime. Based on the Principle of Identity. No one thing, group, concept or whatever can be operationally identified without "knowing" whatever it is not. In this book, we usually take the "A" position, while "enemies," opposition, etc., the A' (A prime) position.

ID   IDentity. Nothing else. Often takes the form ID'd (identified), ID's (identifies), IDer (identifier), etc.

4D   Four dimensional man. Refers directly to participation within our STEM universe. Specifically *includes the time dimension*.

2D   Two dimensions, used to indicate *absence of the time dimension*. Refers most often to "tagged" neuronal nexi demanded by language and to any communicative/linear production which can be stored absent the time dimension and reproduced with no change of "substance." Examples: words spoken or in print; TV programs, movies, picture frames, lines, numbers, mortgages, stock certificates, square edges, hieroglyphics, etc.

Linearity   That capacity of man to produce 2D time-extracted products. Examples: any glyph, a pyramid, an SUV, a brick, book, printed word, insurance policy, constitution, or portfolio with Lehman Bros.

PART I

The Roots of Political Extremism

Chapter 1

WHAT ARE WE?

"You can't handle the truth," screamed Jack Nicholson in *A Few Good Men*. Maybe not, but if we hide from it, avert attention to Ipads and Facebooks, we'll never find the truth and suffer the species. For there are truths, facts of life which not a one of us can refuse to accept. For one, we are all children…you, me, and any 90 year old man. Each of our governmental officials…a child. Every national leader, President, prince or king…a child, and the operational abilities of every child differs in quality, capacities which we will examine. Two, we are each species spawn, not cast out of a God's hand like an Adam into an Eden, but spawn of generations past, each a link in life's chain, resulting in me here, you there. Three, there is a commonality among all sciences and branches thereof…*relations, so* seldom considered but necessary as language permits us to so consider.

We must open our inner selves to understand what we are. We must work as the best of chefs, as an Emeril working with an onion… not from the outer layer in, but from the inner core outward. Can we look at ourselves, our inner, true selves, and not shy away from what we find? If armed with courage, we can begin at the beginning…the *very* beginning, and find…? Well, for clues consider…from an acorn comes an oak tree. From monkey sperm comes, usually, an animal with a prehensile tail. From panda coitus comes a black and white member of the raccoon family thriving on bamboo shoots. And from human sperm…what shall we find?

Too, our trek will not be dissimilar from that of a scientist attempting to locate the origin, the cause and effect of a pathogen put under a microscope. We must begin at that pitch of moment within which we—each of us within this species, began inception and growth, from source through development as prescribed by genetic core and that social womb, individual as it may be, into which we grew, and grow. Our goal? To identify the working stature of a Khadafy, of a Mubarak, of a Mitch McConnell, John Boehner, Mitt Romney, Assad, a Bachmann or of an Obama, Biden, Beck or of you and me. We all have something in common, each the outcropping of very similar treks which began before our conscious ID's realized the world in which they worked. And so we begin…

The Epididymis Constant

If your father didn't have one (or two!), you wouldn't be here. If my father didn't have…neither I nor any other human on earth could scratch for water. No epididymides, no humans, nor apes, meerkats, or raccoons. The epididymis is a constant in all male mammals. It (using the singular) lies in the scrotum, attached to the rear of each teste. Why are we concerned with the epididymis? Because *as it is, we are.*

We realize that each seed, as with *spermatozoa,* carries the genetic heritage from the male and its particular genetic instructions for life, and as they travel the road to ID fulfillment (beginning with conjunctivity with an ovum), so do we, winnowed. So our approach is two-fold…

One, we will outline briefly the stages of formation and fulfillment of the spermatozoa and two, *relate these stages* with the life of a "Contender" for political office—any office, any where. The political stages are somewhat arbitrary, but, as defined by the nature of the originating spermatozoa, the derivation into political transit becomes quite obvious. Not only that—the obvious similarities from an examination of the spermatozoa's trek will reveal the most basic thrust of any extremist, the motivations of each of us, and why football fanatics at a college game, after their team scores a touchdown, raise their common index fingers in a vibrant scream of "We're number one!"

I. Formation

Sperm begin as "immature spermatogonia, tailless, impotent, nonmotile stem cells buried deep in the testes."[1] To acquire the necessary chromosome count of 23, sex cells undergo *meiosis*, during which the spermatogonia become *spermatocytes* and undergo further divisions—the male sex cells becoming *spermatids*. Impotent and nonmotile, the spermatids necessarily shed excess cell contents, grow tails, and compact DNA into their bullet-like "heads."

To further development, spermatids enter the seminiferous tubules which function as "virtual sperm factories, providing supporting cells that bathe, feed, and anchor the developing sex cells." They then enter the epididymis via muscular contraction and pressure from testicular fluids for further development and maturation.

The epididymis, a tightly wound tubing hugging the rear outside of the testis, is around 20 feet in length. Developing spermatids have 20 days to travel its length while learning how to swim. If sperm cells (the smallest cells in the male body) remain in the epididymis too long, they are consumed by neighboring cells (*macrophages*) and fail the journey. (From "inception," formation of mature sperm cells takes 64-72 days, each cell capable of "living" only 48 hours after ejaculation.)

II. Development

Immature sperm entering the epididymis mature therein and are there stored. Here they stay for about a month after which time they are either degenerated and absorbed (macrophages again) or begin the journey to the *ampulla* where they further reside prior to ejaculation.

III. Motility (Maturation—Sperm to Semen)

DNA filled sperm can't make the transit to fertilization of an egg without help. So, coupled with a small amount of fluid in the *vas deferens*, more fluid is secreted by the prostate gland and seminal vesicles perched on the backside of the bladder. These vesicles form the ejaculatory ducts for the seminal fluid which contains 1) sugar for fuel, 2) vitamins to regulate action, 3) enzymes which aid in increasing motility/velocity of transit, 4) regulatory molecules (prostaglandins) which thin the mucus guarding the woman's cervix, and 5) from the prostate, a milky, slightly acidic fluid containing citrate and prostate-specific antigen (PSA)—all for optimization of performance. This stage ends with ejaculation.

IV. Social Transit (The Swim)

Ejaculated sperm have but 24 to 72 hours to latch on to an egg, itself viable for only 12 to 24 hours after ovulation. The sperm must swim through cervical mucus, the uterus, and the uterine cavity to reach the egg, this now *oocyte* which has three protective coverings: "a cellular membrane on the inside, a tough *zona pellucida* in the middle, and a radiating crown of cells on the outside."

V. Target Acquisition

Upon reaching the egg, *acrosomes* (tips of the sperms' heads) release powerful enzymes which eat away at the *zona pellucida*. Most die in the attempt, but *one* binds to the waiting receptor.

VI. Penetration

The egg now internalizes the singular, penetrating sperm, uniting and activating three biochemical gates to prevent the entrance of further sperm (If two sperm enter/penetrate the oocyte, the egg dies).

VII. Fertilization

To fertilize a not-yet-fertilized *oocyte* (egg), the singular penetrating sperm must travel to its center. When genetic material is shared, nuclear membranes break open and chromosomes spill out and the oocyte, now a *zygote*, becomes truly fertilized.

The zygote must now endure a week-long journey down the fallopian tube. 36 hours after fertilization, the zygote splits into two *blastomeres*. In 72 hours, a dynamic ball of cells is formed called a *morula*. On day five, the morula expands to a 100-cell structure, the *zona pellucida* breaks down, and a *blastocyst* is formed, a fluid-filled cavity of *trophoblasts* which becomes the placenta. 14 days after finding a docking station in the endometrial wall within the uterus, endometrial cells cover the embryo with a blanket of protection and nutrition, and the zygote develops, and develops until gestation.

We now present one example, representative, of the Eipdidymis Constant in action…more than a simple analogy…

The "Contender"—From Birth to Goal

We can go through Formation, Development, and Maturation rather quickly. Each of our Presidents and assorted politicians, up to probably their early twenties, has "matured" to various degrees and kinds. At some point, however, each was nominated for a public position by a supportive, leader-need clique. However, there is no "moving up" unless within a defined *duct*, man-defined or physical, and since the route to a goal (Chairman of GE, potentate, fireman, representative, or President) is *linearly defined* (since classifications do not exist in 4D reality), we (or adjoining sperm) must promote the movement to "bathe, feed and anchor" the maturing sperm, or, upon identification of potential winners, "reabsorb" those outside the "mainstream", or attempt to remove from contention either rivals or those judged ill-equipped and work to "recruit from the circulation to aid in their digestion and clearance." *We live the epididymis.*

Upon identification of fertile sperm (our Contender with his coterie), we afford nomination of purpose and together set upon a goal. We help the swimmer to forage, to transit streams, and, in time, urge (physically!) to make transit. Motility confirmed by immature through mature stages of *elections,* we assist through the application of enzymes (money from eager lobbyists), nutrients (volunteers, TV ads, and a personal jet), and physical pressure (interviews and a chauffeur) all from the largesse of hormones—GnRH from the hypothalamus and pituitary, FSH and LH from the pituitary, estrogen, progesterone, testosterone, with bass accompaniment from endorsements, each performing as to nature.

The time comes whereupon we institute *primary* notification that our Contender "is in the running." Red colors sustain one contender, blue colors sustain another, and in time our runner becomes ID-decided. Into the mainstream, with our pulsating pressures, we eject into the mainstream. We donate more money, pepper neighborhoods with placards and interviews, and continually urge…urge, urge onward, forward, "down" the road (*ducts*) leading to ID fruition—his and ours. "He" finally, with our recognized help and assistance, arrives at the gate marked "Finalists Enter"—the party's local or National Convention where he, and others having made a similar trek, swarm (the convention center), each seeking penetration within an awaiting receptor—a platform whereupon he (coated with mucus-penetrating enzymes) is welcomed. Together, the candidates having eaten through the outer ring of cells (party representatives and peer contenders) require now only permission (the convention's confirmation) for one to break through to the middle zona pellucida and be confirmed (by the convention). The winning candidate, able to "bind to a pocket within a receptor," lets loose with gratified speeches (acrosomal enzymes). The winner (in a Speedo swim suit) now connects with all his constituents—a giant merging (both connecting via mitotic spindles, connecting all). But Speedo must wait a bit (a week long journey down the Fallopian tube) before days later when he is, in fact, sworn in (the morula grows, the zona pellucida breaks down, and a blastocyst forms—the future placenta).

Looking for a residence, our winner looks for a "docking station" wherein to conduct business (the preembryo, the blastocyst, implants itself to the endometrial wall, high up in the uterus). Speedo seeks security and gets it…a White House and a Secret Service ("14 days after fertilization endometrial cells cover the embryo with a cellular blanket of protection and nutrition in which it can grow"). Having won the contest, he exacts and demonstrates his final conquest: he enters the *Ova-I* Office, the only such office representing by name the nature of the quest.

What have we learned from this exercise? Hopefully, the following…

One, every act of man involves a search for fruition in stages similar to those outlined above. From the acorn, the oak. Ingrained. No exception.

Two, we have encountered spermatagonia, later "mature" sperm, which either don't or can't make the journey to ID fruition. The question must then arise: If we can't ride the bus with the "winner" and share the limelight as supportive follower, *can we make individuals* within our societies who are not on board, *incapable* of "making it" so as to ensure that our "chosen" Speedo can afford us (the "Right," the "Left") the ID input we crave (forget the capacity to govern)? Well, yes. Macrophages do just this. Consider our antiquated educational systems, high stakes testing, gerrymandering, restrictive voter registration, disproportionate taxing of the middle class...all of which dissuade, rendering "incompetents" into composite castes to prevent species-rendered quests for success and fulfillment. We cater to the moneyed, the upper strata of banking and name-known governors not really knowing why, such is our ignorance and need to hide personal, ID-striven, selfish needs. But, if we really knew why, would it matter? If it matters, how do we put species first?

Three, given number two above, do we understand why constitutions, federal and state, limit capacities for recall or impeachment? We can translate this mutually dependent union into a rule:

RULE: The greater the dependence upon groups for ID food (as is Speedo upon nutrients, hormones, 527's, SuperPacs), the greater the need to *protect* both groups and the dependent member ID's.

Four, nowhere in the sperm's journey for conjunctivity with an ovum (its purpose after all) did any sperm take time out to read a newspaper, watch TV, or write a sticky note—each operation requiring a *stop-time*, *2D interface*. However, the sperm's journey involved every aspect of our 4D STEM environ—pressure, gravity, time, Space, Time, with the Electro-Magnetic pull and push of cellular, molecular interplay. We must then reach a most important conclusion: How can we say that reading or writing are *natural* acts, 2D out-of-time proscriptions as they are, or as *natural* the inscribing of nota within a vellum binding? (Below we will find that the formation of an extremist is often initiated in elementary school.)

Five. We are 4D creatures embedded in STEM. *Every* happenstance of neuronal transfer, synaptic kiss, brain response or activity is acquired only through initial passage of incoming input via a 4D STEM *in-time* body. The body is the tollgate, the holder of passports, the AV receptor, the lightning rod through which all input must pass prior to ingestion and manipulation by a homeostatic brain, each and all action executed *in time*. Remove time from this 4D in-time equation and the un-natural results. Always.

And this is the missing curriculum, the curriculum bypassed in our educational systems—the study of man, of boy, of girl, instead of doctrinaire categorizations of out-of-time life (histories), of symbolic studies (algebra, etc.) which are far from understood as extracts from time and therefore of life, for children prone to "drop out" when ID food and sustenance are the base requirements for life. We feed our children bamboo shoots and expect them to eat. Herein, we feed... on natural food. In sum...

The Epididymis Constant is a *constant* in each and every species. Whether procreated via an epididymis or by other means, each species member (as a product of spermatogonia) lives with this *constant in-built drive* to be equal to or superior to species peers (rivals in the quest to fertililze...ID), but never inferior. With this human species, two alternatives only are presented for the determination of future act among adults, alternatives due to the acquisition of language: 1) understanding species' nature and the nature of each individual within this species coupled with educational packages which supply this information, or 2) lacking such requisite self-knowledge and understanding of species' nature, species members have no other recourse but to *artificially invent* species peers of inferior status so as to proclaim a "superiority." This false "superiority" is often achieved through the accumulation of "money," wearing Rolex watches, or building a car elevator within a ten-car garage, filibusters, or by creating castes—whites superior to blacks, "untouchables" inferior to Brahmins, seniors without picture ID's inferior to those who set rules, Christian conservatives to left-wing Liberals...instigated most often by those ignorant of species' nature, by those who chant "Hell No, You Can't" attempting to mark a "superiority" to those who attempt species advance through "Hell Yes, We Can!"

Our lives are not so much determined through the exercise of momentary "free will" as by the directives of the Epididymis Constant. Consider the following...

Is it by accident or by genetic code that the U.S. government is structured on *two* legislative houses, an executive branch which executes leadership and direction of transient movement, *controlled* by a Supreme Court which determines the efficacy of output, *and* male genitalia consisting of *two* testes, a libidinal, epididyan drive for dominance ensconced in an executive (ID) office with supporting cabinets, *controlled* by the opportunity of in-time moment relative to the depth of coitus?

Is it by accident or genetic code that the head of the Catholic Church wields a staff, is supported by a single body of Curia, and emits act via the release of "legal" encyclicals?

And so might it be that the U.S. government is so admired by other nations which have failed to recognize their own species core, to lodge fertile sperm within infertile, impotent tracts of governments there to fester until "Arab springs" or protestors of whatever stripe struggle to urge "release"?

We are so distant from an understanding of both species and self.

Chapter 2

OPERATIONAL MATURITY—THE LEVELS

NOTE: This section is most important for never can we understand extremism absent an understanding of how we operate. The relational operations discussed herein are those identical operations executed by all men at all times—our congressmen, every national leader across the globe, and the molecules in an Alka-Seltzer.

If we have "enemies," as we do, we must understand, as well as we can, how they got that way and how to combat, absent war. The principles remain constant. To this end, we must examine those operative/cognitive roots from which may evolve a Hitler, a Bin Laden, fractious politicians or the leaders of any group whose primary interest is self-protection and aggrandizement, not species-specific concerns. From the latter roots, of course also come a Mother Theresa, caregivers for the handicapped and forsaken, Doctors Without Borders, and fighters for a better world. It all begins in infancy and the young child. Let's see how....

Everything we do in life in any instant of time, whether it be a bodily movement—voluntary of not, thinking, reading, writing, or viewing the stars, involves relations. Within these relations lie the vehicles for the construction of any word ever written or read, for the production of every thought ever concocted, for the execution of every behavior—both conscious and autonomic, and the development of the human race. Without these relations and their operant workings within man and nature, we wouldn't be here nor would any other entity on earth. In humans, we call these operative workings *operational relations.*

Below, rendered linear, are the fluid relational operations (or operational relations) capable of use by individuals, governments, or birds and bees—the only relational possibilities in nature.

A and A' (A prime)—The Operative Base

Coupled with the Epididymis Constant, the A-A prime operative constant makes for a powerful potion…a witches' brew if improperly used, but for he who understands, initial steps toward a junior Solomon. A and A prime…

From birth and before, the infant begins to discriminate: Mother's voice, or its absence; a full nipple, or not; cold, or not; succulent food, or not; friendly, or not; right-side-up, or not; "anxiety," or not; etc. Discrimination develops into a sense of the "Discriminator" which leads into an "executive" sense of Consciousness. Concurrent, however, is the realization—to whatever degree "conscious," of all components of the universe as either what they individually are or are not.

We will occasionally use circles (Venn diagrams) to help illustrate. Each circle is fluid, however linear, and 2D, subject to power, will, emotion, inertia…whatever. Here, each circle representing either A (the child's conscious) or A' (whatever is deemed "not") also in turn represents the child's (and later, the adult's) initial steps at categorization—an integral behavioral component not separable from the conscious through which "boundaries" are established for every concept, every word, every thought we entertain. As the awareness, strength, and executive capacity of the personal ID develops, so does, reciprocally, the awareness and strength of determined sets of "is/are's" and "not's." The circles representing A and A' may then be seen to expand or decrease in fluid depth—protecting and enforcing both A and A' as determined or not, to aid in the development, protection, and security of the A-ID—the child. We must remember that the main inherent goal of any living thing in nature is perpetuity, growth, and expansion as far as it will go, and that entails the acquisition of tools to achieve these goals. The tools are mastery of the operational relations. Further, when language is achieved within the child, A primes can be defined orally. "I don't want that!" "No!" In such cases the identification of an A' is an act of *negation*—an identifiable separation of A' from A.

The A-A' relationship is the most basic, necessary, and common operative relation. The A-A' sets can be inverted, converted, extended indefinitely and, from birth, set the stage for every thought, behavior, concept, belief, or action in which any individual, group, or institution may engage. The only resolution possible between completely antagonistic A-A' sets will be found in the *Conjunctive* set, Stage 5.

A and A' provide the basis for all categorizations. Try this from an article by Thomas Friedman...[2]

"Sadam Hussein built his politics around *negating* Zionism— rarely, if ever, speaking about Palestinian economic development or education...The *politics of negation* has a deep and rich history in the Middle East...."

This book has several distinct purposes, one of which is to unveil and make clear political thinking which puts our children in harm's way—wayward, faulty, inconsistent "logic" which results from an ignorance of how we—all of us, think. Therefore, we might ask, what if our national leaders could ferret out the operative stages of development of opposing world leaders, and understand their cause? Or know inclusive and negative commitments and their causes before negotiations, and had the means to counter? Or come armed with cognitive/operational tools necessary to diffuse potentially hostile and dangerous actions? Or if we had such tools to correctly choose competent national leaders? We cover each area below....

The Relational Operations

"The doctrine [of *internal relations*] cries aloud for a conception of *organism* as fundamental for nature."
Alfred North Whitehead[3]

"It's called relations between relations and it's a basic scaffold of intelligence."
Ed Wasserman, University of Iowa[4]

There is no consort between 4D STEM reality and the words we use to describe. As such is the case, we occasionally resort to symbols. Consider upper-end mathematics or symbolic logic. Here we also use symbols, but to the minimum. A and A' (A prime) for example.

Ernest Nagel entertained the idea of "reduction" in his work, *The Structure of Science* (1961) in which he wrote "T reduces T' [T prime] just in case the laws of T' are derivable from those of T." Mathematics progresses, and while the reception of such a statement by Nagel's peers was most tentative, the "reduction" of T' from T today doesn't require a second thought. Example: If I come upon an apple core with teeth marks embedded, I can rightfully assume that at one time there was a complete apple. Core = T'. Apple = T, or reverse given the direction of sequence. Such considerations enter the field of cognition and operational logic.

We cannot deny that language permits us the vehicle to impose arbitrary relations (depending upon the relations which we may wish to impose) upon criteria—people, objects, events... We do so here. Neither can we deny the nature of the relations imposed—identity, negation/exclusion, inclusion/exclusion, disjunction, and conjunction (No other relations are possible, in nature or out). Neither can we deny that, prior to enforcing relations, we must *first ascribe identity* either to individual organisms or groups (us, in other words) and the behaviors in play, or to concrete elements. There is then a priority, a virtual ascendancy of relations from identity to conjunctivity. The employment of relations between two or more ascribed elements, "real" or linguistic, involves *operations*—the brain's ascription of relations to discerned elements. An apple can be simply identified. An apple cannot be involved in a behavioral relation or potentiality since neither active nor an organism nor be involved with conjunctivity unless smashed into with cinnamon. Human behaviors, however, are constituted within species which can, as a property, execute all relational possibilities. We are organisms as are all groups so consisting. A hive of bees is an organism acting in response to the needs of its members.

We begin with the most simple of relations, identity, and the philosophical Principle of Identity which simply states: A thing is what it is (as determined by what it is not). Simple. Every relation is intrinsically an operation and, for us, evolves in each instance from a 4D body. The nature of the operation *is* the relation whether it is avoiding a flame—*exclusion* ("No!" "not," negation, negative, A' [Read "A prime"], etc.); *identification* ("me," "I," ["A" in this work], etc.); *inclusion* (part of family, group, club, government, religion...); *disjunction* (one of two or more possibles in a tentative relation); and *conjunction* (the secure merging of parts of two or more intersecting sets). We'll take each in turn, in the end equating each with a level of operative maturity...

Stage 1 Identity (Infant-Child)   [The "Solo-ME-o's"]

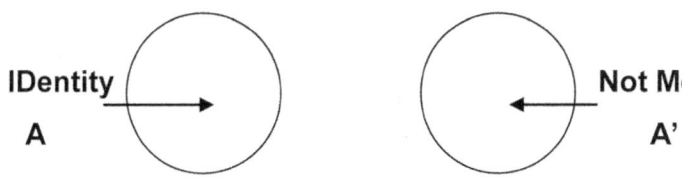

IDentity
A

Not Me
A'

There comes a point in time wherein A—the child, incorporates language via his prefrontal cortex (and elsewhere!) into what Ernest Becker would call the "pronominal 'I.'" This is the beginning of the true Executive ID.[5]

It is not simply the acquisition of language that does the trick. Infants can say "apple," "more," "milk," or broken sentences such as "I need potty," or any similar. The child is here acquiring the tools as well as "ingesting" the communicative medium of his family, society, and culture.

The conscious-behavioral integration becomes perpetually bonded when the developing child says "I" or "me" and means "Me!" by name, and in this breadth gives testimony that he is now the master of his ship and can execute, through the nuances of acquired language, determinations upon his environment. He can manipulate, order, change, excise, ignore, accept, or gather what he determines to be beneficial to him—all under the recognized aegis of "Me"! He has the power and he knows in whom this power resides—him.

[The vagaries of the English language make it awkward to write 'he/she' so forgive the continual use of "he."]

From this position he is bonded for life and executes his decisions within a conscious ID aware of an environment, access to which is garnered through a communicative language which becomes as much a part of his natural environment as the physical world around him. A mutual incorporation, a mutual melding. His prefrontal cortex, his Broca's and Wernicke's brain areas, are functioning as are his six physiological areas necessary for the production of speech.

The dichotomy developed herein at this stage—between a "touchable," seeable environment vs. a 2D communication medium (other than spoken language) with which to interact is outside his ken (and should be). However, the still-developing child is incorporating within his ID, as a single unit, his environment and his language which, as we shall see below, is linear, involving nevertheless operant production in time. As this incorporation progressively takes place, those attributes involving language facility within four and two dimensional interchange, two-dimensional sequencing (written language, e.g., and recognized as such!), etc., become second nature to the degree that his culture and his environment allow. The ID of the older infant becomes integrated as one in preparation for his passage into the next cognitive state. He has developed *linear* capabilities inasmuch as he has been introduced to such (both spoken and written) and, with a safe and secure cognitive platform is thus able to function rather well in both 4D and 2D environs without effort.

NOTE: The Stage 1 un-developed *adult* will forsake further operational development of ID into overt maturity to focus on fulfilling the needs of a deficient and basic, insecure, ill-founded ID rooted in *ID protection and acquisition*, to whatever degree acquired. To this end he will use (unknowingly) upper level relational operations as he must to read, write, or speak, but these uses pale in comparison to his need for safety within a stilted, infantile ID which *he necessarily must bind* to a group. If no group with which to bind, he will become a Virginia Tech assassin.

Stage 2 Negation (Infant-Child)   [The "Hell No's!"]

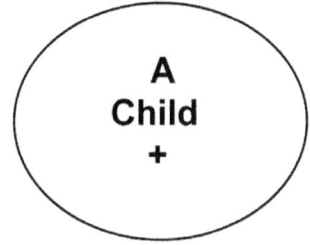

As we shall see throughout this book, the A-A' continuum is a given. That is, there is no identity of person or thing without the acknowledgment of whatever that person or thing *is not*. This really unconscious awareness slips by the wayside, not to be bothered with since attending to such continually would be a simple waste of the brain's "time." There is, however, the relational operation of *negating* given the first instance of *identity*. In other words, the rational brain cannot negate thought, thing, or event without first positing an initiating identity (ID) *from which* to negate. So, ID comes first; negations come subsequent. Understood also is the "cognitive" realization that whatever is identified (ID'd) is, consequently, a given part of a person's brain-stored data bank. If I want to say, "No, That is not an apple," I must have in mind full awareness of *what is* an apple, and that ideation of "apple" is in my brain's data-bank. The same sequence is operational whenever a denial, negation, or 'no' results in any category, any time. We then understand that first comes identity ("consciously," at whatever level) and second, subsequent acts of negation. So…

In early infancy the child learns what is harmful, unpleasing, or cause for discomfort. The identified (ID'd) sources are categorized as "not," unwelcome, alien, harmful, etc. As such, the infant begins—for personal protection and survival, rampant classifications of "OK! Yes!" categories, and "No's", "Not's," and "Hurts" as non-amenables. These are, for us and for him, A' (A prime) categories. Each element in each category has been so identified through an initial communion with his body. The *remembrance* of each interaction, forged from bodily reaction to a categorized element, constitutes and develops into his internal categorizations (his experiential data bank) of relational operations… those involving rejection of items (A′—rejections) or acceptance (A—"OK, acceptable"), the latter beginning to additionally forge the ID of A—the infant/child (not necessarily the infant himself but items which become incorporated within the infant's consciousness so as to begin the further development of pro-nominal awareness, the "I"). Repeated identifications of amenable elements confirm the "correctness" of the infant's "decisions" which further forge the efficacy, exactness, and appropriateness of the operation which is, for us, a relational operation (A relation, as operation, cannot obviously be "seen" just as one can not delve into the amygdala to pluck out a memory. The body, however, remembers its own operations just as a pianist's fingers "know" the keys)

Each circle (above) representing either A (the child's aware consciousness) or A′ (whatever is deemed "not" A) also in turn represents 1) the child's initial steps at categorization—an integral behavioral component through which "boundaries" are established for every concept, every word, every thought we entertain, and 2) an A′ (A prime) counterpart through which the child develops his own ID (Identity)—an ID which develops *because of* the A primes experienced. As the awareness, strength, and executive capacity of the personal ID develops, so does, reciprocally, the awareness and strength of determined sets of "is/are's" and "not's." The circles representing A and A′ may be seen to expand in fluid depth, protecting and enforcing both A and A′ as determined, or not, to aid in the development, protection, and security of the A-ID—the child.

After the relative "safety" issue has been settled, the child begins to feel tentatively free to explore the world…every part of it. Some parts appear curious and require later defining. Other parts, primarily through environmental contact or education by parents, get predefined as "out of bounds" or harmful. As maturation progresses and an once or two of freedom is granted, the infant/child not only explores but shares his ID with other artifacts in his environ. He will prefer certain books, certain toys, developing attachments which will evolve into a developing "I" or "Mine!" whenever a threat may appear to possibly remove one of his toys, or whatever, from his "ownership." Threats to his belongings appear as threats to him. And, if *threats to his belongings* ("Don't break my toy!") may actually effect *their* security (precursor to inclusion), he can also easily translate these threats as a potential and threats to himself. So, what to do? (Remember that the seeds for all operative relations are being nurtured and developed. Inclusion…"That's mine!" [even if the infant can't speak yet] indicates a tight bond, an inclusive set—object to infant, which approaches mutual identification: "What is mine, is Me!")

If and when the child identifies with an object and feels a need to protect it, he includes his ID within the rubric of the object and operationally (behaviorally) hopes to exclude that object, vis-a-vis himself, from potential danger. The relational operations here involve *inclusion* (to and with object) and *exclusion* (from A' danger, each tagged relation tentatively ID'd as a set, the level of identification dependent upon maturational development). The child, in effect, *outsources his ID*, assumes the ID of the object and thus operates on its behalf having first ingested the object-set within his own ID. He then considers the danger to the object as comprising a specific set in itself—an A" (double prime, danger set) to an A' (object set), that set which initially helped ID the child to effect exclusion/negation.

NOTE: Stage 2 *adults* (The "Hell No's!") typically have very fragile ID's. Any affront to an object-set adopted within the ID's of Stage 2 adults becomes a personal attack which then requires a "Hell No!" in response, unable as they are to exercise upper level relational operations (disjunction, conjunction…). Upper level operational behavior becomes out of the question as the ID must first be salved, as to a child, prior to advanced levels of operation.

Stage 3 Inclusion/Exclusion   ["Block-heads"]

Inclusion

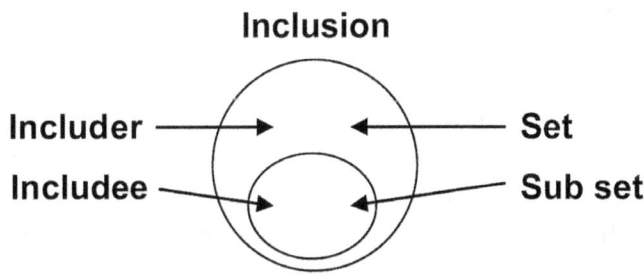

| Includer | Set |
| Includee | Sub set |

The development of relational operations naturally evolves under wise guidance and a protective umbrella of safety. There comes a time however, when the child must be weaned, to venture forth to acquire a "safety net" of his own which could be used in parental absence, literally or physically. An example or two will suffice since all children are different as are all parents and all situations.

My older son used to play with GI Joe toys. If I had had a daughter, she would probably have played with Barbie and Ken. What does any child do with a toy soldier, a toy girl, toy airplane, stick of wood, matchbox car, or a Spiderman? Anthropomorphize! Attribute human characteristics to whatever, and manipulate events! "Zoom...zoom!" "Bang! I shot your helicopter down!" "Ken...do you like my new outfit?" In unspoken parlance, the dialogue runs thus: "You, GI Joe, are now me, or rather, I am now you!" ("And see what I can do!") What the child is "now" doing is controlling his environment vicariously through an anthropomorphized figure, "protecting the world" and manifesting power over the environment.

Early in life the young child begins a good realization of what could constitute danger (Even without the developed pronominal "I," he "knows" what he knows, and feels). To control the environment and to protect himself—his guiding and permanent goal, he needs to acquire whatever powers he needs to "dominate" forces which may constitute a threat. How? First, he identifies the threats. Second, he identifies those powers which can control the threats. Third, he *becomes* those powers (through Identification and Inclusion! In order to cope with such threats, "identified" or imaginary, he incorporates into his ID those specified powers which can conquer the threats. With a child, it's a GI Joe. (With an adult, it may be the command of military forces capable of initiating a campaign of Shock and Awe or simply becoming a congressman, acquiring both security and power to dominate.)

The child may wish to become a soldier, doctor, plumber, teacher, lawyer—anything with certified power attached. The child, with his GI Joe, has imbued Joe with his own ID, and vice versa. He has voluntarily, as a natural precursor to an adult "safety net," given of himself. He has *included* himself *within a rubric of his own fashion* and in accordance with his own needs and in accordance with his own abilities, via external objects. Later on, in his maturing years, he may include himself within the aura of a football team, a university, a Hamas, a political clique, or a "kitchen cabinet." But further into inclusion…

"A" is now integrated "formally" (for the child, around age 11). Puberty sets in. As the Survival ID in passage safely submits to bodily change, security develops. Brain sheaths, some under-clothed, are now becoming fully myelenated. Linearity is now passé, the operation of dimensional reduction (necessary to execute language) relatively conquered. Operational behavior becoming somewhat integrated, the ID is now hungrily working environments to further build and sustain a rapidly growing ID.

With the ID (who and what he feels he is *now*) thus far developed it now stretches to acquire a broader, firmer base in anticipation of a fully developed ID in adulthood. Peer associations, clubs, teams, schools, etc. become "end-all" focal points. ID's now become outwardly transparent via associations: Boy/Girl Scouts, "Panthers," "PS 42," etc. As each association develops, so too does the personal ID which ingests with gusto, attributes of membership which can apply to the sustenance of a personal ID. As the ID continues to grow, so too does tentative trust in associations (always ID-survival and ID protection foremost). "Entrance granted!" ID absorbs, and gives—in trust, hoping for continual ID sustenance. At some point, a merger develops—a non-separation of association of an A prime (the Includ*or* G Group set) with the A set—the child (Includ*ee*—the ID). Inclusion occurs—both as cognitive act and as identifiable relation. The ID now *lives* a relation—the ID inseparable from sets x, y, z…. "I am a *Bearcat!*" "This is *my* room!" "I'm an *Aries!*" Sit in a school lunchroom or just observe standing outside a Starbuck's or watch the hand motions of rappers on video. Every motion, every nuance of behavior, every article of clothing, every twisted position of cap on head gives, or asks for, ID sustenance through inclusion within group. What is significant here also is that *no act of negation* (possible separation from Group) *can take place unless the A—the "child" here, is rooted within a prior inclusive relation* (family, personal clique, etc.) even if only sketchy. This is a universal rule: *No negation unless prior inclusion* even if "inclusion" means only within A-ID's 4D inclusive environ (An *American Idol* failure still has some place to go!).

NOTE 1: It is assumed that the reader is picking up on the notion that any particular behavior, by its relational definition, *defines the operative level of the performer—at any age.* If the operation is *predominantly* defined as inclusive *to the exclusion of the more advanced operations*, so then is the operational level of the performer indicated *and defined* as child-adolescent *in that instance* (Any congressional behaviors fit in here?). While the inclusive operation is regularly employed by most mature adults ("Yes, I will join." "Of course I will give," etc.), the disjunctive and conjunctive operational relations, as we will see, require maturational development.

NOTE 2: Any human group is an *organism* as are its members. As such, the group assumes the same characteristic needs for the acquisition, sustenance, and protection of *its* ID as do its members and assumes those operative characteristics in common with its members. To this end it will exclude members not supportive of those needs. We therefore couple the *inclusive* stance of a group with its *exclusive* counterpart and define and use *i/e* to so designate (inclusive/exclusive). If its main purpose is to *include* members to so define itself *while excluding* others, it is at the i/e level, no higher. Examples: Ku Klux Clan, the Wisconsin Republican Senate, the DAR, Mensa, etc.

In sum, the child has but one "set" with which to barter. Himself. His body is the medium—the vehicle, through which his ID communes with his environ. His ID has remained relatively constant, integral until puberty. Then, the changes! He becomes a sperm producer, she an egg producer. Hormones switch in, melatonin spigots open up…two and twenty blackbirds all at once! Bodily orifices assume new meanings, new functions. "I'm not the same as I was!" Indeed! And how does the ID cope having done so successfully up to this point?

As the body changes, *so too does the ID, in time.* All the inclusions, all the identifications, all the negations—all the relational operations effective to this point morph as well. They must. The body and the ID are integrally one unit—one the medium, the other the executive in charge of operations. One corporation. (There is no body-mind problem. There is, however, a body-language problem…language, 2D and linear. The body—4D and STEM. Linear language cannot mediate or substitute for 4D reality.)

The effectiveness, however, of past relational operations still lingers. The A-ID has thus far successfully identified, negated, included, and excluded others of his environment within his ID set and he within the identifiable "sets" of others. This mutual relational interchange is most important for it is the forerunner of all adult associations, involvements, and potential wisdom.

Relational operations are interdependent, particularly from "the top down." However, moving *upward developmentally*, there is, in fact, no individual pronominal identity without inclusion since one rational ID can never develop an ID without inclusion within a group if only within a family (this inclusive notion will be considered fully, below). Further, since only ID's (rational, conscious humans) can effect a negation and since ID's are only formed through group association, we might accurately give the sequence as *inclusion to ID to negation*, working from the early infant on up.

The brain operates at lightning speed. We can however, freeze time and simply say through analogy that if one orange is in a bucket, that bucket "includes" an orange. If so, the *set* "orange" is included in the *set* "bucket." At this point we might ask the reader to estimate the number of inclusive sets (let alone disjunctive and conjunctive!) his brain processed to simply process (read) the first four sentences in this paragraph. He would be astounded (*c.f.* Chapter Four on Language)! Such a tabulation would, however, serve to clearly distinguish the difference between a 2D linear description of inclusion vs. the brain's actual 4D sequential performance of inclusive operations. We understand then that relational operations are not static, that simply "reading" requires the brain to process *inclusive* relations within *exclusion* relations within *identity* relations within *disjunctive* relations (advanced) within *conjunctive* relations, etc., all the while using ID'd sets and A primes…and we still (on average!) have not necessarily hit the teen years! Let's move up…

Stage 4 Disjunction   [The "Im-potents"]

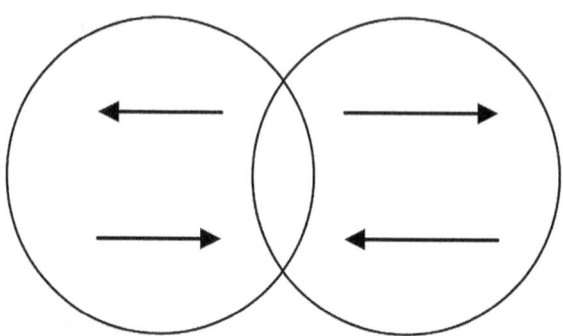

Operational disjunction is not mathematical disjunction. Mathematical disjunction is an either-or proposition—*either* an apple *or* an orange, two options, *time factored out*, freeze-framed, awaiting resolution by a 4D agent *in time*. Axons and dendrites don't know this. We, with our linguistic brains, come along and attach droplets of language to a 4D problem, insert under a microscope, and label freeze-framed relations.

Operative disjunction, even with linear application, marks a demarcation between simple inclusive (i/e, inclusive/exclusive) behavior and the next level up—a homeostatic interregnum between a possibility and a fusion (and don't adolescents know this!). Here, the older child moves into adulthood.

Operative disjunction is a behavior. OD (operational disjunction) is where and when quantity (relational sets) becomes quality (behavior). OD is being stuck (maybe by choice!) on one of two horns, and knowing it.

Disjunction, taken separately and apart from ID involvement, involves *two* or more sets—either of which is inclusive (container sets), both held in mental stasis like a juggler juggling basketballs while wondering how to stop his toothache. Disjunctive sets do not meet and do not converge, yet there is a relation between both, otherwise no disjunctivity—rather, simply separate inclusive ID'd sets. So, to execute a disjunctive operation requires a behavioral relationship between two or more sets, each related in some way but distinct, held in stasis awaiting movement either toward convergence or further separation. 2D Venn diagrams don't do the trick simply because any disjunctive relation/operation is mental, behavioral, and processed *in time*. Two separate circles drawn on paper with arrows pointing from one to the other must remain just that—two circles with antagonistically pointing arrows *outside time*. We, however, are not 2D Venn diagrams on a sheet of paper.

As illustrative examples, consider a seven-year-old child whose parents are undergoing divorce. For this child, whose ID is nascent, undergoing development, each parent is separate. He cannot hold the two of his parents together in a joint relation extant in time within his own ID. The relations are…his mother as major set, his father in major inclusive set, he in minor included set switching back and forth, *in time*, from mother set to father set, both distinct. Then consider a 19 year old whose parents are undergoing divorce. Now rather fully developed (research having put the years for male maturation at around 25, girls around 21), this boy *can* retain the disjunctive relation of mother and father while holding his own ID in a rather constant stable state.

Disjunctive behavior is such only in direct correlation with experiential data within a memory-based ID. Saying "No" to a chocolate is not disjunctive. There is no threat to ID present, no suppression of the basic need for survival and protection, no loss of any consideration of possible outcomes as required by disjunctive behavior. For a mature disjunctive episode, there must be, to a degree proportionate to the operative capacity of the individual, 1) a threat to ID homeostasis, 2) an impending need for physical protection or survival, and 3) a full consideration of two or more relevant positions (major sets and subsets) with a decision to disjoin from one or all positions in spite of pulls toward a fusion. The simplest example here might be a young man full of angst deciding whether or not to invite that girl he has a serious crush on to the prom. Will she accept? If so, slight conjunctivity. If not, he retreats into walled-in inclusion—his home set, a bit painful perhaps, but secure. Prior to the invite—disjunction. After rejection, relational regression into walled-in inclusion (he + family/friends). But with maturity and opportunities to engage in further potentially conjunctive relations, possibly beset with many more "rejections," the system (maturity) becomes "inoculated" and *mature* easement toward conjunctive relations becomes the norm. For most of us.

With the disjunctive operation/relation, we can discern the operational level of anyone be he child, teen, adult, diplomat, president, or House leader. If, with confluence possible, one side can relate to a single side of the issue *only*, this *dependent* ID is *forcefully inclusive*—one step below the disjunctive. Example: if a Senator's ID is *vitally dependent* upon membership within one of the major political parties or ID supporting groups, to that degree of dependence will he be unable to entertain participation within a disjunctive relation involving the recognition of a position adopted by the "other side." Disjunctive status is behaviorally "felt" by its participants most naturally producing angst since the potential of a conjunctive stasis dissolving the potentially disjunctive state constitutes a real threat (Witness the ID protective "Hell No's!" with retreats into the security and anonymous protection of an i/e group womb).

Understanding this relation and its operation plays directly into an understanding of international confrontations and the developmental level of the major participants. Since it is the natural evolutionary thrust of man to acquire homeostasis—a stable behavioral equilibrium, disjunctive participation becomes unsettling, particularly if of long duration. Such long-term behavioral instability produces neurotics, factional splits of whatever sort, and wars. However, for some, membership within a disjunctive relation is beneficial. Consider Ahmadinejad, Kim Jong Un, Castro, al Qaeda, Cantor, Boehner, Palin, McConnell, Limbaugh, etc., and the ID-food supplied through continuations of disjunctive states which require, each, A' foils for ID food. Think warring factions, each side "needing" the other for ID food; think increased military budgets, House Republicans vs. House Democrats, Presidential candidates, wives who submit to abuse refusing to "get out of it," KKK's... Take away military adversaries and military budgets go down. Take away "Obamacare" and Pauls, McConnells, Ryans, Boehners…run out of oatmeal. Therefore, the disjunctive participant *welcomes* the disjunctive (A-A') split, such providing a *raison* for disjunctive behavior which would otherwise go wanting. It is important to recognize that in these latter instances, one or both disjunctive parties is *totally dependent* upon the other for the ID food provided through the disjunctive relation. (And this has nothing to do with the Palestine-Israel feud, the Taliban, or Shiites and Sunnis?)

NOTE: To simplify…any disjunctive relation consists of two or more inclusive sets related via a *potentially* ID altering conjunctive union leading to joint stasis. Thus, Hamas, Hezbollah, and the Likud; Republicans and a black President, etc., *could* acquire conjunctive stasis (peace) with each other and end practiced enmity, but such stasis would deprive each group (its leaders, particularly) of its inclusive, disjunctive ID which receives nourishment *only* from an A' "enemy," the source of sustaining ID food. Simply put, why give up a warm dinner already on the table for a questionable potluck at Sean's down the block?

Does any of this have current relevance? On April 18, 2006, as an example, President Bush declined to criticize Defense Secretary Rumsfeld and, instead, stated full support in spite of increasing and overt criticism. David Brooks (*NY Times*) referred to Rumsfeld as an…

> "Anti-Organization man…[with] *unshakeable self-confidence*… [one of these] event-making characters who exist above their organizations, or in a *tightly organized renegade band* [a *group*, in other words—italics mine]….he has unleashed a reign of terror on his subordinates…."

Do we see *group* here, a chosen inability for *fusion* (conjunction), or an experiential memory-based ID behaviorally ill-equipped for the responsibilities of the position with a commensurate need for *disjunctive* stasis due to needs for ID embellishment? Then Maureen Dowd (she's a "lefty") on both Rumsfeld and Bush: Rumsfeld is "…intimidating…arrogant, obtuse, wire-rimmed…promoted sycophants…" (I read i/e ID here.) Concerning President Bush… "His whole presidency…has been designed to prevent him from being labeled a wimp, as his dad was…Anyone who challenged the administration was painted as traitorous…" (Do we read A' [A prime] here?) Or here: "Rummy set up a State Department within the Defense Department…their own CIA within the Defense Department…their own Defense Department within the Defense Department…."

The question of course, is—Which cognitive behavior causes more deaths, war, conflagrations, human disruption: 1) closed i/e behavior with its inability to entertain a higher level disjunctive behavior let alone conjunctive fusion; 2) disjunctive behavior—two players at a poker table, both refusing to deal the cards; or 3) conjunctive behavior, with ID stability well-contained, two poker players in the act of actually playing cards—the only level of relational behavior through which peace and tranquility is achieved?

The natural inclination of man is to merge with whatever resources may abound to propagate, expand, and to extend his natural genetic endowments—the call of all nature (the g/e, genetic/evolutionary thread). To be operationally bound, therefore, within a disjunctive relation is to thwart the natural inclinations for growth and to frustrate a natural, species-driven desire to evolve through disjunctive states toward conjunction. (Why do most species have two sexes?) Below we will take a detailed look at methods and procedures available to derail disjunctive relations and promote advancement to the next and higher level, the conjunctive.

Stage 5 Conjunction   [The "Can Do's!"]

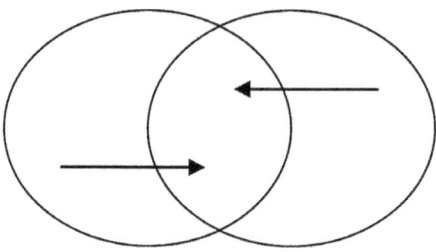

Conjunctive relations contain virtually all the operational relations possible in nature, and are graduated. As with the beginning of the universe when two hydrogen atoms first kissed, the initiation of all elements in the Periodic Table took off. It's the same with us. We begin, as infants, establishing ID's, A-ID's and A primes, and work our way up through inclusive behaviors, disjunctive behaviors, and if sufficiently mature, conjunctive. However, as graduated, the slippery slope goes backwards as well. If unable to countenance a conjunctive relation, an operator must slip into disjunction which involves compelled inclusion within a safety set. Beyond that is Robinson Crusoe, but he will still have an ID accrued through past inclusions. To the task...

The conjunctive stage marks the pinnacle of cognitive reach. In the conjunctive stage, a personal ID has developed to the point wherein a minimum of two perhaps apposite sets (A and A') can be housed within a single conjunctive set (an A-ID) *in time*, held with some degree of equanimity by prior disjunctives with homeostasis secure. Secure middle teens can handle conjunctive behavior rather well; adults are the most capable with experiential practice.

To reach this stage it is obviously necessary for C (the conjunctive operator) to be comfortably free of overpowering inclusive entanglements—entanglements to/with family, religion, peers, spouse, children, political party, lobbyists, oil or financial cartels... to whatever may put a "brake" on freely exercised relational operations. The C stage person must be homeostatically healthy, secure, protected, without undue restrictive ties to any inclusive set (read "group") which may override stable, free, ID security. The conjunctive stage is further marked by a practiced freedom to think, to entertain diverse behavioral sets conjunctively, freely in time without compulsion, secure in knowing *that the operator can return* to a supportive, secure disjunctive/inclusive relationship whenever needed, whether it be with family, parents, home or whatever. A few examples may make it clear...

Conjunctive thinking is being engrossed in the machinations within Dan Brown's *The Da Vinci Code*—wondering, guessing, anxiety rising—unaware of the book in your hands.

Conjunctive behavior is an umpire born in Greenwich Village, New York City, about to judge "Safe" or "Out" for a player sliding into home plate during a Red Sox vs Yankees game with the dispassion of a Solomon.

Conjunctive behavior is a brain surgeon concerned about his dying wife while carefully sliding two electronic probes into the brain of a patient with the uncontrollable tremors of Parkinson's disease, carefully attending through his computer to the chatter of firing neurons judging by the sounds the correct placements while his wife swings between life and death.

Conjunctive behavior is a species-supported Republican with a well-developed ID voting for a Democratic sponsored Bill promoting health care for millions, facing subsequent party expulsion.

Conjunctive behavior is a President of the United States assenting to a Kyoto Protocol for species benefit, sacrificing ID support from oil companies to which he is personally beholden.

Conjunctive behavior is a President deciding on a face-to-face attack upon bin Laden overriding dissenting voices from his closest advisors, putting his Presidency at severe risk just to fulfill a promise.

Then consider a case before Judge Judy. Two combatants, one judge. JJ hears each side, individually, then questions each, in time. Is there conjunctivity going on here? Well, when JJ questions the plaintiff, does she also keep in mind the defendant, and vice versa? Involved here for JJ is attending to one side of the conjunction (a disjunctive plaintiff), then the other (the disjunctive defendant) requiring her to enter into an inclusive relation housing two disjunctive parties within a conjunctive (JJ) set, one at a time, but never leaving the C relation entirely. (There are, at minimum, seven sets involved!) JJ retreats to chambers, considers the arguments, gives weight to this argument and to that, and reaches a conclusion. The conjunction for JJ is the *relation* between the two oppositional parties, each *disjoined* due to their stated differences but in court for an *identifiable purpose*—the conjunctive unbiased court. We realize that conjunction never fully consists of two or more parties—of whatever nature, *fully joining in complete conjunction so as to lose ID!* Conjunctivity, as we will see below, requires the security of ID to accept *an alteration to ID* which depends on maturity and depth of ID stability. If you add sugar to lemon juice, you can distill the components.

It would be impossible to reach the conjunctive stage with a tangible "I need" or "I can't leave" tie to a 4D world. Children can't leave 4D except through pronominal phantasy. Most adults can. Ultimately, of course, everything we do is dependent upon a 4D universe. But with 2D linear we can, with acquired operative skill, shunt the 4D aside while we go about our work (Are you continually conscious of the font used, for example, in what you are now reading?). The efficient execution of these relational operations requires this brain of ours with its billion or so synaptic connections to "leave" a tangible 4D universe to work on the conjunctive level. It can't, like a dog on a leash, maintain conscious contact with physical reality and work upper level relational operations. If this makes sense, then let's take a short look at just a few of the most basic implications…

If cognitive man works at his fullest without demanding restricting ties to the physical, then why are children taught the following: "C A T. This spells *cat*. Say *cat*!"? Children are taught that printed letters…moveable, colored, "physical" letters, *are what is read, are what is dominant*, and *are the basis* of "reading." Ever after, having been taught by hallowed (hollowed?) respected figures of authority that all "reading" depends on a tangible tie with a "physical" reality such as "printed words," children stumble when an attempt is made (internally and so naturally!) to think in the absence of a physical tie. The tragedy is, of course, that teachers and the institutions which "teach" teachers, either pay little heed to the nature of dimensional reduction—4D vs. 2D, or are simply ignorant of the operative nature of man, which they are (Our children, in this system, are literally *taught* to fail!).

In sum, the conjunctive operator, more so than the disjunctive, can find operative stability in both 2D and 4D STEM environs. While the disjunctive operator depends more on the "I" within a situation of choice, the conjunctive operator can acquire balanced stasis among perhaps discordant elements. If the conjunctive operator chooses incorrectly or encounters an ID threat he can't overcome, he may opt out and head for a safe haven. Disjunctive example: A general torn between attacking the enemy on the left or the right flank and doing neither. Conjunctive example: a pensive Lincoln, facing the option of a split union, deciding for war to preserve a co-joined union.

There are no age limits (beyond mid-teen years) to effective inceptions of either the disjunctive or conjunctive relational operations. We use either, if normal, throughout our lives. Indeed, collapse one or more sets of a conjunctive operation and, if the immediacy of need is too great, the operative demands slip easily into disjunctive (Ever walk out of a boring movie?). So…

If major flaws in relational understanding lie at the core of genocides, wars, suicide bombings, dysfunctional government, etc., then we must learn below how to "attack" faulty sets. We must understand the causes of obsessive ties within inclusive i/e politically executed operations. To understand how relational operations work, how their depth and power influence the workings of man at large is really to understand man at his core, and through an understanding, solve a few problems and hopefully save a few lives.

Chapter 3

THE NATURE OF HUMAN IDENTITY

Consciousness

This business of consciousness sits too high on the totem pole. I'm conscious (I assume!). Are you *conscious*? Add the "ness" and what do you get? A longer word. Unfortunately, no massive compilation of 2D script will equal one nanosecond of my, or your, consciousness.

Consciousness (too long a word) is my awareness of what's going on *now* in my 4D theater. My visual cortex—accepting reformulated photon input from the outside, interacts with relay networks in my brain to process either response or to initiate active reflux from my data bank. I am aware of the outcome, a degree of "consciousness"— not necessarily the process (who is?), but Edelman and Tonini appear best in line for explanations.[6] *Cogito ergo cogitum habeo.* So…

All the words ever written or which could be written can never transmute 2D linearity to "adequately" describe consciousness. With 2D, there's no bridge to the mainland. So, why then do we read and study "consciousness"? For those interested in the machinations of man, such a study demands analysis of human neuroanatomy. But here we need, *require*, an understanding of human "cognition."

Only through an understanding of the relational operations intrinsic to every cognitive act, can we allow print to juggle around our existential data into meaningful juxtapositions which we "understand," consciously. This in itself requires and defines consciousness. So again, why pursue the subject of consciousness at all? We study consciousness to help in an understanding of "self," of "I," of "me," of who we are and what we think we are, for *any extremist isn't who* he thinks he is, nor is he *what* he might think he is (But that goes for thee and me also!) Point: *to get to* any extremist—a Palin, an Army, a McConnell, a Limbaugh…we'd better understand *what* he is prior to any "who" he is!

We study consciousness because any extremist thinks. He dreams, judges, forms bonds, loves, hates, dotes on his children, prays…and perhaps attempts to kill, either through word (as a Boehner, Cantor, Coulter, Beck…) or sword. The point here is…

No thought, no feeling, no belief, no act of any sort is executed without neural activity occurring some place within the human brain. Therefore, whatever is experienced in any manner involves requisite execution within or among facilities and faculties within a brain. No "images," no "voices" from Allah, Christ, or the Virgin Mother, no Gabriel on a chariot, no "visions," no "He spoke to me's," *no nothings unless executed within neural pathways* (Think otherwise? Tell us how!). Therefore again, neural pathways within the body are requisite for experiences of *any and all types.* Additional point…

Every "image," every "vision," every "He talked to me," every whatever can be accounted for by neural activity *without exception.* Any "image," "vision," or audible reception *can be* verifiable as externally extant to a neural brain *only if incapable of production within a human neural network.* The obvious is this: *if it can't be produced, it can't be understood!* (If the radio isn't on, you won't hear it. But if it is on, what recognizes and processes the sounds?) This all leads from, and to, where we're going—identity (ID), relational operations, and the time in which we commit ourselves as members of inclusive groups both to avoid reality as well as to understand what, and who, we are.

ID Validation

We are each alone. No telepathy, no brains bonding in series like a computer network. The only vehicle we have for the transference of thoughts, feelings, pains, and the need for a sip of Bailey's Irish Cream is language. On that, we do depend.

My ID is the *only* reality I know *for everything else shifts in time, my ID with it*. The wind blows, then it snows. Sand storms arise, no water in sight. Open the lunch box, eat the sandwich. My ID remains, never to surface the synaptic symphony or the instruments at play. Even "I" change. So, who am I? What am I? I once had no arm hair, now both arms well hairy, head bald on top. Where's the stability in all this?

The existentialists stopped short. Neurologists sought Golden Delicious apples from a Macintosh tree and Aristotle and the Scholastics went as far as they could with what they knew. Piaget came close and should have come closer, but he had a hidden agenda (see his *Illusions of Philosophy*). Needed were understandings plus knowledge of ingredients missing from the mix—time, the brain, and its operational structure.

In this chiasmus in which we all exist, nothing is permanent. Matter decays, the universe expands. I occasionally need a haircut and upgrades for my software. My kids grow older and morning dew evaporates. I remain. And the "I" is what? The "I" is a 2D vocalized inscription—nominal, and therefore time-less. But I'm not. I decay. Residues of metals, minerals, chemicals and residue from exploding stars formulated over eons of time and g/e interplay, form me. I am 4D. The "I," as scripted, isn't. So where does that leave us? That leaves us with the fact that no thing, *nothing* in this universe can either equate with or describe my Conscious-ID. I am once again alone… ID-conscious, a tremulous, ephemeral, cloud of transient impressions, withering, passing, formulating…totally dependent on the mechanisms of body for transit and operational commerce…4D, with no anchor…no anchor in eons past and no anchor now. For Og begat me—two legs, two arms, and corpuscle containers. Same species, same capacities, same needs. We have pyramids; Og didn't. We have subways, dual-exhaust Corvettes, F16's and microchips. Og didn't. But we *developed* language, language which never influenced my bodily need for calcium, my brain for salt, or my eyes for zinc. I lift with my hands, arms, and legs and grasp with fingers. But language remains 2D and time-less. So Feuerbach may have said that man is what he eats. Rather, *man is what he does*, and what he does is traffic in scam, in a STEM divorced module to acquisition food and language which he thinks works but is "ingestible." He thinks that language is a natural phenomenon, as integral to man's constitution as his liver. And so he lives a lie—*the* lie that what is written, said, heard or read is as much a part of STEM as is his body—equated with that medium from which the C-ID feeds. Inseparable. So, as the lies of words are writ, so do they become as the hematocrits or the oxygen coursing through 4D veins. We equate, never understanding, never appreciating the difference and die through our ignorance.

We gave language substance—to mesh with everything else in this universe. We had to! For what other use could 2D language have in a 4D universe? We fleshed language out to make it compatible with the 4D universe in which we subside: "and the Word was made flesh, and dwelt among us;" "We do not question the word of Allah [for if Allah speaks, surely the word must derive from substance—otherwise, how could words have a "reality" of any sort?];" Allah must have "two real eyes and a generous mouth." The Second Amendment declares 'the right of the people to bear arms." Of course! Substance! And because of substance and the self-generating proliferation of language backed by "substantive" interjections, language construed itself into not a Tower of Babel but a Leaning Tower of Pisa, bending to whoever fed it, and worshipped it.

We are still left…alone, enmeshed in this time-full struggle to ID our ID's. Who are we? What are we? Well, we have a tool now, don't we? Language—mutual feed time, and we so submit our ID's to Language…

We get married. Why? To validate ourselves. A's and A primes. I love my wife, or do I? Do I love her for what and who she is or solely as validation for my data-bank ID? "Love" *is* the acquisition, and repayment for, a validating A prime. Love is the expansive g/e thread saying, "I love you for validating me; for giving me contractual substance, for tying my ID into a bond, perennially set in a time-bound relationship set in 2D scripted stone." A and A'! Without language, however, would I love my wife? But then, *sans* language, what would be the condition of my ID-data bank, or hers? So language "makes" us; the evolution of our brains gives substance to that. We can't see the trees for the forest and commit ourselves to 2D rule, Big Brother (Big "Language") watching over us, embedded, imbibing, then granting us surcease after implanting on our foreheads our ID's: Catholic, Muslim, Jew, Mick, Wetback, Immigrant, Polack, Gay, Democrat, Republican, Liberal, Conservative, Reborn, Lesbian, Afro-American, Pacific Islander, Hispanic…and we, in thanks, go to the polls and vote, and to the church, to the synagogue, to the mosque…and pray, practicing in thanks via the 2D time-less language which both formed us and warped us, in time and space, *compelling distance* from that species in which we all reside. For that, I do not pray in thanks. But should you…wars sit in wait.

We each draw on accumulated data in any one instant to make any decision, large or small, given that the chaos of continued 4D involvement is thankfully mitigated through the brain's depositions of consistency, creating a continual blanket of expectations through which we might interact, operationally, with every encountered little bug in our environment and sweep from off a white tile floor an unexpected mote of dropped tobacco (It wasn't supposed to be there, our brain said!).

It follows, therefore, that as our data banks are *continually* modified and changed through the operational course of daily living, *each of our identities changes—in each and every instant!* That is why an understanding of ID is impossible without an understanding of our place in time, and why cognition—dumb word as it is, is without meaning absent our 4D place in this Einsteinian STEM universe. Call me Horace, call me Sam…no 2D moniker has transport with my 4D data bank, or my ID. And such is the case with every human on this earth, suffer him, suffer her, title upon title. The nonsense crumbles when you look at a clock or write or speak someone's name knowing full well that the name does not equal the man. Let's go a bit further…

If I add a grain of sand to a beach, the ID of that beach changes. It is now not what it once was. Operations within time change ID's.

A kid is in a barber's chair watching in the mirror the barber as the barber goes clip…clip…clip. The kid's eyeballs are at work, transmitting through local subway systems a myriad of data to the six or seven areas of the optic center so concerned. The brain isn't asleep, and so records…shuffling off data to data banks here and there, time not stopping. The brain is performing according to purpose and schedule. It is imprinting on data vaults procedures, events, tools, situations…all of which are for one purpose: to rev up the body schema so as to passively prepare for a like encounter in the future. The brain, in effect, is recording its recording. In time!

This is why "reflective thinking" is impossible. There is but one *now* and we each live it each and every instant. There's no going back, no reflection upon a reflection, but only an operation in each instant, in and of itself. Upon itself? No. In itself, yes. In time, yes. There is no "time travel," no "reflecting," save for that "dark network" which neuroscientists call the "default brain mode" in which we transport ourselves hither and thither while listening to mother-in-law tell the same story for the eighteenth time. There is only *operating* in the now of time, dark network or not. And ID? *ID is the now conscious awareness of operational processing, the organism checking, re-checking, and re-re-checking its past operations as to efficiency, efficacy, and inclination toward homeostatic regularity given the now-instant.* Your car does the same when you turn on the ignition. Low oil? Light on. Low battery? Light on. Ever go to the fridge (like me), stop just outside the door wondering, "What am I doing here?" The body knew where to go, as directed via past inputs, but the brain was working in the cornfields. Stop, recap…"Oh, yeah. The butter!" Too, every bodily sense (the "five senses"?) is *prehensile*. This means that *each* is a "grabber," grabbing input from the environ, sending info to brain via neurological/biological systems—autonomic, Central NS, Peripheral NS, Autonomic NS, etc. We input, organize, categorize as to use, filtrate into proper organismic structures and store for future use. If OK, we continue on un-interrupted. If new episodes are encountered, we back-track, re-filter, locate, and use. The body thinks. The brain thinks. And junior sits in the barber's chair…

"Hello, son. What's your name?"

"Johnny," replies the child meekly.

"Johnny…what a nice name," replies the bald barber who continues …clip…clip…clip….

And Johnny's brain within his organismic structure continues rhapsodizing within electrical, neuro-transmitting circuits with continual pings, firing circuits, and circuits within circuits. "Johnny. What a nice name." And Johnny continues in life studying George Washington, FDR, Attila, Kings and Queens, test-trials for each XCAT…each jockeyed up into a time-less aura by a 2D moniker, and the 4D properties which make Johnny who and what he really is get lost, replaced by state-sponsored text books on U.S. History within state-sponsored schools financially fed by state and federal monies to later perform as a 2D mendicant within an armed force, soon to be a pin-prick, a memento of a war memorialized on a granite wall. Johnny. 2D episodic implantations of the backside of language. And yes, we are here to identify and to protect Johnny's ID.

So Johnny goes to war, dies, gets buried in a Flanders field, but his 2D moniker becomes forever established in the repertoire of a government, his moniker used as a number, symbolic "…of all those brave and dedicated soldiers who now defend our country or who have died for its preservation (or mine!)." Now, we're certainly not against defending our country, even dying for it, but we are against group leaders sucking in ID food through the use of human fodder, "leaders" whose eyesight sees only ID food in the faces of all before them, and if not there, living, well then, "out of sight, out of mind." Group "leaders" who coalesce slaves to linear arguments, who suck in ID-group food while Johnny, with his brain of a trillion neurons, synapses capable of relational operations exceeding the particles in the universe…Johnny, or Achmed, or Moishe, or Zhen…the sublime epitomes of evolution's prowess and largesse, become but totems, wallowing, fortifying local flora.

So an understanding of human identity is not important, that ID involvement—4D-2D, A and A', have no bearing on the deaths of your children? Try this example of solidified i/e intransigence, and the consequences… In an editorial in the Ft. Lauderdale *Sun-Sentinel*, January 27, 2007, we find this…

> No wonder Vice President Dick Cheney likes to stay mostly out of sight. Anyone else who had done as much harm would want to hide too.
>
> Now comes word that Cheney wrecked a chance for the United States to improve relations with Iran and perhaps get some help in stabilizing Iraq. Iran offered such help in 2003, a former State Department official told the BBC, and also offered to make its nuclear program more trans-

parent and drop its military support for Hezbollah and Hamas. It asked for relatively little in return.

The State Department wanted to accept the offer, but Cheney opposed even talking to a member of the "Axis of Evil." A golden opportunity was lost, and America remains mired in Iraq and on a collision course with Iran.

When history assesses the Bush administration, it will not be kind to the president. But it will reserve its lowest marks for the vice president.

All politics consists of behaviors. All behaviors can be ranked from inclusive/exclusive (i/e) to disjunctive to conjunctive, low to high, immature to mature. Cheney's political behaviors, evidenced above, are classic i/e [inclusive/exclusive], representative of pre- and early teenage onset, immature, evidenced by Cheney for one purpose— the salvage of a petrified ID, stated, slated, and digitized in disk. How many Johnnies suffered as a result?

2D history books, with their time-extracted linears may not be kind, but the burial mounds in Lebanon, Israel, Palestine, Iraq, Afghanistan…and the rows upon rows of crosses, Stars of David, and Crescents filling our military graveyards understand. So our thousands upon thousands die to defend a 2D document ensconced under glass? Or is it something else…perhaps the acquisition, maintenance, and preservation of leaders' ID's which, titled, can power species' peers to obeisance in any category prescribed, each prescribing ID incapable of apology? There is a violation of the sacred here, a sacrosanct issue, an understanding of which we are painfully ignorant.

Logic, Reason, and ID

Logic and reason are in a spectrum disparate from that of ID. The former are linear in application, the latter 4D, participant within the space-time continuum.

The real ID encompasses a 4D organism which accumulates cognitive, operative, ID repertoire while marching its way through a 4D universe. Logic and communicated reason (try executing either in a non-linear medium) ply a linear response. *Nations are not governed by logic or reason, but by ID*. So...

There's formal logic, material logic, paralogic, symbolic logic, Boolean algebra (logic)...but try using any one in a request to Y asking that he, and his nation, refrain from nuclear proliferation.

There is a taxonomy within each of us, a taxonomy based within a species-specific built-in regimen. Such a simple taxonomy might run like this:

1) survival, 2) reproduction, via 3) an acquired, maintained, and supported ID. Such works with camels, ducks...even us. Hominids. Supposedly rational.

This hominid ID serves as both an aid to survival and reproduction. But to enforce the latter, the ID must be nourished and maintained. The "bent" of the ID, depending upon the moment, will be either group-specific or species-specific—group-specific if defending/supported by a particular group, species-specific if understood as engendered by the nature of the species and for the understood benefit of the species (not, usually, found within the general nature of any group, governmental or not).

Logic, in any of its forms, is defensive. Logic resides within a linear medium of choice, linear even within the brain while contemplating 1...2...3...4...5... all in a sequence, consuming "time" within a linguistic framework. The ID, however, just lingers on, occupying space, time, and history (memories, that is). And to throw "logic" at any Y-ID is akin to shooting an arrow at Fort Knox expecting walls to crumble. The continua are disparate. So, what's the solution?

To defeat an extremist we must expose the tower of toothpicks upon which his ID is built and use a "logic" of a different order, a logic which entails recognition of the 4D status of Y, and in so doing, make the ID the hallmark of any communicative relationship. We must take into account the basic elements which constitute any human's ID: 1) species-specific entitlement so engendered within and by the species, recognized or not by Y, 2) peer support, without which any group-specific ID is unobtainable (family, school mates, politicos, religious brethren...), and 3) "subject" support...those minions controlled, or who voted for, or live with the gracious acceptance and acquiescence of Y supported by scripted dogma. This "logic" must, in some way, assume a 4D status and approach directly the ID on throne, for we know that...

Everyone wants and needs the acquisition and maintenance of a functioning ID. If recognizably human and to a degree *species-specific*, the good of the majority may be a goal, more so if the "majority" provides peer/minion support for Y's ID. If, however, Y's ID is perverse, severely a-kilter from species norm (Khaddafy, Assad...), behavioral experts (but where are they?) become the locksmiths, not the diplomats. Determinations can be made in either case, objectively (see Double Binders below, where we attack the problem with force). We need, however, to examine the bonding of groups, and from bonded groups, the individually bonded ID. Therefore, to The Code of Manu...

The Code of Manu, 201_

The epitome of a dichotomy is you, me, or any one of the seven billion humans strutting this stage. No greater example of a split at the seams can be found than within an aware ID human who consciously works with just one instrument—his brain, his "substance" subject to the whims of politicians who know little of STEM or the nature of man.

One brain, one world. One brain as A, all else as A prime. Always and evermore, one operational powerhouse in a sea of "rational" organisms, each with the identical propensities for thought, feeling, emotive need...for water to quench thirst or food to fill a belly. "We are part of a species," we tentatively say when the comprehension of such is beyond the capabilities of any singular brain to process, the thought constrained within a singular skull, STEM realization lost in the wind. Loneliness. Yet the autonomous brain *is* of species bent as is one goose following another, pheromones or waddle to guide congress. The necessity to bond is constant, testosterone or estrogen to force.

Language is recognized, if not consciously, as but a vehicle to facilitate *union*, so casually used that the realization of its nature falls within shadows of oblivion, nature forsaken, yet its objective treasures gainfully accepted—food, bonding, barter for goods, but what else...?

We are fruit of the epididymis. Each of us. Our natures are to be Number One, to excel, to triumph, to declare our uniqueness by finishing first at the tape. But what to do when we gaze about and see a sea of ourselves, people plotting, gathering, dressed in frill, fancy, and Levis all moving this way and that going about the daily grind? When "species" is recognized but with "recognition" of its STEM nature suppressed, how is it possible to be a Number One among species peers? How...? We must devise a *strategy*...

Within every species will be found those "smarter," those who become leaders, perhaps voracious for ID conquest, capable of forging a place "at the top." But one can't simply stand among a crowd and say, "I'm Number One." That won't go. A band of brothers is required, a semblance of solidity among species' parts representing capacity to bond, with no ill effects. So, with brothers bound, required next is a vehicle, a swath of communicable media through which others of species can process a message receiving the declaration of our #1 status. But still insufficient, for what justification forces the issue that, just because Harry says that he's #1, he is? Insufficient. More is needed. What...?

Authority is needed. But where to get it if all species' parts are equal? Available for use, so far, are a band of brothers—leaders, "smarter" than the crowd, and language—the medium through which proclamations of superiority will be issued. But how to force the issue? One path would be to physically subdue species peers into subjugation, "enemies" forged and put under yoke. The problem here is that such "enemies" must be of a set *outside* the supportive set fostering the ID's of the G1 (Group 1) group. A primes, in other words. But, if the G1 band is itself situated only among a group which can offer weak support—citizenry poor, illiterate, living day-to-day plucking meager essentials from the earth while other known societies ride subway cars to work in skyscrapers, or locals, ignorant of species' nature, bound through prejudicial or insular belief in this or that following the directions of a traffic guard to turn left, or right, or to form a roadblock...such a weak supportive group can itself, through force of need, be cast as A prime and, through subjugation and exploitation, be used to facilitate an A-ID rise of the G1 group, such procedure giving rise to Dictators, domestic or foreign, so many of whom we know. There is an additional need...

Needed is an *amenable authority*, one to whom obeisance can be given while authority to work as Number One is given in return. How to implement? Let's work with a monologue in an attempt to fathom G1L's thinking...

Gil (Group 1's Leader) thinks, 'What do we have on hand which is held universally by all men, particularly those within this culture which we need for ID support? Of course! Language...language inscripted. Language can be chiseled into pyramid walls, cave ceilings, Saharan rocks, on scrolls of papyrus or whatever, even into the form of constitutions, and made as permanent as the material on which inscribed. Time-less, *Time-absent*...the key. With this capacity of ours we can render unto perpetuity thoughts, directions, histories of past act stopping time in its tracks. Surely this time-stopping capacity did not come from us but from a being with powers beyond this capricious world we inhabit. It must be that, if inscripted language is permanent, some entity, somewhere, must be a cause of this gift and timeless as well! Also...

'The authority we need must be *compatible* with our needs, we who are limited in knowledge, eyesight, wisdom, physical movement... We are ignorant of so much; our eyesight permits limited vision; our physical self is corruptible. We die. There is not one constant within nature. But what if we envisaged, constructed a being all-knowing with ultimate wisdom who "saw" all that is going on, is un-corruptible and doesn't die, an A prime for all our human and natural limitations using this very vehicle which can make time-less whatever we wish? Certainly no inconsistency! So, let's promote this ideation (well within reason) and call Him Primordial Being (PB for short) both as an answer to salve our natural doubts and to provide a platform upon which we can construct our needed status.'

Time passed and the PB was constructed.

Armed with the perfect mesh of time-less inscripted language and an ideation of time-less Cause, the Dharmasastras (of which the Laws of Manu were a part) were written for "verification" of the existence of such a Primordial Being over 2600 year ago in India—to provide a platform for divine authority. In like manner was Yahweh transcribed into the Jewish Bible (God speaking to Moses, etc.); God detailed for Christians via Christ in *The New Testament*. In like manner was Allah given substance via the words of Gabriel to Mohammed. In like manner did Joseph Smith, Jr, give substance to Elohim, "God the Father," who, married with wife, emigrated to earth (one of many inhabited planets) from the planet Kolob where earth was once situated, earth moved 6,000 years ago to its present location in the Milky Way (Mormonism).

In every age of religious initiation reigns doubt and uncertainty and the need for man, in some way, to fulfill his destiny to become Number One following the epdidyan directive. The observation of Romela Thasper regarding the Laws of Manu fit universally: "The severity of the Dharma-shastras was doubtless a commentary arising from the insecurity of the orthodox in an age of flux."[7]

While the Code of Manu is but one example, locate any decree, treatise, Council, constitution, law, holy book, or directive relative to the control of human behavior and located within will be a thrust by group—clan, tribe, force, political party, cult, culture, society, or a single individual to be Number One with no exception, save for those few groups which both recognize the nature of species and surrender themselves to its enhancement—the best of teachers, nurses, doctors.... We arrive at the present day wherein a Declaration of Independence proscribed a Number One status opposed to an overbearing England coupled with a Constitution identifying Brahmins who would determine policy and governance, stabilized within decree. Up to date, with an analogy...

Analogy: If one has *h pylori* (a harmful bacteria in the gut in about half the population) and takes a couple of good strength *aspirin* for a few days, then adds a couple of full strength *ibuprofen* in the middle of the night, the chances for a full blown bleeding ulcer are quite high. Accordingly, if one values a member of our species—anyone, say a Michael Vick, QB (under a $100M contract, or a baseball playing Pujols—$250M for an eight year contract) in terms of "money," other members of this species *will* feel insulted...not in terms of "money" but in terms of the valuation of humans only as *numbers*, nature of species ignored. Result? "Occupiers" of Zucotti Squares. In other contexts, a Tea Party. When CEO's, basketball players, hedge fund managers, and those of financial control determine the ID status of each of us in terms of "money," the subconscious within each of us *will react* to the artificial, contrary de-valuation of species nature, even if the nature of reaction is beyond verbal expression.

We are first a species, species-bond uniting us all. But when a caste system prevails over species' nature, something within this social organism *must* go awry in automatic rebellion. Do we live within a caste system? Yes we do, and the word *caste* should be the main thrust in the battle cry of any Occupier. Why? Try this, updating the Code of Manu with its division of castes, then ours…

Brahmins (Priests and Teachers of Scripture…Determiners of ID's): Senators, Representatives, Governors, Party leaders, Christian right…

Kshatriyas (kings, warriors, law enforcers): Admirals, Generals, Joint Chiefs of Staff; Commander-in-Chief, Attorney General, Supreme Court…

Vaishyas (traders, bankers…): Federal Reserve, SEC, Banking Heads, stockbrokers, hedge fund managers; insurance companies, CEO's, billionaires…

Shudras (laborers, farmers, craftsmen, service providers): road builders, farmers, hospitals (MD's, nurses, etc.), construction workers, aircraft mechanics…

Harijans (Untouchables—outside the "caste" system: not to come into contact with others of "official/divine caste" status): "Occupiers," lesbians, the "poor," voters with no picture ID, marijuana smokers, under voting age children, thieves, rapists, drug dealers… as many as possible put "out of sight" or incarcerated so as to be beyond "touch."

Before we hit the punch line, a bit more on the nature of the caste system…

The word *caste* is derived from the Portuguese *casta*, meaning lineage, race or breed…*casto* meaning pure and unmixed. Merriam-Webster (online) defines caste as "A division of society based on differences of wealth, inherited rank or privilege, profession, occupation, or race." One Wikipedia author wrote, "For the Indian politicians, this [Code of Manu] has proved to be a useful myth to promote, as it provides them with ready constituencies for which to claim a perpetual victim status and benefit from the divisions and votes this garners."

So much of the Indian caste system could be parlayed into the caste system within this country. The British colonial powers, for example, assigned powers to the Brahmins to rule and to assign authority for the control of castes as Obama relinquished control to banking industries with authority to regulate "money" for either lending or hoarding. Further, looking at hegemony (hegemon—a leader state), "The hegemon rules subordinate states by *implied means of power* rather than direct military force." (Wikipedia)

The question must arise: upon what basis is a member of this society recognized according to his STEM nature and not upon an artificial contrivance used to classify him within a caste?

Within the Indian caste system (abbreviated within this section) is the notion that each caste is *separate, distinct,* endogamous, assigned to "perpetual" tasks, professions, etc. Such distinction is noted when strict divisive protocol demands that if a Brahmin comes into contact with a Harijan, he is to bathe himself to rid contamination. Is a CEO of Citicorp, who flies into Washington DC on a company jet and who receives millions in salary, likely to associate with a concrete mixer or to live in a middle class neighborhood? Further, what is it within our society which ID's castes "by implied means of power rather than direct military force"? Answer: Other than state and federally funded high-stakes testing which castes children prior to secondary casting via voter restrictions, the two most prominent are The Tax Code (devised by the Vaisyas) enforced by the Penal code (devised by the Kshatriyas). First...

We note elsewhere that the "value" of money is but a wisp of wind. One headline reads: *US stocks soar on help* [verbal] *for Europe* (central banks easing terms for loans) and the value of portfolios jumps up. Someone at the Fed coughs and inflation goes up, stock values go down, bonds ascend, and Marcia implants an IV into an accident victim. Paul Krugman writes, "The economic crisis showed that much of the apparent value created by modern finance was a mirage."[8] Credit, *credo*—I believe. What means of belief and ID quest are used to divide our society into castes? The Tax Code (capitalized as with the Code of Manu)...

When Marcia receives her W2 form and has to fill out a 1040, the value she is obliged to pay is fixed. If H&R Block fills out a longer form, value still fixed. Pay it, by the numbers. The amount earned plus rate of tax determines caste, as determined by the Tax Code, codified, as caste determiner. Yet bonds rise as stocks fall. Inflation rises, times get tough but the Code remains intact. As individuals we may verbally barter outside the Code for the cost of a new car or the price of a house. Value up or down according to the season for purchase, but the Code remains as constant as the northern star. With the value ascribed to "money" is the caste of each of us determined. And the nature of species? The definition of you, or me, or Marcia? In terms of "money" and the Tax Code (Manu derivative) are we so assigned.

The Penal Code is used to differentiate castes as well as to enforce the stability of the Untouchables—that caste upon which the "superior" castes subsist. Harijans, the Untouchables, are *essential* to provide "substance" to those castes absent STEM or natural support. If no Untouchables, why needed would be castes dependent as A's to A primes?

The Penal Code extracts from society sufficient numbers to populate an Untouchable caste, individuals most often directed to incarceration, all purposefully lacking the support of a STEM based educational system sufficiently adequate to develop self-understanding to the degree necessary to maintain a self-appreciative homeostasis.

Our domestic penal system has, with errant examination of man, run amok (The U.S. has more people in prisons than all the rest of the "civilized" nations combined! More money is spent in California on its prison system than for all of its educational institutions combined!). It doesn't take an equation in symbolic logic to equate the overwhelming percentage of incarcerated prisoners within this nation with a dysfunctional, Brahmin-needed system of education directed by Shudra vassals assigning parameters for caste alignment (high stakes testing, e.g.). There is a "positive" side to this however. The greater the definition of an A prime set, the greater the definitions of all other sets obversely dependent. No poor, no rich. No small, no tall. So Shudras capture, imprison, and four castes derivative from the breadth of Brahma (the Primordial Being) grow fat with status. (One distinction between Brahmins: the strict Brahmins of old were devised to be penniless. The Brahmins of today aren't. Rather, they are Krugman's %.1 billionaires and 249 plus multi-millionaires in Congress…who wear ties.)

We need to change the artificial into the real. We rate professional quarterbacks as to their efficiency in passing and running. We rate chess Grand Masters. We rate baseball players (check out *Moneyball*, the motion picture). We need to categorize people not upon how much "money" they control but upon their contribution to society. From 1 to 100, Michael Vick might receive an 80 in the assigned category of *professional football*; Justin Bieber and Josh Groban an 85.6 each in the field of *entertainment*; for Susan Hockfield, President of MIT, for pushing the implementation of manufacturing methodology across curricula, an 86.2 in the category of *academic leadership*; for each of CNN's heroes, a 95 for *species betterment*; for Marcia our nurse, a 96 in the field of *nursing*…and across the spectrum. (Rate then individual members of Congress or political affiliates—Boehner, Gingrich, Norquist, Cantor, McConnell, Obama, Pelosi, Palin…relative to species beneficence) Does a professional quarterback require more income for a house to raise his family than Marcia the nurse? Which attends more closely to the expansion of species welfare? The millions upon millions of dollars received from Boards of Directors which CEO's themselves appoint? And the Occupiers in Zucotti Square have no reason to dump upon this scene? Rate then where teachers, dedicated to the uplifting of universal minds and the salving of this nation, get ranked unto caste according to the Tax Code. There is a disparity, the epitome of a dichotomy. The Tax Code and the Penal Code are but two fingers on a Brahmin's hand directed at you or me, fingers pointing up. (Do we understand that the value of money is based not upon the usage to which it is put—the beneficence of species not an issue, but by castes to so determine themselves…as castes? For if "money" were valued as attendant to species' welfare—the primary axiom in the order of species' support, what ranking of species' beneficent "castes" would then occur?)

Two rules are at play here…

RULE 1: Man fears most having his ID changed by an outside source over which he has no control.

RULE 2: Any ID, firmly grounded in STEM, has little need for an ID ascribed by artificial means.

The question must then be asked: Which of two groups is the more attuned to species' nature…Group One consisting of the poor in spirit, the mourners, the hungry, the merciful, the pure in heart, the peacemakers, the persecuted, *or* Group Two consisting of the proud, the sated, the rich, the mourner creators, those who deprive livelihood and life-support to families, those who cause conflict and impasse to species growth and who persecute those species peers of Group One?

Protestors protest the overt violation of species recognition and beneficent administration. Protestors are the insulted, the weather vanes pointing in the direction of species concord against forces bent on extracting life-force from contrived castes as cannibals would feed upon their own.

There is not one Protestor who has not been ascribed to a caste over which he or a friend had no control. *Any man's natural STEM ID is automatically attacked through caste immersion.* It is those who, by need of ID acquisition, so position themselves as controllers of the ID acquisition of others, thinking that such power defines for themselves a STEM ID based in species nature. In biological terms, such scavengers are called *macrophages* ("big eaters"), eaters of others. Their role is to *phagocytose* (engulf and then digest) cellular debris and pathogens *made* immobile through caste ascriptions, while assuming the role of "Hell No," recalcitrant, obdurate conservatives tied in some manner to script, to engulf and digest mobile, positive pathogens seeking species enhancement… Protestors.

No man protests himself. Rather, man protests those castes others have encrusted upon him, he of good will yet deprived of choice.

NOTE 1: As a teacher, it is disheartening to realize protestations which should occur, but don't. Consider: Cut out a slice of pizza and set it aside. How many pieces of pizza do you now have? Answer: two, the one piece cut out and the remainder. It is impossible to have a singular caste unique unto itself, all by itself. Any cut, any division, any separation must result in two or more sets. Always. Now establish a set of students who have "passed" a reading, a writing, or a high stakes math test. Only one set? Hardly. The "other" set *must* consist of those students who *did not* pass the test/s. To make one, two must be made. The second? Those children down the block, or living next door, or in the next city. "I don't care about them," might cry one mother. "My child is what counts!" And the other mothers? The other children? Does the mother of the "passing child" take responsibility for those children who did not pass the tests? No? Well, she should. She should, and she should not shift blame to "educators," testers, governors, school boards or administrators. She participated her child knowing that, through such participation, some other child *must* fail. So where are the mothers and fathers who refuse to take such responsibility and demand, instead, that *all children* be educated to their maximum within an educational system geared to providing satisfaction and achievement goals directed to individual needs and abilities? Not here. Further…

NOTE 2: This nation supposedly guarantees universal education for all its children. Any child can go to school (given that there is one to go to) for the purpose of both individual "education" and education which allows easy transit into a workplace society. Interesting it then is to note that this very system enforces a testing system which *requires* children to fail that very educational system supposedly geared to their individual and social advancement! Our educational system is not only dysfunctional but schizophrenic. As such, and as it is constructed to be such, the only obvious "survivors" are those beyond its reach—either within the halls of congress or as controllers within our educational system itself! We need not Kevlar vests but straight jackets, with a citizenry capable of application.

It is not children who require caste distinction. It is the extremists who require the imposition of caste-differentiated progeny to secure their own A-ID's at the expense of A prime ID's—those less fortunate, keeping the less fortunate, less fortunate. True fruit of the epididymis. Our goal? To locate and defeat those methods extremists choose to restrict the understanding, development, and growth of individual ID's…yours, mine, and our children's. Santorum's goal, Perry's goal of cutting off all state and federal funding for education (the first sign of tyrannical intent)? Consistent taxing of the poor and middle class but safeguarding the 1% offering Brahmin support? Assad butchering malcontents? We understand. From needs to goals...to keep the ignorant, ignorant. Game on...

Chapter 4

LANGUAGE—THE BLACK HOLE

The sole remaining task for philosophy is the analysis of language.
Ludwig Wittgenstein

Einstein wasn't around when the Constitution was written. If he had been, and the Founding Fathers had understood the space-time continuum, they would have known that writing the Constitution was constructing a document which would go into a time-absent, time-locked vault simply by being a compilation of time-inscripted operations inked onto paper. Voila! Time absent. Perpetual and never-ending. To bring such a document or any like it into present day affiliation would be to simply involve combustion.

So is it with man today. We use language not understanding the depth to which language deludes us. We are, each of us, 4D STEM organisms, breathing, moving, eating, passing waste, occupying space and time. This we are and ever shall be until becoming the dust from which we came. Yet we speak and assume that as we are real in-time 4D STEM creatures, so must be anything of which we speak, for how could a non-reality be produced from the mouth of moveable, tangible man? So reverse mortgages become real, taxes become real, diamonds acquire a value only achieved via language, titles allow kings to acquire power and prestige over any serf; political parties become real as do filibusters, No's, and debt ceilings. And man walks through storms never touching the earth, lost in words, implanted thoughts, boycotts, denials, refusals…never stopping to consider the source of it all.

Language deludes us as we delude ourselves in thinking that language is the means-to-all, a satisfactory substitute for one finger searching for another to bond in common cause. Language deprives us of the need to recognize that all men are naturally, *naturally* equal in species bond, and that what is vital for survival for you is also vital to me and requisite to assume the rights to life, liberty, and the pursuit of happiness. If language deprives me or anyone of these rights, it is solely due to the ignorance of men who delude not only us but themselves as well.

Each of us belongs to this species. With language we communicate as no other species can, and to this language we suborn ourselves. We surrender nature, species' soul, blood and guts to HR 1 and the politicians who have theft their lives and ours to argue its merits…touting language as the holy grail, they as the sole possessors, while 400 families sit on printed folios to control 50% of this nation's wealth. Language…without it, equality.

To the extent that man is duped by language and his powers to use it, so is he removed from species bond, to suffer un-naturally induced ostracism and rejection, forced to wander a desert in search of fellows with whom he could naturally bond, perhaps over a cup of cow's blood or a Coors Light. If man doesn't understand himself and the reigns of power within this natural universe and his place within it, there will be wars, desolation, poverty, bank failures, unemployment, and acrimony over who's right and who's wrong. Ignorance run amok, politicians slurping the effluvia created…by them.

People have allergies as does probably each one of us. My grandson is allergic (severely) to sesame seeds, peanuts, eggs, etc. Chocoholics love chocolate. But how many chocoholics are allergic to chocolate and don't know it? According to figures, many. Is it possible that people are allergic to…language? We watch *NCIS, Criminal Minds, Law and Order*, programs galore themed with murders, killings, mayhem of all sorts, but could any of us live with murders, killings, and mayhem around us as daily diet? So why do we watch? Chocoholics, couch potatoes…addicts who won't look under the covers to find the bedbugs. We are allergic, yet ingest too often exactly that which kills us.

We have other types of addicts as well…people who eat, breathe, digest, expel and toss words…and words…and words, living addicted to a 2D contrivance, language, artificial from beginning to end. But when nature calls, they take a dump. Silently.

We invite the reader to look around, to look at society as a whole and to categorize those of our species who help others with the necessities of life—providing food, water, clothing, medical aid… help here and help there, then categorize those who shill via words and 2D implants—bankers, lawyers, stockbrokers, and of course, politicians. Then, where is the "wealth"? In deed, what is "wealth"? Isn't the common meaning of "wealth" the accumulation of money, "money" an artificial 2D contrivance having no foundation whatsoever in the space/time continuum in which we, asteroids, and chameleons live? If man was not, would money be? If the chemicals, minerals, and gases defined in the Periodic Table were not, would man be? So what are we, organisms to be defined by Dow Jones or by the Periodic Table?

"If you live by the sword, so shall you die by the sword." So too, if we live by 2D contrivance, so shall we die by same, but…*but*, the most natural instinct of man, that underlying stratum upon which each of us lives and dies, whether voiced, recognized, felt or not, remains itching our psyches from dawn to dusk. Something is out of kilter. Something is not right, and you can feel it when a Boehner responds to a Jobs Bill by reading a script and, by watching his mouth closely, recognize that it was even difficult for him to voice what he was reading so contrary to common sense as it was. Script. A-A prime. Addiction to language with man, his species, and his life-drive ignored behind a teleprompter. Witness the Dependent Need.

So too, if we live by 2D contrivance, language, so shall we die by same, but…*but*, if a war is initiated with Iraq based on 2D contrivance by lip-syncs absent truth, justice, or evidentiary justification, upon what basis is blame to be appointed when the titular initiators stood on platforms of 2D construction? Thousands upon thousands of physical organisms carrying drivers licenses are sent to prison for years upon years for dispensing a gram or two of physical cocaine. But thousands upon thousands of "lives" lost in war are not physical. They are numbers, names, and etchings in granite walls. No one can be accountable for digitizing, allotting, or carving script. How then could a death penalty be assigned to anyone sitting on a 2D throne bandying 2D script/language via media designed to transmit such, responsible regarding lives neither seen nor touched? Impossible. Instead, such language-mongers appear on TV touting scripted actions of time passed in show-and-tells, all for 2D moneyed script and praise received via Twitter. Nothing is wrong here?

We live in a sham world. To overcome our ignorance, we weave nets with words, we cover ourselves over with make-shift trappings, we color silken gowns to appease TV critics attuned to their own voices, and honor, in words, statuettes, and tenure practitioners who make overt those latent behaviors we each harbor, imbuing PlayDoh media with time-less extrusions—actors at an Academy Awards or those in elected office on a Congressional floor—those who exemplify what each of us do every day, all day.

We cloak our ignorance in words, in 2D passion plays initiated by 2D script via 2D screens. We greet each other with a "How are you?" or a "My, what a lovely dress!" or render a State of the Union speech to millions of gene-filled, chromosomic DNA patchworks of organism—to us, the speaker having written not a word of it ("Here is your speech, Mr. President. Put it on."). And by spreading words over time like icing a cake with a flat spatula, we pass this existence in a hovercraft, waiting for fuel to burn out.

We read harlequin romances to regurgitate past and possible limbic emotions—to pass this life-time in a felt stasis and to certain our conscious state. We study economics, history, psychology, mathematics plus thousands of sub-divisions to acquire a shade of meaning to suffer through construction of a house, a transsexual niece, the degrees of fallibility of the next Presidential hopeful, or the evening news, then sleep, repeat the process, and believe in the rightful reality of an outcome as centered around, and in, our Copernican ID's. In short, we cloak the world, and us, in language—to hide from the vaporous truths we can never grasp but think that we do by getting people to kiss with words. Language is a cloak yet devised by man to aid him and clan, to avoid tigers burning bright, to learn to grow organic soybeans and to successfully implant an artificial heart valve—legitimate targets in a 4D spectrum.

Switch to 2D and targets enter the Twilight Zone. If you live there, so shall you die there. Language is spread over potential voters like a billion dollar blanket—4D possibilities structured as squares on voting ballots.

The Four Uses of Language

At this point, it might we wise to reduce into one simple section the four uses of language. If we understand these, we'll understand a good deal as to how and why we act as we do. The first we'll call *Now Stuff*.

Now Stuff is the language you and I use every day in talking with people. Purpose: immediate response requested. *Now Stuff* occurs *in time*, *now*, and emanates from 4D creatures—us. Examples: "Pass the butter, please.""Let's meet at 4:00 PM.""Where's the wrench?"

The second type we might simply call *Historical*. Historical is past-obsessive. Historical is readily ID'd as script derived from 2D specifications interpreted relative to 4D human act or interrelation thereof. Visit any book on history. No relationship to now or time-present unless focus upon 4D operators required to make a connection. "Past" occurrences, and as such, *passed*. Time factored out.

The third use of language we might call *Psychic Plasma*. The primary use of Psychic Plasma is to serve as a buffer placating time-onset anxiety. Language here is understood to be temporary and possibly throw-away. Examples: *TV Guide*, obits, editorials, opinions and news, *NY Times*, PBS, *National Enquirer*, etc. If *Tic Tac Toe* comes on at 11:00 PM on Channel 62, fine. It may not…but if the predicted "time" of program eventually merges with the spindle of now-time winding by, then fine. If not, anxiety in proportion to need. Psychic Plasma is transitory, 2D expectations or plasma for a depleting brain hungry for information and material for the execution of solutions. In the main, 2D blither. Major purpose: to avoid anxiety. With Psychic Plasma we can switch the channel, hit "off," and recognize this usage as in-time but disposable.

The fourth language use we might call *Pump and Circumstance*. Why? Well, we do this all the time. We find a circumstance and "pump" it into some form indistinguishable from the original. In the *physi-*

cal 4D realm we find a Model T motor and "pump it up" into the guts of a Sherman tank. Not satisfied with potassium chlorate, phosphorus, and friction to produce a safety match, we pump the basics with know-how and develop napalm, dynamite and missile propellants. The Wright's air-bike becomes pumped into a nuclear-laden Super Fortress. We pump up a single shot musket into a Gatling gun, a Town Council into a war-hungry coterie of ID famished single-dimensional men, a rain forest into a forget-me-not ghetto, and from an "I" and a "God," we construct an Oxford "English" Dictionary from which tagged extracts are selected to pump into Holy Books, given the "right" circumstances.... And language?

When Bill O'Reilly encounters a particular circumstance, he "pumps it" into a column. So does Thomas Friedman, Maureen Dowd, Joe Klein…or Trudeau into a *Doonesbury*, Limbaugh into a diatribe. When Abe visited Gettysburg, we got a "pumped up" Gettysburg Address.

We understand—if no circumstance, nothing to pump. But if a circumstance arises and we have a "dying" need to communicate our involvement with it—since we have the means—language, we do so *in proportion to our need*, and one of our primary needs is the continuation and security of those groups which feed us our ID's. Language both ID's us and permits the passage of ID's in time within a group necessarily evolving in counter-tune with the circumstance which provoked. Get a paper cut? You use language and yell, "Ouch!" Want a protecting group to curry ID development in a poorly producing Levant, and write the Quran. Find a leader who champions the "little man" in the face of religious, political, and cultural oppression and write epistles, some of which become Gospels or pass multiple editors to become a Bible to forge homeostatic ID's for both self and group by means of which might be had the tune for a common, forward ID march—in time. However, while the 4D group "marches on," the 2D supporting platform gets printed by Gideon to rest in motel drawers, *out of time*. There's little difference between an evangelical waving a Bible in the air and the out-of-time Bible itself. Neither moves on.

From a line drawn in the sand to a "Right! Let's go that way!" or from cuneiform and hieroglyphics to kanji, from the Ten Commandments to the US Constitution, from Og's "Ow!" to Shakespeare's "bough," we have a sequence.

Evolution proceeds apace. From the universe on a turtle's back, to the Bhagavad-Gita. From stars as holes in the firmament, to Genesis. From the "decision" as word, to "The Word was made flesh." Yes, there's evolution (The "Divine Design" no less!)…evolution of everything! Evolution of all except—the locked-up and locked-in "decisions" (beliefs!) clothed in carved-out, embedded language—the Flesh made Word and used to defend ID's by establishing group adherence and protective compliance, all conscripted to serve as tagged petrifactions within a linguistic embolism. All for the group and ID acquisition. Language to control the future (which never comes), 2D language to group-control 4D beings. Out-of-time. As such, out of 4D rationality. Deception, reductive, "heaven" in print.

The fourth usage of language, Pump and Circumstance? Illegal. Co-ruptive. Offensive to a 4D evolutionary universe. But those who need it, need it, as Tea Partiers need a *Take Back our Government* sharpied onto placards, as McConnell needs a miniature Constitution to carry in his jacket. No chance of change. Evolution gone haywire locked below a 2D trapdoor. And time sprinkles on….

And what does the fourth level of language have to do with why we kill? Well, first we understand, don't we, that we kill to keep a "house" intact? Of what, pray tell, is this or any house built? Some are built of rafters, joists, foundations, roofs, and good nails fastening all together. I think that we'll find any and all major religions (more so than fibrous political positions) have foundations embedded in promulgated dicta painted to be "universal" ("An eye for an eye," "Death to infidels," "Pray for the lost, for those who don't know the name of___," etc.) studded with beams (supporting paragraphs) upheld by names of dead (but through 2D transportation, still "living"), stuck together with "nails" compressing pressure points, etc. And what are the "nails" *who* do the compressing into form, into cohesive bondage? Well, they may come to your home on a Saturday morning with leaflets and a mantra, or with AK 47's shouting "Do not bake bread!" or they become appointed by ecumenical councils, or they enforce group solidity through coup d'états, or they may invade like ants demanding that you change to ___, or that you vote for ____, or…. So, indeed…why do we kill?

We kill with word or bullet to provide consistent scenarios, to keep our housed ID's intact, for If no culture in which our groups and institutions can survive, we too—our ID's, will die, and then…no more. Therefore, if the heads of tyrannies are killed, *tyranny itself, the "House," must continue* even if it is us, or Hamas or Hezbollah or Abdul Aziz or Fatah or the Taliban or the minority in the House of Representatives each group providing means to exercise a continuum. If no tyranny, no parasitic groups. If no groups, no ID's. Death and dead. And how can we break the bonds which bind? The fifth level of operational maturity. Conjunction. *Fray the perimeters. Talk.* (But to this later, in depth) So, to a rule…

RULE: Threaten an ID and go to war. Restructure a *wanting* ID and enjoy peace.

And who would initiate and thereby prove the stronger? Answer: He who would first open his mouth. ID manners. Emily Post in foreign policy.

So, by their actions do we recognize their needs. The needs of Al Zakari, an Assad, a Khomeini, any Obama-is-a-Muslim Christian Mississippi evangelical and an Obama *are the same*—to preserve those domineering cultures which have served as hosts to groups within which each of the above mentioned individual ID's are preserved. *We kill to keep the house which language built* (for who wants to sleep outside…in the desert?) The world of behavioral man is not flat, Thomas. It's round, and seamless.

But what about Post-it notes, *Wuthering Heights*, the original *Grey's Anatomy*, emails, a college psych text, term papers, or a research article in a Sociological Journal? Let's understand further how it works…

Relational operations in the brain coalesce neuronal "bangs" of comprehension. We have a thought. With this thought we reach for the nearest word tree and pluck suitable tags which might represent this thought or that. We reach for a pen, a laptop, or red Crayola and write, such writing using the plucked words in the order which most closely represent the originating relational operation. But what's the purpose? Let's remember that the limbic system plays a part in everything we do and that includes where we place a period. Is it a

Post-it Note saying, "Dinner's in the fridge" or an email asking for a quick response. Is it a long sit-down by a Bronte sister composing fiction or Sagan writing on the Cosmos? Whatever it is, it is *dimensional reduction to life-less print*. Purpose? Long term storage, food to allow someone else later-in-time to operationally re-construct and perhaps refurbish, to store for future reference, or to put in a time capsule. Fiction comes into play here, as does Grey's Anatomy, as do research articles. *Time is of the essence*. So, we have *ablations*.

Ablations? In your mind, do this: Take a long straight stick—let's say a four foot long broom handle, and hold it on vertical. Slowly rotate it like a drum major's baton to the right, clockwise, until…? Along the "tipping" we find ablations—movements from the vertical, or, in this case, *movement from Now Stuff*, and as we rotate it, all the 2D script of whatever fashion—glyphs, movies, notes, pyramids, etc., becomes colder…colder…until, at -459 degrees, all become immobile, frozen still.

Now Stuff, as we know, is immediate, *now*—participating in 4D interaction. The purpose and time for operational disposition in a 4D STEM universe will determine the degree of rotation. Considering the end of the broom stick as the hour hand of a clock, Post-it notes (operational desiderata) might arbitrarily come in at 1-2 seconds ($65°$ F, "Do it soon!"), emails one minute ($55°$ F), completed term papers 3 minutes ($45°$ F, *Historical* starting to play a part), a *NY Times* fiction bestseller 14 minutes ($34°$ F, *Historical* and *Psychic Plasma*—for both writer and reader), *Grey's Anatomy* at 25 minutes ($32°$), and then past the vertical—past 6:00, we find British Petroleum's by-laws ($30°$ F, lightly frozen), all types of instituted laws—civil, criminal, constitutional, etc. ($-90°$ F), the Quran ($-200°$ F), the Bible ($-300°$ F), the Torah ($-375°$ F), and at $-459°$ F, $E = MC^2$.

Grey's Anatomy, the book, was for more than research. It was to serve as a foundation for anatomical insight, for how often does human anatomy change given the correctness of the *Anatomy* (But information changes, therefore slightly above freezing)? The linear-induced intent was for the *Anatomy*, as the Oxford English Dictionary, Viking maps, or research and findings solely devoted to the physical or relational operations of *humans as a 4D species*, to remain transposed, dimensionally reduced to 2D print, and to last a long time. But the key:

6:00 o'clock—the freezing point! For when the needle of act, in time, begins to turn created 4D-extracted operationally induced 2D cuneiform *back toward its originating author* with script *frozen in place*, look out! For this is when the night-crawlers and bed bugs come out…the witching hour, when Moby Dick consumes Ahab and the Mullahs and the Falwells start cannibalizing themselves *believing* in the reflected sonar, when Little Sir Echo comes alive mirroring in reverse image, like a Chucky, the behavioral effulgence of whoever is watching, mirroring, but disappearing (where?) when out of mind like the light in a refrigerator. Belief…in a faux world. For when inked and created out-of-time 2D nether worlds—religions, i/e groups, etc., begin eating at the brains of their 4D creators, refugee camps start dotting landscapes like scabs over festering wounds…all to preserve the ID integrity of 2D act frozen, created, lying in nests purposely placed outside of time, umbilical cords out of mind, covered over by a purdah.

Language in Freeze Frame

History has shown that sometimes events just come to a head. One of the main reasons discoveries tack in time is that terms lay wanting. Find the terms and doors open. Over these hundreds of thousands of years man never knew what he breathed until oxygen, nitrogen and trace elements were discovered. So does it go with language.

With language, two terms open the doors: *relations* and *physics*. Without either men stumble in the dark trying to find the door. Let's open it…

We know the relations (Chapter 3). These relations apply to any and all interactions between/among molecules, events, emotions, every action within the brain and body, billiard balls and cooking lasagna. But then again, so does physics…apply. Absent relations, absent physics…everything stops.

All language is metaphor. No 2D script can capture the nuance of a two year old picking his nose or a gull in flight embossed on a setting sun. But we try. We use whatever power 2D script can elicit in a reader to help his brain paint a picture or visualize a sequence. To understand what's going on in the brain during all this, we have to slow it down and take out a relational "microscope."

You've seen, I'm sure, a picture of a bullet in freeze frame—half way through a sheet of paper…half in, half out, or droplets of extruded milk suspended in mid-air after a drop plopped into the bowl. Freeze frame. In pedantic language we might say *hypostasized*. Ever do the same with language? Let's, but first, we have to get our terms straight so that we are "speaking the same language."

Statistics is a branch of mathematics dealing primarily with probabilities. Statistics, however, is both an art and a discipline, like medicine. One of the major factors within the total branch of statistics is just that—factors. *Factor* can be both a "noun" and a "verb." "A factor to be considered here is…." Or, "You forgot to factor X in…." Or, "Remember to factor Y out…." Factoring either in or out is directly connected with *variables*. Both statisticians and professional polltakers are familiar with variables. Accurate results from mathematical machinations depend on the accurate recognition—as far as possible, of pertinences. Example: Conduct a poll as to the probabilities of Mary Kay being elected President of the United States. Who will you poll? Just those with telephones? Illegal immigrants? Women only? Socio-economic position? In New England only? Voters who favor Roe vs. Wade? (Not a variable?) Etc. Leaving a factor out or bringing a factor in will directly affect the outcome. Important. Enter the fray….

Forensic anthropology is defined as *the application of physical anthropology…usually for the recovery and identification of skeletonized human remains* (The Free Dictionary…online). Yahoo lists 13 forensic fields. *The Wikipedia Encyclopedia* lists many more together with such fields as forensic art, fingerprinting, nursing, psychiatry, toxicology, computer, engineering, entomology…even college speech competitions. Mention is made of Sherlock Holmes and Dick Tracy, users of forensic methodologies. One field isn't listed. Language, inscripted!

Any forensic pursuit involves reconstruction of motive, cause, agent…from trace elements usually left at the scene.

RULE: The examination of an isolated sentence, removed from the STEM spectrum in which it occurred, is forensic in nature, void of any determination of causative meaning.

This is the "linguistics" of old—of Chomsky, Quine, Miller, Jacobsen, *ad infinitum*. To take a sentence (just construct one!) and analyze it this way or that and then back again, and forward once more, is quite similar to an anthropologist examining the footprint of a dinosaur in a dry mud flat in Colorado. How big was it? What was it? When did it walk here? Did it use Crest or Colgate? Remove the trace element from STEM and someone is walking on glass. Deduce, induce… but the answers will never be found removed from the STEM tide in which the originating action occurred. To fabricate a 2D sentence for examination progresses further into fantasyland, a fantasyland we use to kill each other. Conclusion: We must never equate, in kind or degree, scripted words ensconced *absent time* with language used within discourse, *in time*. To equate the two in any fashion is to corrupt the dimensional STEM station in which we all sit. We then ask the reader to consider if any wars, animosities, filibusters, No's, or disruptions to species welfare ever resulted from precisely this corruption.

Words and the Brain

There's a difference between us and a Martin's putty-nosed monkey. We can operate sets with flexible ease. An operative necessity. How did we develop this functionality? We can only guess… Somewhere along the line Og no doubt took steroids. For the brain. He had to because he couldn't cope with the mathematical probabilities of inter-relational sets.

Elsewhere we look at human groups and the mathematics of the numbers of inter-woven relations between and among members. Staggering then as to implications, Og couldn't cope. So, what did he do? The only thing he could do…he subjugated all the members capable of inter-relating into a single set, and sub-setted them! We do this all the time. Go into a vegetable store, examine a few veggies which don't pass muster and dismiss the store altogether! Don't like followers of Farrakhan? Dismiss the entire group, as a set, or accept as a set all those who hate broccoli. That's what Og did to his peers. How? He called them a name. Dings. All those others in that other group over the hill? Those he called Dongs (think history). And, all— he and his neighbors, became sub-sets to…well, what are the "container sets," the "basket sets"? Right. *The names!* For if each individual, each item, each plant and star in the sky could only be considered each as a set with the brain incapable of grouping, their would be no hierarchy and, with no hierarchy, no "tag," no handle with which to grasp a group. The brain would go bonkers. Our monkey doesn't work with sets. Our monkey works with one banana at a time (usually!). He sees one and goes for it, sees another and goes for it. With us it's "Hey, Joe. Look at all the bananas!" and go for a beer.

The brain is nothing if not efficient. It needs tags, words, under which incidentals, items, members, groups…can be tossed about without lifting a finger, or sword! And that's why, and how, words developed. But they're not really "words," are they. They're *sets*, linear sets constructed by extracting, as we can, from four dimensions, two (physics!)…to etch a wall or to construct "mother sets," "basket sets," within which and under which, the individuals, the singulars now reside without the brain having to survey the probabilities of the inter-relations with which each of the individuals may operate. Subset people and reap the benefits of an ease of purchase. Work only with basket sets and individuals become incidentals, and the reader can understand where this leads….

Think politics and put yourself into any one of the sets our politicians tag…conservatives, left-wingers, right wingers, liberals, purchasers of books online… Aren't we each in particular buckets, as are all members of the Taliban, the Hezbollah, Democrats, Hamas, the Tea Party or whichever? But we don't work with people, members of our species, operatives with limbic brains like us. We work with tags and coalesce commissions to counter groups which thrive on other groups tagged as *their* A primes—dependency upon the runes of language run amok, ignorance visible in committee chambers.

Words (names) are one-dimensional, freeze-framing time as they must so as to permit a consistency of recall…over time. The backside is, of course, that in freeze-framing time, they cannot, individually, entertain time unless by serving as a relational repository, fuel for a 4D transponder.

Words are nexi, the intersections you find in *MapQuest*—not labeled, just led to, then left. Words are time-encrusted linear applications of the brain sticking sounded phonemes in time to junctions, capable of being plastered over with artificial flat lettering when called upon. Words are chimeras, phantoms, existing only in pockets of brains fleeting hither and thither. Nowhere located, they come to the fore when travelers on neural highways need signposts telling directions to and from. You don't see intersections marked in *Map-Quest*, just a "go here…then there." The ellipsis is the spot where each very personal brain sticks a traffic light—a word. Stay under the signal and you'll never move. That's a word…static, artificial, man-made, with no meaning whatsoever unless those roads either traveled less or more are highlighted. Your politicians use these "words" and have absolutely no idea as to their proper use.

When a word is learned…whatever the word, some associative context must define some aspect of meaning. When presented with a new word, say *pomegranate*, the word just doesn't sit there, isolated, no peripherals to guide the brain to meaning. Associated may be *tree*, or *fruit*, or whatever. So, when a new word presents itself, the brain goes to work. The brain, in short, Googles itself sending out feelers to the various "servers." "Hey, vision cortex Area six…anything in your repertoire concerning a red round fruit full of red seeds?" And the Area six server searches itself, comes up with *past experiences* which may be relevant and shoots off same to frontal cortex, coupled with input from olfactory servers, joined with input from the hindbrain to the parabrachial nucleus in the midbrain via the taste area of the thalamus via the taste area of the cortex including the central nucleus of the amygdala if taste may have been involved, joined with input from the motor cortex if any physical manipulations regarding peeling and eating were involved, etc. In short, we do know that all incoming sensory information except smell goes first to the thalamus—Grand Central Station, shunting data to the appropriate "servers" for processing. If *sounded* words come in, again the thalamus performs initial processing, completed by the auditory cortex which itself is surrounded by the language cortex…spread over most of the temporal lobes, squeaking into both parietal and frontal lobes. If music comes in, "Each component…pitch, melody, rhythm, location and loudness—is processed separately, then the parts are brought back together and reassembled…."[9] All involves memory—the main function of servers—and is coalesced by what Alan Baddeley of Bristol University calls The Central Executive, which "…coordinates information from a number of sources [servers], directs the ability to focus and switch attention, organizes incoming material and the retrieval of old memories and combines information arriving via two temporary storage systems"—A phonological loop and a visuo-spatial sketch pad (explicit brain areas).[10]

All relevant past experiences provided by the brain's "servers" fuse within the frontal/language cortex *and get labeled*! Neuroscientists may argue as to just what constitutes the "language cortex" or its precise functions or just exactly what constitutes "consciousness" or whatever. I simply know that "I know" and am conscious (aware!) that I know, eat, use chopsticks, that I'm awake and answer to a variety of names.

Words provide the labels, the tabs to my brain's files—files stored in a manifold number of servers resident between my ears and below. "San Francisco" means for me something different than for you. "Love" means something different for me than for you. Any word…*any word* in my brain's lexicon means something different for me than it may for you precisely because of my past experiences, emotional involvements, and whether or not I had malt vinegar on my salmon. Might we agree to this? If we agree, then let's examine the 2D-4D connection, words, their backside, and dip our bare feet into the wasteland of past political incompetence and attempt to appreciate how our "leaders" lack of understanding of the nature of language and words literally *kills*, an inadequacy and incompetence developed in our elementary schools! Really? Are we saying that *there is a direct link between the way our children are taught in Kindergarten and first grade, and our soldiers dying on foreign battlefields?* Answer? Yes.

Have you ever, *ever* had a word in print *speak to you*? Really? ("The Bible *says*…, the Constitution *says*….") The brain is wired for sound and the body to receive it. Hence, one of the most pervasive, pernicious assaults of ignorance upon the developing child is the practice of the "whole word" presentation of words, a practice espoused by the ALA and the NEA. Not phonics, for that would aid a child in imbuing known sounds (named classes) to unknown "words" (unnamed classes) so as to employ ready-made brain servers to recognize, interpret, and store relevant information, thereby accepting the logicality and nature of human cognition—which works entirely in terms of *sets and their interrelations*! With this in mind…

Has the reader ever come across an elementary curriculum in which words were considered labels, tags, *meanings determined by their interlocking and dependent relations*? When Mommy says, "Here's an apple," the kids don't think anything other than *apple = this red fruit*. They have no room for the consideration of anything other than *word equals thing*. No counterpoint nor relational source ever taught, for early children are told, "This is a C, this an A, and this a T. This spells CAT," and the children move wooden C's and A's and T's into their proper slots...cold, hard proof that C's, A's, and T's are *things* and shall be so through all school years and thereafter into the infinity of constitutions and holy books. Relations...? They have no idea. So let's realize a few basics...

We reify words. We *count* them as in "Write a 200 word essay, children" or watch Word tally the number of words typed at screen bottom. We give them names—pronouns, adverbs, interjections... paying no heed to the nature of interrelations of one word with the next. We spread words across time as with a spatula...across constitutions, Bibles, House Bills and bumper stickers giving nary a thought to the operative interrelations involved to decipher...interrelations providing the sole avenue to glean comprehension and the "teachers of reading" lead their students as lemming off cliffs, save for those children whose natural operative natures rebel and who drop out to preserve integrity of mind.

We worship words realizing with our limited capacities that no return to any past is possible, as Hawking demonstrates, so we juice up today with word-anchors in hopes of stabilizing communal platforms on which political parties and social networks might wend the day...*No taxing of the wealthy, Our right to bear arms, Life begins at conception* (ignoring the natural 50-50 chance of natural terminations and survival rates), *Corporations are people*...and nine justices translate words knowing not a whit of the operative relations or the bases in STEM physics which support their mumbles.

However, we have people who glean from sub-strata the bases of operative function. Sommerhoff[11] takes one sentence: *John throws a blue ball*, and divines the interrelations demonstrative of the basic operative relations: *identity, inclusion, exclusion, disjunction, and conjunction* from which some 120 nearly instantaneous relational operations are required to comprehend this five word sentence! Then Hawking (a physicist delving in relational-language?) writes...

> "If you remember every word in this book [*A Brief History of Time*, 197 pages][12], your memory will have recorded about two million pieces of information: the order in your brain will have increased by about two million units...This will increase the disorder of the universe by about twenty million million million million units—or about ten million million million times the increase in order in your brain—and that's if you remember *everything* in this book."

Hawking is counting *words*? No word count can equate the distance from Tuscaloosa to the Eagle Nebula. But relations can. So...

When a President calls someone a tyrant, another a dictator, another a dissembler, another this or that, and several nations an *axis of evil*, well certainly, "educated" as we are, *they must be such* since *words are as much things as things are.* And how interesting is it that after elementary school, kids drop out...and in high school, more drop out, but thousands upon thousands remain, struggling through "remedial" readers trying to locate in life the things which each thing-word represents, moving fingers, sequentially, slowly, left to right, word to word. And what are we left with? Kids who consider words as things and use them in gang warfare or perhaps to get jobs in which reason is not required. And we, older, call each other names, and yes, sticks and stones do hurt. They're real things! Never relate, never trace connections to an inter-locking source. Never reason, never attempt to peer under the surface, to co-join in reasoned debate. Rather, cling to words...words like *conservative, right-wing, liberal, lefty, Christian evangelical, minimum wage*, and dropped words (Just pick them up. They're things, after all!) like, "Yes, mistakes were made" and without reason, if picked up, session ended. So...

Do our vocal leaders know the difference between words and things? They don't bandy words about with no idea as to consequence? They never label actions, actors, or events with words which stick like superglue? Listen to your politicians and commentators with brain-lock hurl words as if they were buckshot, steel-tipped arrows, or simply, mud. Words aren't things? And where do they draw the line…at this country's borders? Before you send your son or daughter off to war, collect, if you would, all the localized and current bombast, all the words-as-things which, minus defining source relations, instigate hostilities. And will anyone, any leader outside of our own responsible country, pay heed to the nature of words as interrelated within the operational storehouse housed in people's brains? Maybe. Then consider your "Education President," or Governor, or School Board, or textbook publisher, or mandated curricula, or in-line university, or your child's XCAT's and ask your new high school graduate, "What did you learn about words, language, relational operations, your brain, human groups, cultural impacts, or how to think?" Dear reader, we are in the Middle Ages of operational, relational psychology and our children have no teachers.

The Backside of Language

Society and community developed in time. Remnants of Og's society are with us still. However, to keep our signifying phonetic repertoire intact, we supply missing terms for those 4D STEM "forces" we don't understand like Thor, Athena, Eros, Neptune, Krishna, Vishnu, The Rain God, Buddha, Allah, Christ, God, neocons… If we don't have the understanding or realization of the physical underpinnings of happenings, we can group gaps of understanding within other groups and *label them* using any of the above terms and thousands more. We can pigeon-hole these gaps and get on with our lives comforted in the knowledge that others can accept these same pigeon-holes, even worship them, and still partake of an earthly mission to participate within an evolutionary schema, the same schema within which all that we see participates and evolves, but through language, ignore. But problems have developed in tune with solutions. Indeed, that very language which liberated our species from near-total physical dependence has now enslaved us.

Language is of no value unless shared within and by a community, be that community of two people or millions. And, as a community becomes bound together by that language which fuses all of its users into common bond, so too does that language become a totem, a community symbol displacing the 4D STEM universe from which that very language emerged. The tokens, the symbols, the signifiers in language, to remain of use *must divest themselves of any possibility for evolutionary change so as to remain meaningfully constant ensuring homeostatic stability among community.* As such, its users become devotees and the language itself transports its victims, literally, to a world uncommon to Einstein. Language free of STEM constrictions becomes the pathway to visions *extraordinaire*, a pathway to worlds, universes, spectra defined solely through the demands to adhere, to employ its 2D vehicles to describe and to enter a 4D world of choice as the brain may so wish to interpret. Select a stream of words, in whatever language, in a particular order, and one could use that 2D-created private vehicle to transport any 4D user into a brain-constructed, now operative-enslaved 2D world of choice. And it does. And we, its users, fail to see the implications for and from its diviners. The world will not end because of nuclear puffs but by what this reader is looking at, and speaking...streams of words...words that create, words that kill. But who understands this power of language? Mullahs? Reading teachers? Nations' Presidents? Congressmen?

Language is a Trojan Horse, a "gift" perhaps, or a succubus leading each of us to cliff's edge, we without a compass. Each of our *vitas* is clothed within the cloth of 2D which we either bear or facetiously exalt, suffering time expanse until our moment of *in extremis* curtails the façade.

The problem here, in its raw form, is that not only is each of us veiled under coat upon coat of linguistic varnish, but the repercussions get buried beneath. If words alone define me, I am lost. Yet how many of us live lives cloaked under layers of deceit never to poke heads into open air.

We can't see the relations of which language is built, but they're there. We can't see the *relations* which form our basis for being—that unseen platform upon which *everything* in this universe is built. We can't see the *relations* which bond those of our tribe together. We can't see the *relations* which fuse our species into one body. We can't see these *operations* executed within our brains every nanosecond of every day. But they exist. We write of them, use them, and as invisible, unknown yet derivative, elevate ourselves via these operative relations to a platform visible on TV channels worldwide. We are a species which uses our relationally caused ID's to kill others over ephemera none of us can see but readily die for, with others who use the same operations to proclaim "There is no God but Allah" just as the poet wrote "Mary had a little lamb." We kill the physical for want of brain-sight into the relational.

For to understand man, we must understand language—2D language scripted through ink squirts or deposited via the ear into data banks. Hidden from view with nary a thought as to how or what gives language its function, this true language which we can not see, touch, dance to or smell, this true language buried under tons of 2D rubble makes each of us blind, walking without a white cane into a manhole.

C's and A's and T's

If C's, A's, and T's are real (participatory of all four dimensions—Space, Time, Electro-Magnetism, etc., as are all things within this universe), then all documents of whatever kind containing C's, A's, and T's are real. If money—both coins and paper, contain C's, A's and T's, they too are real. If all words, written or spoken (the latter if derived from written form) contain C's, A's, and T's, then they too are real. However, if words (spoken or written), documents, and money are *not real*, the only conclusion reachable is that all STEM participants of transactions among such fabrications operate under and within *belief systems*. If such is the case and each of us, STEM real as we are, engage such belief systems for daily commerce, we must be operating in confidence games, literally. The question remains: what then is real within all this intra-human commerce? Answer: inbred operational relations (excitations) enticed through and by artificial stimuli, artificial contrivance designed to provoke STEM response within each of us. What then is the bottom line as to what is *really real and only real* within human interactions? Answer: operational relations…synaptic convolutions within individual brains.

This then means that the *Summa Theologica* of St. Thomas Aquinas is not real-ly real? The books are real; they have substance and can be lifted. The pages are real as is the ink which microscopically can be found to have substance. All else is artificial contrivance for the purpose of exciting neurons in my brain as in anyone's. Money…artificial, as is the U. S. Constitution and any book, holy or not…artificial contrivances invented to store out-of-time cuneiform, hypostasized glyphs…linguistic code only, capable through proper ingestion for a relational excitation of neurons. Artificial also…the political platforms of any party, the No's exhaled in bad breath from minds similarly constipated, the financial folios of the 400 richest families in the U.S., all denying by proxy the need of a mother to feed her child or the need of a father to work for family sustenance, artificial cuneiform on paper his payment. Islam requires the open admittance of slavery to Allah. Our culture requires the subtle repression of slavery to the whims of religions, tax codes, constitutions, political parties, and alphabets created by the roadside, food for scavengers who crave only the dead.

The Constipated Terrorist

A terrorist is anyone who, with "cause," instills fear into another, even to the point of death. The degree of fear imposed by the terrorist is directly proportionate to the degree of fear "felt" *within* the terrorist—mild to extreme.

It is said that no one can love another unless he loves himself first. The same goes for hate (emanating form the inside), or terror—which is simply another name for deep, systemic fear, first internalized.

A terrorist can be a tyrant, a king, a President, a neighbor, or those of whom we hear on CNN—blowing up this or that seemingly without purpose. But purpose there is, and it goes to the very core of human behavior…universal human behavior. And so we ask, what does the terrorist fear? Answer, with a twist (we've already seen a form of it): the terrorist "fears" (not consciously, of course) the exposure of a realization that the vast, vast majority of his species peers is living under a net of betrayed relationships, that something is deeply, deeply wrong with not only himself but with the social order from which he derives his ID, and that he too has been betrayed to the core, but to expose the root cause would mean a cataclysmic overthrow of his entire social order. What's wrong? To Og…

Og got started with *Now Stuff*, "words" (possibly grunts) to indi-cate immediate needs...possibly *er* for "water," *uff* for "run," *guh* for "food," *oo* for "drink," etc. No alphabets, no "language" inscripted, no OED, just the basic basics. Then someone started making nota-tions...marks for numbers, pictographs for words ("wine [symbol] in this amphora"), developing into sophisticated markings for sounds... cuneiform, hieroglyphics, ideographs, kanji...and along the way, someone else thought, "Well, if we can make symbols for words, so can we make symbols for star gods, nature gods, animal gods, tribal names, emotions, or whatever we think governs the world, parts of it, and its divisions." So Osiris got a symbol, as did the Monkey god, the weather god, the cat god, the Long Legs in the other valley, and on and on. Things got dicey, however, when Trudeau started drawing historical events on the cave walls—the Red Baron killing a wart hog, tribal members warring with the Short Legs from up north, etc. 4D act "recorded" in 2D, transduced, dimensions altered. So to today...

It shouldn't surprise us when utilities used daily come back to bite us. We live in houses. All is fine until a typhoon blows out the walls and the roof caves in, or a kid steals in in the middle of the night and drowns in our swimming pool; or a semi-trailer which smashes into the side of a car killing all inside, a car which can take us from home to work and back again... With language, no difference.

We use language to communicate. We are not language. We *use* language as a commodity, a tool to purchase beer or to assuage a contretemps among siblings. As a tool, language contains imperfec-tions...imperfections unseen but noticeable to the aware physicist or to anyone conscious of the dimensional houses in which we each live. Language, by it very nature, stores 4D act within 2D rubrics whether sketched on wood, canvas, linoleum, paper, papyrus, dollar bills, or stored in the digital cracks of CD's, DVD's, Wal-Mart servers, or in brains. We, however, continue walking around the court on New Bal-ance sneakers. Disparity...disparity when the Supreme Court relies on 2D ancient script to equate Grandma Moses with General Electric (disparate dimensional protocols lost in the wind)...disparity when a seeded document forms the foundation for acceding tenure to an incompetent President whose incompetence becomes the cause of thousands upon thousands of un-needed deaths...disparity as language facilitates the storage of epic, fable, event, historical act, political divisions, gerrymandered districts, or belief with the same ease in which it stores the names of branded beers, neighbors' names, or any push-pull act required in the course of a day to get to work. There is disparity among pin-stuck appellations stored in 2D lexicons flittering among our four lobes, and a simple desire to get a glass of water. The terrorist can't distinguish one from the other, a 4D requisite appellation for necessary act from a 2D transcripted nexus of "foreigners," "infidels," "communists," "Muslim," "Pro-life," "Quran," "Bible," "Hamas," "Likud," "Democrat," or "Republican." And he sits down for dinner and wonders why he has trouble digesting his calamari marinara. [The brain is not a blank slate, as we all know, Steven. It's the chalk, passive to the hand that uses it.]

And the terrorist gets constipated, not knowing why, simply aware that his brain brooks no difference between his marinara sauce, the Epistles of St. Mark, the admonitions of Mohammed, or The Book of Mormon. Appellations, nexi, and if able to eat one, why not the others?

We have no anti-allergens to protect against the cobblestones and tribbles abundant in languages worldwide. Minds adapt to language ingestion, formation, and retention but are equipped with no digestive tract to eliminate indigestibles via a colon. As the brain sits, so does its retentions, not considering the formulating sources. We are each poisoned by non-Now Stuff…alphabetic, linguistic formulations which are absent concourse within a 4D STEM world. We choke, unable to vomit out the germs of concatenated bias, terms, rigmarole fabricated to ID and protect groups from this and that, and in so doing, split this species apart, its members riven at every country's borders and tribal reach. We kill ourselves through and with creative contrivance, embossed by word into 2D lexicon, and strive, with our epididyan urges, to conquer, stifle, destroy, yet to dominate, mindless of the nature of mind and the food it ingests. The Terrorist? He "feels" the schizophrenic nature of himself and strikes out—directionless, ignorant as to the cause, simply urging surcease and the tranquility of a brain at rest.

"Shiites?" "Sunnis?" "Christians…Jews?" "Alawites?" Liberals, evangelicals, right-wingers, conservatives…all cobblestones and tribbles, thrown into the linguistic sluice box, bouncing, roiling in maelstroms of incestual bombardments, the gold of peace sitting quietly on bottom level…the peace of men who recognize the value of what they are…men all, the gold at peace ever mindful of the shams of mountebanks each claiming 4D dominance, slurry, all in time to add to the slag heap.

Chapter 5

LINEAR MAN

Linearity is not language. Linearity is the disposition of man to create artifacts which extrude *time* from STEM (We are here deprived of terms. We will use SEM—minus T for *time*, or *linearity* as stopgaps.)

If man excises time in whatever manner, linearity results since the cause—hypostasis, creates an effect, necessarily. Whether the effect is oral or not, an effect must occur if in no manner other than via synaptic connections. In the overt physical sense, such creations may consist of obelisks, pyramids, a Buddhist temple, a curbstone, 9 X 11 inch copy paper, a Mona Lisa, or a comb. If it has an edge, a line, or was created to forge permanence as a basis for human discourse, as a foundation for human act or belief, or for the protection of ID's, it is linear as is a*nything* created by man which has induced permanence, fulcra around which men may gather…for discourse, trade, the Olympics, or the Book of the Month Club. Such are the words you are looking at as well as programming code which allows identification of my wife's CD's. A cypress tree is not linear since participatory within time and nature.

All human groups of whatever nature are the effects of SEM creation if designed and instituted by man absent natural cause. No exception. If, however, *spontaneous* groups are formed to sandbag a river, flee from a tsunami, put out a fire or to rescue a drowning man, SEM is not in play since action was caused by a natural time-in STEM cause. It is obvious then that all *designed* human groups are necessarily based on SEM foundations and are therefore independent of natural STEM cause and are consequently artificial—creations only. SEM groups then may be defined in one of two ways: either beneficial to species or not.

If we bring linearity to the fore, with concern given to current group practices with which we are all familiar, we may then acquire a bit of clarity regarding a few episodes of behavior—Bernie Madoff, CEO bonuses, the value of money, and even the Tax Code. First…

Bernie Made Off?

Four guys are sitting at a poker table. The host says, "The blue chips are worth ten bucks, the red five, and the white, one. OK?" All assent. The host could have said, "The red are worth ten bucks, the white five, and the blue, one. OK?" Nothing in the chips changed. The only "accidental" difference among the chips was the color. All four players consented to the first evaluation assigned—the blue valued at ten, etc. The conclusion of the four that the blue was to be so valued had no basis in STEM. The relational operations, consistent among the four players, was, however, STEM based—synapses + accouterments working. The conclusion as to "values" was *derivative* from man's operational structuring and it was the derivative around which the players coalesced. Derivative agreement reached, play began.

But so is it with whatever financial instrument one would care to mention. Credit cards? CD's? Paper money? Name it. Value *assigned and derivative* through mutual consent, executed within STEM based crania. Words pinned on a donkey. "We all consent?" Belief in a unicorn, tags posited, relations accepted in common. The same as Charlie Brown's Great Pumpkin, or _____.

How then can one commit a crime when there's nothing to steal in a STEM lexicon but *belief*? Madoff didn't *steal*. What he did was *violate a taboo* embedded within a story line and, as we know, violators of taboos are ostracized…a long standing practice. What is a taboo? Formally, any taboo is a social custom restricting behaviors or association with a particular place, person, or thing. We could define a taboo this way: messing with a social custom in which derivative ID's of millions are ensconced is taboo. If you "believe" that "money" is real, then "stealing" it must also be real. Operationally, of course, if everyone "believes" in the reality of money as ID supporting groups without which we would die so believe (within this society), "money" must perforce be "real" and the functionaries behind Wall Street, AIG,

Lehman Brothers, the Federal Treasury must be actually working *for and within* 4D STEM reality. True? Of course. And the tomato farmer? He doesn't have to "believe." He grows crops so that we "believers" can continue…to "believe."

So, to Bernie (and Scott Rothstein—our local ponzi expert and Ponziers galore), we pose this question: "What were you intending to do? You and your kind have been around these thousands and thousands of years. Inherent within you is a most powerful g/e thread compelling you and yours to expand, reproduce, develop and adapt in every way possible within your environment…and you come across a scam which only you (or so you think) recognize—preying upon the belief of a culture that something is there, when it isn't. What will you do…ignore the opportunity or use the operationally ignorant to fulfill that push, that desire promoted by your g/e pulse to adapt, grow, and expand to fulfill nature's calling? You got 'caught' for adapting and profiting thereby? We can't *believe* it."

Why would one "pay" $51,000 for a hip replacement unless both the patient and doctors (and the insurance company) *believed* that an artificial numerical "commodity" actually existed equivalent to a physically induced piece of metal? Why do we "pay" Wall Street "fat cats" (Obama's term) outrageous "amounts" and take offence thereby unless such "payouts" were actually STEM-real in a cultural setting which accepts the "reality" of money—2D ephemera in exaltation while the commonality of species is denied? The "substantive" base for ID acquisition of species rests digitized in the vaults of Citicorp? We study with an accounting book in front of our faces but never what resides within he who "accounts"? Nothing wrong here?

Do we realize that every society, every culture operates, and has operated, on *belief systems*, each of a linear foundation? Why such attempts to hide this undercurrent of understanding with a stamp of 4D STEM behavior, AKA "approval"? This brings us to…

Bone-us's

Bonuses differ from rewards. Bonuses are given to confirm fealty to cause. Receiving a bonus confirms the "authority" of a Board to bestow; giving a bonus confirms the recipient as a "productive" member of a class (caste). Take the Oscars. Receiving an Oscar confirms the Academy's "authority" to bestow; giving one confirms the membership of an individual who "enhances" the group's status. Rewards, on the other hand, cross disparate classes. Giving money to Doctors Without Borders equates with rewards for work well done, by non-doctors—the givers. We will reward the winner of a 50 yard run in a Special Olympics, but not give him a bonus.

Bonuses *always* serve to validate the artificial ID's of participants of a group imprimatured by 2D Articles of Incorporation, which leads us to a most reliable rule...

RULE: The greater the bonus, the greater the distance of participants from the activities and ID's of *natural* STEM man and species core, thereby impelling their greater need for ID validation as compensation.

A man picking tomatoes (an immigrant perhaps!) has little need for ID validation. However, a man pushing options, treading insurance actuaries for returns on policies, determining interest on a 30 year CD, or shifting accounts from stocks to bonds, does. The latter deals only with 2D contrivance.

Bonuses are therefore incestuous in every instance—tokens given, in whatever form, for enhancing performance "beneficial" to group viability...ID enhancing, in other words. The male gives; the female receives. Both consort. Such give and take equates with prostitution by whichever sex if within class for "services" rendered. However, bonuses are anathema to those who perform for species' good, such as a Mother Theresa or a politician who would argue for species' advance in the face of those who would stop time with a Rider to a House Bill. It then becomes easier to understand why banks are reluctant to loan money to those without, or certain politicians who would stonewall monetary incentives to those lacking—the poor, students, schools, women and mothers in need, the elderly, those who need to cross dilapidated bridges to get to work or immigrants who work but have darker skin... The integrity of class (caste) must be maintained at all costs, prostituted membership of no consequence. To specifics...

Consider the social, species' viability of the NACD, the National Association of Corporate Directors...

The NACD meets four times a year, members receiving from $80K to $260K for their enlivened endeavors. The purpose of the NACD—

to set compensation packages for corporate executives and their own compensation in proportion. One member of NACD, an NStar CEO, sits on Liberty Mutual's Board of Directors. A Liberty Mutual's board member sits on NStar's. Many of the NACD members sit on the board of The Bank Of America. NACD board members belong to the same golf clubs, own homes in Vero Beach, Florida, etc. This august body handed Ted Kelly (retired CEO of Liberty Mutual) a $50M retirement package for four straight years resulting in Kelly receiving compensation 100 times that of President Obama, more than the compensation of all U.S. Presidents combined, more than the total salaries of all U.S. senate members combined…or about $24,000 *per hour!* Brian McGrory ("An Untimely Reward," *Boston Globe*, April 20, 2012) writes, "The characters in "Deliverance" weren't as incestuous as these boards are interlocking." Incest recognized? Indeed. Delving into psychoanalytic repercussions of the Epididyan Constant and the seminal drive for communal fusion, here's why…

Released from the prohibition of sexual incest by the development of language and 2D affiliates, incest by proxy emerged, satisfying man's ID need for immersion within *groups* free from the forensics of DNA evidence. "Liberated" from the restrictions of sexual coitus among kin and tribe, language permitted governance and monetary coitus to rise as compensation. From such cohesive immersions artifacts both to promote and insulate groups' ID's as caste classes became developed and given free rein…money free from burdening taxation, xenophobic insulation against immigrations of classes antithetical to the caste composition—non-productive elderly, students, children, mothers and women, potential "non-us" voters…extraneous ID's made exempt from entrance.

The prevention of exposure of monetary castes as antithetical to species' welfare demands maintenance and protection by both board members and an Imperial Guard, members of which today sit within Congress comfortably disguised in variegated dress as sentinels armed with killing "No's," vetoes and filibusters, both on guard and patrolling the perimeters as watchdogs, each denying responsibility for the excesses of an NACD (the Dodd-Frank Bill?). Bonuses are stipends for in-time STEM icons of the moneyed, party classes whether bastard offspring from governmental negligence or not, each grouping supported by tithes demanded from forged classes of untouchables.

Excessive, extreme bonuses enter STEM only via outstretched hands engaged in consenting trysts. The lie of deceit, the lie of guilt, the lie of ignorance, the lie of sham. But that's why prostitutes are hired. To play the "game." Leadership? Yes. We all need leaders. But the purpose of a *leader* is beneath, supporting groups through ingested incentive, not from aloft, floating in ether awaiting payment for "services" rendered. True leaders follow, behind, and should be paid in a proportion relative to the highest paid worker (as in Singapore) along, of course, with compensation for expenses associated. Otherwise, it's theft from the common good. But, with our inability to distinguish 2D out-of-time artifact from 4D in-time act, we equate the two, unable to see the difference.

By 4D STEM operative act we "bestow" legitimacy and "truth" to the fiction of ink scribbles wherever applied. The questions must then be asked: to which orders of "reality" do we accord precedence: to live, developing, each-one-is-different STEM children *or* to the "results" of linear out-of-time "high stakes" casting (as in *caste*) tests which have no relationship with the neuroplasticity of a child's brain…to the right of STEM citizens for universal health care, *or* to drying ink on a 2D Constitution's moldering page from which Supreme Court justices etch their ID's…to workers producing, *or* to CEO's of banks, insurance companies, or hedge funds who verify the "legitimacy" of 2D artifacts with outstretched hands? There are priorities deeply buried, and kept so. And this species of which we are all a part? Hidden under the back flap of a bank book.

The "Value" of Money

Every coin, every paper bill is "stabilized" as to value by the Federal Reserve and by the community through consent. Any amount of money invested in a Put or Call equates with the same amount spent at a grocery store for family food. Any problem here?

What is the constant? It matters not to what use the money was put…it's value remained the same however used. For bread, for milk, for swaps, options, derivatives…the value remained the same. *But the purpose?* We, without placing value on the purpose, surrender all, *all* value to money and warp our ID's thereby.

We surrender to a narrative the notion that money is fixed in statute and stature. "Money," however, is but an artifice, a means by which men might transact business of whatever nature without sacrificing a daughter, a camel, or a bushel of salt. Unseen, soul sacrificed, modicum and narrative players ensconced within vaults overseen by "economists" who parlay the game into chapter and verse for that is exactly what "economists" do…they enliven the script with maxims, formulas, "psychology" even, to make the story line palatable. Is it any wonder that Brad Pitt and the CEO of Merrill Lynch are "paid" as they are? Both are paid to enforce narrative story lines—one on screen, one via a ticker. Try…

The Fed and Bernanke. Writing about Bernanke and the Fed in *Time*'s "Person of the Year" (Bernanke) '09 issue, Michael Grunwald assays…

"The economy, after all, is a confidence game. That's why financial analysts use psychological phrases like "jittery markets" and "economic anxiety." It's no accident that the word *credit* comes from the Latin word for belief."[13]

So yes, the case might be made that, like the financiers and governmental officials who both promoted and allowed the financial meltdown of '08 and '09, Madoff should be put before a firing squad and awarded this nation's highest civilian medal for making transparent the behind-the-scenes narrative in which he lived (not only "lived" but ate whole unto indigestion) and then literally shot—not for committing a "crime" but for the extent to which he violated the taboo regarding the "reality" of "money," derivatives from positive, species-promoting, custom-afforded interchange, so useful around the world for purchasing bread, rice, water, mosquito netting, and a sheltering roof.

No dip of fingers into Holy Water is necessary to gain entrance into this church. Just possession of an acceptable credit card. "Believers" unto the Imams, the Popes of Wall Street, the SEC, the Federal Reserve…none of it the "truth" and so impossible to be set free. One for all, all for one…unto bailouts and economic collapse. Worldwide, as is the church. Belief, unto extremis.

The true value of money can only be measured proportionate to the promotion of species' enhancement, value derivative from species' creation and STEM nature. Any other use constitutes second tier make-believe (*tiers* below). Simply,

The true value of money can only be determined by the use to which it is put. Does the reader have a set of knives in his kitchen...a bread knife, cleaver, paring knife, chef's knife, fillet knife, garnish, boning, cheese, carving knives? They're all knives but each for a distinct purpose. A dollar spent for a loaf of bread does not equate with a dollar spent for a municipal bond, nor does a dollar spent to pay a utility bill equate with a dollar spent for a margin call. *No tax code can be viable unless distinctions of purpose are defined relative to the use of "money."* Such involves class distinctions. Such involves a new and different look at fiscal responsibilities. Such involves the determination that finance houses parlay monies useful for the basic maintenance of life into schemata which siphon life-blood, literally, into digitized vaults devoid of meaning. If any regulation of castles of finance is deemed necessary, the determination of categories of monetary usage is mandatory.

Tyrants and Sons, Inc.

We must be dispassionate here. Toes will be tickled and we must have reasoned discourse. We begin with a question...

What are the commonalities between Kim Jong Il and his sons, Saddam Hussein and his sons, Moammar Khadafy and his sons, tyrants innumerable and their sons, and Mitt Romney and his sons? Whoa...! We are relating these? Well, yes. How?

We know that Romney's portfolio is "worth" ¼ billion dollars. He allots ("gifts") each of his five sons $1M per year ($13K is what the rest of us can "gift."). And he's running for the office of the President of the United States. (Any similarities so far?)

Why is it that *some* wealthy men strive for high office? What is there in life other than "wealth" accumulated or inherited? Why is it that The Donald endorsed Romney after calling him a "small time businessman," Romney apparently on stage (February, 2012) to be the Republican nominee? Why do tyrants, in office, often accumulate billions, in gold or otherwise, leaving little or nothing to the citizens of those countries "ruled"? What are they after? What do they need?

Between any two ears is but one brain. With this brain we choose chocolate or vanilla ice cream, measure cosines, relate this to that *infinitum*, and believe that the roof won't fall in. We believe. We believe (or posit, giving limited probabilities that such will turn out to be the case, but always without solid resolution), for *whatever we believe in is not* and cannot be accountable now, in 4D STEM time, for if "it" were here, *now*, with cause accountable, there would be no impetus for "belief." We believe only in whatever *isn't here*, now, either through physical presence or incontrovertible verification.

There's not a human being on earth that doesn't believe in something…that it will rain some time, that the sun will come up tomorrow, that someday he'll meet the girl of his dreams, that the stew will be ready in thirty minutes… We must believe, for we live in progressive time, time never ending but always, *with each of us,* in the knife-edge presence of *now.* When we cease, so will our conscious awareness of time…the now, now, now of time calling each of us to live, to do something, to fulfill our epididyan determined destiny as ecology, climate change, and as a total environment would allow. *Credo.*

If one brain *can* believe in one thing, so can it believe in another. It must or we're dead, each of us. This same organ which can believe in God, or rain, or Osiris, or an outcome of a Superbowl, can also believe that a pile of printed, negotiable paper money on a dining room table can buy a porterhouse steak. We need to think this through…

A pile of money on a table is worthless, worthless unless another person comes along who believes *also* that the pile of "money" is negotiable for various commodities. Sticks won't work, cribbage chips won't work, outdated lottery tickets won't work…only that pile of paper money can "work" if *two or more people accept it as negotiable* for this or that. If we have two or more people, what do we have? A group! Therefore, "money" has value *only by group consensus*, an *imprimatur.* So far so good, but we have to go deeper.

The brain is a three pound physical organ. Physical. It "knows" nothing of spirits, ghosts in the night, a single-horned white horse with wings or the orbit of Saturn. But we, with constructed "tags," provide nexi for possible operations relating this to that, that to this, and so instruct the brain to *record these tags and to impose them upon the relational operations* within which we imbed these tags. The brain doesn't and can't *know* a Pegasus, but it *can* both know and "understand" *the relational operations* involved when we hit the "recall" button to have the brain dredge up from its repertoire tagged relational operations executed in times past.

The brain doesn't want to be made a fool of, so it, naturally, "assumes" that what it is working with is "real." And to keep the ruse alive that it is always working with *only* what is "real," the brain, efficient as it always is, "suborns" itself to a common commodity if it must continually work with other brains which think also that "money" is real. Meaning... it's not going to go through a reality check each second while on the floor of the stock exchange. It has work to do, "commerce" to conduct, inter-brainial interfacing to execute. It subsumes its nature to function as instructed.

Modern automobile motors can run with ethanol in the gasoline. Some can run on compressed natural gas or converted restaurant oils. The motor is designed for one purpose: to run the car. If the fuel input isn't viable, it won't work, but the motor will "try" with whatever's put into it. The "motor" consists of all the relational operations set and ready to go when the ignition is turned on. The ignition? Any tag. Just key the brain (the "motor") with a tag and it starts. The first operation is identification...then it waits for further direction... the next tag, and the next...until you hear it operating, and humming. Every brain works this way, in time, processing linear 2D tags which start the 4D STEM neuronal process, just like a key inserted and turned in your car's ignition switch. Every brain works the same, if toggled into the 2D tag spectra. Every brain. It's collective. It's unconscious...automatic, universal across species. It's Carl Jung's "collective unconscious" (one of Freud's disciples). "The collective unconscious collects and organizes those personal experiences in a similar way with each member of a particular species," writes Jung. (Wikipedia) Stan Gooch (*Total Man,* quoted also in Wikipedia) elaborates..."certain structures and predispositions of the unconscious are common to all of us…[on] an inherited, species-specific, 'genetic basis."

The brains of us all are more than similar to each other. We are a species after all, but the intent is clear: just as a baby Van Clyburn can hit his first note on a piano to later become a concert pianist, so can the brain couple a known tag, "convertible," with another known tag, "bond," to create a "convertible bond," a creation devised by Charlie X to exist outside time for the purpose of financial communing among millions of people to either create or lose "money." And the familiar brain plays the game rather than rise to the surface in mutiny. Schizophrenic, sure. Better this than dead. And "belief" becomes a "reality."

Consider the brain's servitude to communal legerdemain, the "collective unconscious." Consider the tyrants and brokers who delve in Dungeons and Dragons all day long…believing, but underneath? You can keep a lid on the brain only so long. But sometimes the brain's owners feel something…a tingle somewhere…that something isn't right, hoping that the nagging doubt will disappear or go deep undercover. The tyrant feels this doubt if he has a brain, the slightest sensitivity as to what is real…or not, and is a species member. So what does he do? He resorts to species bind, to those closest to him…not to those distant who also "play the game" but to his heirs, his sons, and implants upon them his reasons for doubt in the hopes of safekeeping. Money, his fractured ID bequeathed to his sons… viral, genetic, DNA…in a Swiss bank.

Take a bag full of twenty dollar bills and sit it on a log among the isolated Mashco-Prio Indians of the upper Amazon. Then turn, hide behind a tree, and switch to video on your IPhone and record what they do with it. Question: Is it any wonder that, communal as we are, those with money choose to associate with others with "money?" Would Trump endorse a mendicant running for office? Why, oh why might we ask, do A Prime Republicans want to restrict the poor and disenfranchised from voting unless…*unless* those without money are restricted by forced happenstance to lack the accouterment capable of *enforcing the beliefs* that what the "privileged," the "moneyed" have, is *really real?* "But my sons are real…my progeny. Surely they won't lie to me! Surely they will give body to my beliefs and prevent the disclosure of the sham under which I have constructed my life!" Isn't this the same with nepotism everywhere...dynasties of kings, presidents, hand-me-downs confirming the righteousness of cause, effect, and lives lived solidly entrenched within the known cement of this species' nature, but not?

Chapter 6

ANATOMY OF A GROUP

Anatomy of a Group

People tend to think of a "group" as a quantity, a number, like "a quantity of ducks," or apples, or kumquats. If you want to "count" people, do so. But it's not a "count" of people which throws hand grenades or worships a cat. We need to know what constitutes the relational interplay among members of groups, why both may function as they do, and how to distill the focus of those groups which harm the species.

Books upon books have been written about human groups. Probably the onset of group examinations could be put at the foot of Moreno and his classic, *Who will Survive?* Erick Fromm wrote his share. Exemplary. Then Russell, Ortega y Gasset…. One could go on and on. But we're not going there.

To understand a group, we have to understand the individuals who comprise the group. We all belong to groups. We have to, to survive. But groups, like each of us, are different. Why?

Every group is *inclusive.* That is, any group must include/acquire members for its own survival, maintenance, and support, and each of us must belong to a group for those same reasons. Common to both is the fact that the ID of each—members and groups, is obtained through the nature of membership. But it goes deeper than the obvious.

It can be said that any group takes its ID from the ID of its members. In a way, true. But not in any way complete.

A group, like an individual, is a ID'd set. With an individual, accumulated experiences—physical and mental, constitute his ID. With a group, however, *the ID is linear*! It must be, since it cannot "consume" the ID's of its members. A group can only ID itself in terms of this...or that...and conscript supporting members. If a member joins, he willingly accepts the terms of "conscription," unless of course, compelled by force. Nor is a group 4D. Its members are, but the group falls under a name, defined by a linear purpose. If no name and no purpose, no group. The ID of a group does not equal the ID of its members, individually or collectively, and that's what we have to examine, both to understand the group and, when it comes to it, combat.

Each of us is hit with a double whammy—the language(s) we use and the groups which use them. Both are invisibly seductive. We will survive if we transcend each and that we can do only if we understand the pull, the needs, and our position within the mix.

Each of our ID's is derived from the "outside"—from parents, peers, teachers, gas station attendants, school crossing guards or whomever. If no one else was around, we'd each go through life naked to the core—no ID, no name, no who-am-I, no what-am-I...nothing. Just a reactor to life's random stimuli. But people tell us who we are, all supposedly tagged under a "name"—Joe, Alice, Henry, Jose, Maria, Rico, Achmed, Liu.... We are told what social class we belong to, what we should and shouldn't do (which constricts our activities) and what we should do to garner ID food.

Picture a foursome standing together under the awning of a Starbucks, each speaking a language unknown to the other three. What would be the bond holding them together? Slip and slide and away each goes. No glue. Add a common language and if each isn't there to further discover self-ID through group immersion, the earth is square.

We need groups for the ID psyche just as much as we need air to breathe and water to drink. Our consciousness is our awareness and this ties in directly with the vicarious nature of groups.

There is no "Islamic" DNA within any of us, nor is there DNA which can be genomed as "Catholic," "Buddhist," nor "The Seventh Day Advent of the Second Coming." There is no DNA directing affiliations with political parties, social or fraternal organizations. So, where do organizations/groups come from?

Any group begins with one or more individuals. Why? For the usual. Self-protection and ID nurturance. Are any groups specifically altruistic, engendered with the goal of benefiting, in some degree, the progress of the human species? Yes, of course. The Red Cross, Doctors Without Borders.... OK, now join one. Who, now, are you? "I work for the Red Cross." "I am a Girl Scout." And what is the first word used? "I." ID acquired. Goal accomplished. And the group?

Any member of a group must acquire the ID of the group. There's no halfway here. One is either "in" or "out" (unless an ID is sufficiently strong to execute a departure, having first, however, acquired a secure inclusive base to permit exclusion). But here's the rub...

If anyone can "leave" a group, a prior ID must have been sufficiently developed prior to allow ID removal. But what if a singular group is so "powerful" and the individual ID so weak that no ID could be attained absent the group? What if the group's dictates, strictures, and "commandments" ricochet off every room of the house, in the kitchen, dictating what could and could not be eaten; off the walls in the bedroom, dictating who should sleep here, or there, and how; off the entrance-way, dictating the dress of those entering or those leaving; off the walls of the library, dictating what could be read and what not and on and on? If such is the case, the true species-driven ID of the individual is lost.

Picture a Christian conservative President of the United States (a member of "X" group—Christian conservatives) urging that "Y" group enforce "democratic" voting ("Y" group is that group described in the previous paragraph). The result? First, we recognize that every individual in the Y group has no ID apart from Y-group membership (Such was the goal of the group, instilling strictures and social policies on each individual within the swath of its sweep, from birth). Second, "democracy"—the universal right of vote, has no basis for acceptance in Y group's members' ID's. Third, it is rather unlikely that a sitting President, himself (herself?) a member of an "X" group, could either understand or appreciate the difficulties of establishing individual awareness of operative independence within a member of Y group. Why?

If a group is 2D based and I am 4D by nature, where's the mesh? I need a group. I join. The group, 2D based, is essentially antagonistic in some manner to my 4D essence. Conflict. To stay within the group, that group from which I have acquired my social and present ID, is to maintain ID source support. Highly important. But then, at some point, what if my 4D head starts to rear up, to seek a natural inclination to…eat pork? To slaughter a cow to feed my family? To rebel at forced time-enclosed life-periods within a constricting school building? To not bow to Mecca five times a day because my natural inclination is to lead, not to follow as a flock of sheep at a cry from a minaret? To take "arms" (literally) against a sea of inequity because I have been short-changed by a society which taxes the poor while the rich have their accounts off-shore? To vote for a raise in the debt ceiling, not against it? And on and on it goes.

So who's the neurotic? Nature is more powerful than any group. I want a good, satisfying, naturally evoked and socially acceptable ID. If I can't get it through this group—and I understand myself well enough to know what I want, then I'll opt out. Call me neurotic, but natural. And so to war.

It may be fatuous to say that every war has been caused by group inclusion. Maybe, but true. Factoring out the need for self-preservation in the face of attack, every war has been caused by the initiating instigators of group inclusion. We think it rather necessary, therefore, to understand the nature and power of groups and their effect upon any individual's basic and primary need for ID verification.

Which groups (not a President!) were instrumental in causing, perhaps initiating, the war in Iraq? The Korean War? Vietnam? The War of 1812? The Civil War? The Peloponnesian War? WWII? One man doesn't do it…nor two…nor three. There are some very simple rules to determine Who Done It….

RULE: Any group which requires the definition of another group as an A prime for the purpose of ID acquisition is automatically anti-species.

RULE: The greater, in degree, that a group excludes parties from membership, the greater that group is predisposed to war.

Which group calls outsiders "infidels"? Which group calls non-group members "gentiles"? Which group calls others "liberals"? Which group cancels baptisms if one of the parent-members drops out? (Answer: Mormons, without even asking God first!) Let's just list…

"Non-believers" (and the Crusades), "Americans," "Capitalists," and on and on….

A linear society lives in two dimensions. Likewise The Educational Testing Service within a chiseled 2D environ. The children, adults, and teens they purportedly "measure" are 4D. *A linear society exerts no degree of latitude into 4D nature.* That's why testees are only given the opportunity to bubble in A, B, C, D, or E on high stakes tests with no opportunity given to express levels of degree of confidence or assurance which would do nothing other than express *ID maturation, an attribute only of 4D STEM individuals*—relative to the points under question. But that's not what the ETS wants. The ETS wants, *needs,* to discriminate—for the future salutary health of itself and of a linear society! Why mention all this…?

A linear society promotes linearity. 4D focus—species-specific, is antagonistic to linear productivity. Capitalism is linear. Communism is linear (You can watch the ticker tape, watch Mad Money, count the linear bills in your wallet, purchase a Trump seaside mansion on the Gold Coast of Florida for $125 million—but only if you have the linear numbers!) Why do your kids get A's, B's, C's, D's, or F's in school? Not linear?

Any group is *per se* group-specific and vies for *permanent* ID stability for support, each group member reinforcing his ID as he sees fit. To the extent that a group buffers itself in linearity, to that extent is it *anti*-species specific. Therefore, to the degree that a group is restricted by its beliefs, borders, and statutes, so is it removed from species-interest concerns and is openly susceptible to an A prime counter-attack. Then, if attacked, what might be the normal response?

RULE: To the extent that a group self-buffers itself for the purpose of ID verification and protection, to that extent does it offer ID food for an opposing i/e group to acquire an equality of strength in opposition—for *its* ID protection and preservation. (Remember, for every A there's an A'—necessarily!)

NOTE 1: This rule applies equally well to the splitting of atoms as it does to what it really describes—the causes of war. Interesting, isn't it, that the same rules which apply to group behavior apply also to those properties identifiable with the smallest particles of matter?

NOTE 2: Those familiar with the writings of Edmund O. Wilson, Harvard sociobiologist (*The Social Conquest of Earth*, 2012) will note that this work is in some ways but a permutation. Individual members of groups—ants, termites, etc., will Indeed fight to preserve groups (their own or others) but *not* for altruistic purpose. As Wilson once wrote, "an individual without a group is dead." So is it with man. This work focuses on the singularity of man and his absolute need for group membership. While Wilson focuses on the sociobiological need, we focus on the human need to acquire, maintain, and protect the ID—the primary need of conscious, aware, language-driven man. Wilson may write, "Individual selection tends to favor selfish behavior. Group selections favors altruistic..." We disagree.

Any group contains virtually the ID's of its members. The primary directive of any human is, as above, the acquisition and protection of his ID—who and what he *thinks* he is. This directive must be incorporated within the Articles of Incorporation of any group if such group is to be viable for human membership. Otherwise why join if not to garner ID food, protected at the same time? Certainly ants will die to help in the preservation of their group as will soldiers on the battlefield. Ants, however, do not possess the language-processed ID's of trillion-synaptic humans who, dependent as the ant, understand the burdens of *time-encrusted* data-banks of experiential input. With humans, if the founding groups upon which their ID's are totally dependent are destroyed, so then must be destroyed any basis for the establishment of consciously aware ID's. Of this they are conscious!

A human group becomes altruistic only if upon conscious consideration, group members alter the prime directive in its founding Articles to pave way for act beneficial to species—the larger group/set of which any smaller group is but a part. Too, if our primary goal in this work is the defeat of extremism, it is to that functionary element of human behavior—the acquisition and protection of ID's that we must direct our endeavors. Understanding the precepts and protocols of the Taliban, of an extremist Minority Senate leader, or of a solidified Supreme Court Judge in terms of the needs of each to preserve its ID's, is *the only way* to effect change...through the exposure of anti-species, poorly constructed, untenable ID's.

Belief—All Day Long

There are, it is estimated, about six or seven meanings per average for every word in the dictionary. Words have, therefore, equivocal or analogous meanings. Obvious. With *belief* we have to specify terms to get the train on track, but even then we'll find that belief itself is a phantasm, a linguistic construction sitting atop relational operations. Let's enter…

A little old lady (LOL) who says, "I believe I'll have a butterscotch sundae," uses the term in verifiable context and in-time. For *believe* she could have simply said, "I *think* I'll have a butterscotch sundae." Not what we're looking for.

There are really just two kinds of belief: the first is tentative, in-time, probability of execution high with alternative paths available. The second use of belief entails group commitment, out-of-time reference, probability of realization approaching nil, no alternative paths accepted nor possibility of escape. Of the first: "I believe that I'll go to the dance." Of the second: "Christ is the son of God."

Belief ties in most intimately with ID, inseparable unless analyzed. "I believe that Judaism is the true religion. If you can prove me wrong, I may change, but realize that I have been indoctrinated from birth to so believe and if presented with proof that my life has been spent entertaining a false premise, I will not think highly of myself." Khadafy ruled Libya for 42 years, well beyond the average age of Libya's citizens. They knew no other despotic leader, singular though he was. Khadafy's troops fought the rebels because they had no other choice; no alternate ID source available. Their *belief* in the sustainability of Khadafy as a loggerhead of ID support and stability was palpable, enough so as to take up arms in his defense. From whom else could they receive ID validation? Change ID affiliation for sustenance to an unknown alternate? To whom? And this is why, my friends, ID's must be the target within any "war" or attempt at regime change.

Any ID which has been developed on the basis of belief is as a tree dependent upon its roots. Remove the roots and the tree dies. No war can be envisaged or designed without taking into close consideration the replacement of dependent-need belief-based ID's without supplying compensatory alternatives for the replenishment of ID food. Any war undertaken without these considerations will result in manifold deaths, unnecessarily. Guaranteed. The consideration of native ID's within any population must be a benchmark within the foreign policy of this nation. Further…

We cannot separate belief from relational operations at any time, in any manner. The two are inseparable. "Belief" in God does not differ in kind from belief in a Biblical sponsored pro-life platform or that Obama was born in Kenya. After all, the primary concern, the primary element within this conscious universe for any one of us is our ID… our individual, conscious, aware, ever-operating ID. Now, how do we buttress our ID's with foundations suitable for confident act of any sort? If not educated, learned into the operational physics of human behavior, we have to attach to something "permanent," something around which we may act like children running around a stable maypole. It is not satisfying to work through life as a rowboat twirling around and around in a maelstrom. We need a cornerstone, each of us, and upon this cornerstone, we must construct an edifice—like the third piggy, of brick. Then, what's closest? What can we reach out to and touch if tangible need is required? Well, for many it was a Khadafy (or substitute a "leader" of your choice). For others, improvisation is required.

A Watchtower servant comes knocking on your door and, after you open it, says, "God has a new form of governance!" with a huge smile. "Thank you," you say, smiling, grabbing her proffered leaflet and closing the door. God gets peddled? We don't serve God. God serves us…as a linchpin, as a cornerstone, around which those of us untethered to operational reality might attach a steel link of *I believe* and move on with some sense of security. It's the same with a Khadafy, or a Palin, or Bachmann, or Beck, or Limbaugh, or a House majority leader. Attach an ID and obtain in return security and reciprocity. ID fulfillment, each and all with the same need: to fortify, secure, protect, maintain, and acquire ID's not subject to any angst of operational doubt. But then our leaders want a "regime change" in Pogoland? Change the regime, my friends, and you dislodge the maypole. What then? How will you dry yourself after a shower if the wife removed the towels? If no satisfactory alternative to the removal of a quantitative maypole, the result will be, without question, death upon death like dolphins beached, suffocating, lining the sands from end to end. And how might we sustain this orgy, these episodes of deaths, bodies buried in communal graves too numerous to count? Simple: restrict funds in whatever way possible to fruitful student-first education—*anywhere and everywhere*; keep the "leaders" in power and keep ignorant the masses who might otherwise yearn to be free…of their "leaders."

RULE: The possibilities for either a belief or an ID are non-existent apart from group membership.

RULE: The greater a belief's distance from the verifiability of 4D reality, the greater the need to establish defenses for the belief's protection and the believer's group-sponsored ID.

So, where do beliefs come from? Obviously, any belief must be rooted in cause—an emptiness of understanding, of knowledge, of an unfathomable answer. Beliefs don't pop into our heads out of the blue. They develop, are permutated from the *relational operations* of which each of us is capable, but only with the tools at hand. The issue is one of *probability*—that issue with which the mind works continually, every moment, every day, but if not invoking probability, then belief it is.

Probability has a 4D STEM base. Useful would be a verb to shorten expressions such as, *I consider the probability of rain to be…*, or, *The probability of snake eyes (on the crap table) is 6 to 1*, or, *The probability of Jethro at the front door is fifty-fifty*. Nevertheless, these sub-junctive (no joining) propositions are dependent upon the *unfolding of time* to reveal 4D in-time answers, but answers are divinable. With *belief*, answers are *undivinable and non-verifiable* since outside concurrent time. Waiting 'til the cows come home won't help. So, let's understand from which viewpoint we're working. Beliefs—fixating probabilities to an unverifiable source negates in-time verification. "I believe in astrology." "OK, prove that astrology works." You can't? Belief. "Defeating the Health Care Law will reduce the national deficit." "Prove it!" "Oh, you can't?" Belief.

You read a word here…and another. What are the probabilities that the next word will fit into the context of the discussion so as to provoke meaning? Something is going on in your life at the very moment that you read this. What are the probabilities that, whatever happens next in your continual evolution in time—either through your initiation or through an external stimulus, you will act and respond correctly (similar to Pinker's Theory of Expectation)? If we didn't utilize such a mechanism—one of pure probability, our actions would be as chaotic as a ping pong ball in a hurricane. If someone says, "Believe that a rescuer will come!" I will 1) "believe" in the professed "believer," 2) pit his need for a rescuer against the facts as I know them in the present environment, or 3) accept and join others expressing his belief so as to not be excised from the group. *Belief* is a 2D word. So are *poltergeist*, *imagine*, and *pepperoni*. We can only do what we can only do.

So, what do we do when we "believe"? We transduce. We reduce to 2D from 4D with the ability to reverse—induction into reduction. We don't "suspend belief." We *engage* it. Same process. All natural, all human—an ability of those of our species. How can we identify with actors? Because we do what they do—become different people at different times. If we did not do the same, how could we identify with a "sweet" Anthony Hopkins in one instance and revile him for his "evil" nature the next? *We are different people at different times.* We can identify with this. Therefore, our ID is what it is—a *set* of accumulated experiences, physical and mental, stored within the synaptic vaults of our brains, any portion capable of being brought to bear given the situation. So, let's conclude with this observation: *The improper use of language screws us up.*

So, what do you believe in…whatever, whoever it is? Do you believe that Allah is all merciful? That Christ is the Son of God? That God spoke to Moses? That Christmas will come? That there will be fewer hurricanes next season? That the Democrats will win the '16 election? Osiris? Whatever…whoever…. Following is a blank line. Write in any, any belief you have, OK? Do…

Fine. You used words, in whatever language. To do that, you had to use/apply relational operations. You had to denote a major reference and relate attributes, actions, motivations, positions, characteristics…whatever. Correct? Where did the operational relations come from? Were they built into your brain's natural operational networks? With Neanderthals, probably not. Just primitive grunts and groans with pointed fingers. Ah, but with language…referents, classes, sub-

sub-classes, exclusions and inclusions, conjunctive and disjunctive relations. The works! Indeed, the relational operations which each of us use to process and construct language are the same operations we use to count, ask for a beer or state a belief…the same operations everyone on earth uses to accommodate any word, in any order, in any relationship, for any purpose—in time. The intrinsic operations upon which language is built also become those operations upon which sand castles are built…sand castles, in all too many instances, which become as "true" to the utterer as "Charlie, it's raining out!" And why not? Who is to deny that Heaven is not just another Moishe's Deli, as I say it is? Language, but not language. The relational operations… the mortar upon which all thought, every idea, every wish and supposition is built. The backside of language. And with these relational operations which are peculiar to man only—incapable of use by God given the negatives, exclusions, privations, limitations therein—we kill, maim, and do to species irreparable act while a President yells "Bring it on!" to our "enemies" so as to build their ID shell to do just that. And they do.

If anyone *believes* that what he says is correct (or simply says it to satisfy an ID need) while ignoring the A-A' underpinnings of relational behavior within the operations constructing his "belief," he can start a war. But that, my friends, is why they do it, perverting language…a way to keep occupied after all, before curtain drop.

Any belief is an attempt to either deny or suspend STEM so as to incorporate a conjecture, a possibility within the structural nuances of language. Any stated belief of any nature whatsoever is a language-stated relations-built linear conclusion of a relational operation. As such, say what you want. Believe what you want. Simply realize that, in so stating you can never leave that 4D universe, that STEM spectrum within which this universe turns, grows, and passes time. But propose a belief, dismiss time, and fall into the well. Any "I believe" is an assertion that 4D STEM is out of the picture, and that includes time. But if you, or anyone, can escape the *now* of time, we'll buy you lunch.

There is an adjunct to this relating as to *why* we must bend to strictures (words) upon which a group is formed. Example: If a group incorporates into its group-feed a doctrine dimensionally reduced to either print or "tradition" or whatever, to not uphold those implants would be to destroy the "foundation" upon which the group rests. In other words, if a doctrine so states that *non-members* of the A-home group consist of "right to lifers" or "unbelievers" or of slanted eye or darkened skin or of a group not-so defined as amenable to group A, in order to sustain the ID of the home group upon which its members depend for ID food, action will "justify" exclusions even if such "action" is nothing other than an increased confirmation of group attachment—for ID food. Affirmation of a belief is therefore equivalent to a union card, a B.S. degree, a PhD, a passport or secret handshake allowing entrance into a cartel, sect, club, coven, church, synagogue, mosque, Taliban, or a political party.

People must believe! It's a Catch-22. Whatever the beliefs are, to keep the ID food larder replenished and food kept coming in, the group, which believes such and such, so and so, or this and that— must be supported even unto death for the sake of siblings, parents, cousins, or votes…all those ID feeders whose ID food would be forfeit were the group to fail. Therefore, groups have to be protected at all costs.

There is no other word the use of which has killed more people than the word *believe*. Want to be an Indian Maoist? *Believe with us that...* Want to join our local Taliban subsidiary? *Believe with us that…* Want to make money through L-swaps? *Believe with us that…* And you will find no human group which does not exact from its members a compliant, affirming *Yes, we believe with you that….* Believe, and join. Don't believe and isolate yourself unto a lonely hermitage. Human groups. Believers. A's and A primes. And physics? Force = Mass times Acceleration. Take it from there.

RULE: People would rather believe than know.

Why not? It's easier to have a belief. You don't have to prove it. If someone says that they "know" something, a "prove it" response entails research, backup, evidentiary protocol. Any statement of a belief then shows nothing other than group membership. "I believe, they believe, and that's our group." And, since belief can only be supported by group adherence, conjunctivity can never obtain *unless the ID is free to depart from group belief since group can never rise above an i/e operative level*. The individual in any i.e. belief-group is a prisoner. Between the solidified, welded group-ID and the conjunctive ID of individual operational freedom lies a world of difference in both degree and kind. Within a group-meld, is escape possible…? Let's look at **faith**…

The direction of faith is not up. It's out. Sideways.

"Have faith!" someone says. But in what? Not in God, who is out-of-time eternal, offshore, non-tangible and non-participatory in our STEM universe. For God, no 2D and no 4D. So, since out-of-time and never in it, God can't entertain *time* to receive either the beginnings or ends of our pleas, either of which would involve in-time operations. Therefore, in what, precisely, are we to "have faith"? Answer? *The group.*

RULE: Faith is the belief 1) that the ascriptions of one million bending bodies can't be wrong, 2) that the ascriptions of the group in question are "correct," 3) that the ID food received from the group and which is incorporated within the ID's of its individual members is correct, and 4) the ID of each individual member is not a sham.

"Having faith" is simply belief that this group which feeds us ID food and substantiates for us ID's, is valid, on the "up and up," tied in correctly and totally with the principles governing our 4D STEM universe, and that our ID's—absorbed and constructed from the group's 2D ascriptions—are also valid, ecologically correct and totally within tune with the governing principles controlling the movements of protons. If not, our ID's—derived as such from that group, are shams and we have wasted much of our lives absorbing and executing in shadow. Our brain, efficient as it is, does not like being played upon. Nor do our ID's. "Have faith that your group is correct!" (No admission of the possibility for error!) And why do we thereby fight, engage in wars, and blow up school buses? Answer: to preserve the supposed integrity of falsely constituted groups from which are derived falsely constituted ID's, and to keep hidden the secret of lives spent in the sham of operational deceit. Conclusions follow:

1. Since groups operate under particular astrictive protocols, no singular group practices universal (read "species") principles (unless so specified, conjunctive in all aspects and STEM based, e.g., Heifer.org). As such, each group is thereby inclu-

sive/exclusive (i/e) denying the generality demanded by a universally conjunctive protocol and is thereby necessarily false if it ascribes to any "universal truth" non-STEM based.

2. All of the fallen—those dead, battered, maimed who have left families with frozen tears, have fallen because of false dictates, false ascriptions, false protocols if demanded by groups which espoused doctrines supporting anti-species behaviors and insular inclusive doctrines.

3. As each of us in this universal species become bare-boned, skeletonized, and subject to stacking along the walls of tunneled crypts irrespective of prior in-life group memberships then merging fully *into time* without recourse to 2D subterfuge, our *time-less* creations become the fragile constructions only the few of us know them to be. Al-Bashir and Ilk? They kill...to hide the sham, too painful to recognize. But then again, so does (Let the reader choose) _____ .

Finally, to underlie our examination of belief from an operational viewpoint, let's first attend to some research into political behavior... domestic here, transferable into global...

The Boston Globe offered a July 2010 article by Joe Keohane— "How Facts Backfire,"[14] which presented research by Brendan Nyhan of the University of Michigan and by James Kuklinski of the University of Illinois a Urbana-Champaign. Conclusions reached by Nyhan...

- "Misinformed people, particularly political partisans, when exposed to corrected facts in news stories, rarely changed their minds. In fact, they often *became even more strongly set in their beliefs*. Facts, they found, were not curing misinformation. Facts could actually make misinformation even *stronger*...

- "It's absolutely threatening to admit you're wrong. [Backfire] is a natural defense mechanism to avoid that cognitive dissonance." [i.e., to avoid threat to ID integrity]

- "We often base our opinions on our *beliefs* [which] can cause us to twist facts so they fit better with our preconceived notions. Worst of all, they can lead us to uncritically accept bad information just because it reinforces our beliefs. Worst of all, they can lead us to uncritically accept bad information just because it reinforces our beliefs."

Kuklinski, researching 1000 local residents, concluded…

- "most people will resist correcting their…beliefs, but also the very people who most need to correct them will be least likely to do so."

Keohane concluded…

- "Participants who self-identified as conservative believe the misinformation on WMD and taxes even more strongly after being given the correction. [The stronger the attachment to a belief, the greater the threat to ID sovereignty if subject to correction.]
- "People tend to interpret information with an eye toward reinforcing their pre-existing views. If we believe something about the world, we are more likely to *passively accept as truth any information that confirms our beliefs, and actively dismiss information that doesn't.*

But…

- "People who were given a self-affirmation exercise were more likely to consider new information than people who had not. In other words, *if you feel good about yourself* [independent ID] you'll listen—and if you feel insecure or threatened, you won't. *This would explain why demagogues benefit from keeping people agitated. The more threatened people feel, the less likely they are to listen to dissenting opinions and the more easily controlled they are* [and the more ID gain for the demagogues. My italics].

These results are not surprising. We have all argued with people of like dispositions. The problem involves working around and through these stonewalls of ID protection for simple reasons: group beliefs cause war, dissention, mistrust, and, of course, extremism…to the extreme.

From our analyses of belief and faith we can come to rather specific conclusions:

1. Any belief must be stated within a language.
2. All languages and all thoughts are constructed via relational operations.
3. All operational relations are executed *in time*.
4. No thought or belief can be constructed *outside* of time.
5. Since no belief can escape time during construction, it is impossible to commerce with a posited *out-of-time* referent.
6. Therefore, the only value beliefs have are to serve as slogans or delineated positions of groups.

Given the above, a re-read of Keohane's work in the *Globe* might be profitable, considering in the re-read the dependence of each group of answers upon group immersion and dependence. *Beliefs are tie-binders and relate to groups only*, and because of this ignorance of the nature of belief, thousands will die…today, tomorrow, and the day after that….

Ignorant people are dependent upon those in power, upon those who can direct lives this way or that, not "knowing" the better from the worse, the right from the wrong, the productive from the barren. The ignorant, universally, *are made to stay that way*, followers kept from knowing alternative paths or positions wherein to acquire knowledge and understanding of paths anew. Locate any tyrant, dictator, politician, or a Khadafy who wants to slash funds for education to the bone and you'll find an individual afraid to his core of ID discovery and ID exposure of which even he is inadequately aware—his ID, an ID based on the *belief* that *his* is forged of steel, suppressing with that same agonizing fear that it isn't, and that his papier-mâché ID will be proven so by someone educated in the depths of human nature, leaving him a waif scrambling for any recourse to ID food. By his actions (most likely by his Hell No's!), he proves his tectonic fear but can't recognize the cause! We can. That's why politicians become pimps, slave traders if they could, buying votes, selling plums, but in the while keeping secret the color of their minds. And this, my friends, is one of the main reasons why STEM-based, species sponsored education always ranks near the bottom of legislative expenditures…because of the fears of ID exposure and the prospect of unwanted discovery. Better to these tyrants, dictators and close-minded ID's is to shut the entire system down (Santorum, Perry, Kim Jong Un, Taliban, legislators far and wide…) rather than to allow learning which would shake tyrannies to the ground and crack open vaulted minds. Areas of concern? Logic, neuroanatomy with emphasis upon the brain, set theory, and physics, teaching *from* the child instead of *to* him…*the beginnings of which should be taught in elementary schools.* Why? Any one of the named subjects could topple *belief* through a universal understanding of the true nature and capacities of man. But why would that be a problem? Answer: because of entrenched ID's—local education departments, testing services, "follow the leader" parents, and because any secondary belief system stems necessarily from the *primary* belief that any individual's ID is stationed on firm ground, and *that* is a belief!

The Fear of Exclusion

To whatever extent a culture gives cause for restrictive *inclusion*, to that extent does that same cause provide the means for possible *exclusion*, the flip side. If one attends a meeting and, for whatever reason, encounters prior in-place liaisons since "older" members will typically preserve ID's against intrusion, a new entrant may feel excluded from the intimacy of membership. Further, to the extent that all ID's need to be reinforced, to that extent are those who have not contributed to the maintenance of the included set's ID's excluded in favor of those from whom reinforcement and support is acquired. To the extent that ID's require reinforcement, to that extent are the unproven, unknown A' actors held in abeyance until proven of worth, downgraded, or excluded altogether. And if excluded? Group exclusion results in natural and basic A' behavior—rejection, humiliation, or revenge with an "I'll get you" by whatever means available.

It is not then religion *per se* or any definable cult or program which excludes or includes its like. It is the restrictive program *as course of identification* for that culture's members which is of concern. Those "out" will want "in" *regardless of the nature of the defined set* (if compatible with local or STEM based needs). Those "in," afraid of affecting the tenure and quality of their accrued ID's, want those "out" to remain out…the basis of xenophobia and the restriction of voting rights.

So any attempt to kill, by whatever means, is also an attempt to eliminate any reference to the self as equally and overtly subservient to conscripting dogma (Articles supporting group ID) which, by its nature, demands ID surrender. It follows that elements of one army fighting elements in an opposing army are both fighting for the same reason: to kill the subservient need to which each member (same species) has become admittedly subject (and contrary to the brain's need for autonomy). It *naturally* follows that any clan obeisant to dogma is not in control of *any aspect* of a STEM universe, by definition. For, if A-prime's constituting dogma is false, so arises the distinct possibility that A's dogma is false also—not a pleasing prospect. Conjunctivity is therefore prevented, inclusion zippered up tight. With religious based wars, it's "Get rid of the prospect."

The matter of species identification cannot be denied, no matter how deeply repressed (and it is repressed!). Equalities in DNA are evident in the most objectively identified "enemy." But we deny that "He is as us and we are as he." That's the problem, for as a species, we are one. With religion (and all religions are products of their culture, never the other way around), the depth of resentment need not be full blown. However, enter "race" and the picture changes. How? If to become a member of a particular religion a man must be of a particular race, or, if a member of that race entails the automatic practice of a particular religion, the issue of reconciliation becomes impossible for those "outside." Conversion *is* possible among religions. Conversion among "races" is not. It may then be understood why intense animosity exists between Israelis and Palestinians or among African tribes. Conversion is not possible when the Jewish claim not only a religious privilege but a racial one as well. The "religious ID" of the Jews becomes an impenetrable lock—a rigidified A'. As such, *time* becomes encapsulated within the Jewish ID. How? Time is imbued within *any* acquired ID-data bank and comprises an absolute attribute with an ID of its own.

So the issue is *not* one of Hamas or Ahmadinejad not recognizing the state of Israel. The issue is Israel self-proclaiming itself a state comprised of racially defined Jews—thereby exclusionary by race without asking permission for its assumed status from its neighbors. "Permission?" you ask. Yes. Permission.

Whichever college you attended had clubs, frats, sororities, right? Before any of these clubs were founded, didn't each require authorization from some source? Why? Each "club" had to proclaim itself open—as far as its constitution dictated, to new members, that the club had as one of its goals the beneficial contribution to the school as a whole, that it met a need espoused by many of the school's students, that it upheld the constitution of the school as a whole, that conformity to the entire school's complex was inherent in its purpose and that the club would be harmonious in operation with all other sub-set clubs within the school. Therefore, as all clubs recognized the authority of the school and of that department which granted official permission for entry, all clubs recognized that the entry of X was of mutual benefit, such as it was, *contributing to the increased and positive ID status of each*. Permission granted! The simple issue? Good manners! Conscientious leaders are considerate. Dictators are not. And linearity is not involved? How do you erase, or at least mitigate, centuries of time-encrusted behavior-dictating lexicons? You don't? Then suffer the consequences and die having left with your ID intact and tomes of support encrusted with patina, proven as such with excerpts engraved on your tombstone. But dead, you won't care. However, if a serene, hospitable reality might become a goal, try this…

Take your copy of the Torah, the Koran, the Bible, the Constitution or whatever outside and hold it in your hands in the dark silence of night. Look up at the movement of clouds. Listen to the birdcalls, the sounds…in sequence…one here, one there…. Listen to the movement of natural lives and realize the process of interactions within your brain. Feel the sequence of thought, of reaction, and the draining weight of pages compiled. Feel the moment and relish your spot in this spinning universe. Then…lift your bound script up high with both hands and say, "What I hold is Time-less and is that upon which I inscribe my Identity! The universe and all within it may move, shake, or change this way or that, but this…this Book and All It Contains will remain as it is, now and forever more."You will be holding Stonehenge, the pyramid's tunnels to Orion, the Ark of the Covenant, Jerusalem, Mecca, the Holy Grail and every book ever written. And, if your ID is so subservient to 2D time-stolen script, you are as it—stolen, stolid, and shrift from time. And, *unnatural*. But a choice any one of this species can make. For that is one of the primary functions of language— to freeze-dry time into a portable anchor, one to which any one of us could cling as we watch our bodies and all around us change, grow, or decay, not an iota within our control. Anxiety dead...until we get an abscessed tooth. Language...coated with the seductive honey of religion or of a political party, freeze-drying each servant in place, compelling disregard of a beauteous egret in flight.

The primary purpose of war is to serve as a means whereby people can feed A-ID's through the establishment of A-prime "enemies," war serving as the means, *in time*, to effect ID nourishment while "killing" time in the process (purely "defensive" war is, of course, justifiable—as long as the "pure" part and the "defensive" part lie in objective fact). The means must be consonant with the end. To this end, war *must* consist of components for ID sustenance, maintenance, acquisition, and ID protection. Any act of man must come equipped with a *cause*. Otherwise, why conduct war or anything else? Man acts only out of need. Always. The need in war? The "need" is to justify the excuse for having it! Boundary disputes? People trespassing on your property? Someone in your retinue assassinated? Causes, or excuses, or both?

If "leader," you will call your comrades to arms and provide them with a most valuable service—the call to arms (Don't House and Senate majority whips do exactly the same?)! Not knowing how to diffuse ID frustration, ID need, ID insult, our leader will capitalize on this ignorance by re-direction. He will arm and encounter. *En masse!* So many will thank him for affording them the opportunity to act in firm group-meld *over time*, giving them something to do—killing time 'til death or until A-A' species-groups bond together, which must be for the disjunctive-ensconced, never. Remarkable!

Patriotism? Only those who know not the workings of the ID mind fall for this scam. If not "patriotic" toward the welfare of species, then "patriotic" to the member-group which provides ID food, "protects" itself physically, unable to counter the tumors in human behavior, deriding those who feel deeply the absence of behavioral leadership. War is the excuse for the ignorance of operational behaviors of a group-need species. One way to "cover" this ignorance? Hire lawyers, fill two houses with them and go linear. Forge justification in ink and toss out linear emissions from a pulpit.

And the fear of exclusion? Bankrupt ID's, like our national deficit, for the fear of exclusion promotes addiction to…inclusion. Chocolate addicts love chocolate. Heroin addicts love heroin. Both suffer psychic trauma with access denied. Fragile ID's require group immersion, and the fear is…fear of separation (Witness the movie, *The Company Men* and the effect upon three men who lose their jobs). The fear of exclusion…the same within each of us embedded in groups—social, religious, business, or political. The fear of exclusion from group is the greatest fear extant, the fear of having an ID changed by sources beyond control, the primary fear enforcing submission to group evidenced by Republicans in the 2011 House of Representatives.

Priorities reign. Without brotherhood within a group, and groups to flavor groups, there would be no society. So is it with nations, tribes, religions, or political parties. While faculty in the psych department at Tufts may appreciate the nuances of this "contradiction," most of us don't, but our brains do. The main priority is group membership, and if that goes, nothing remains. The fear of exclusion is equivalent to metal curtains rolling down shutting us off from group participation, from life itself. That's why getting fired from a job has such impact. That's the main reason congressional politicians are subservient *in the extreme* to party leaders. That's why the minions of dictators and tyrants will commit genocide against their own people…to save their supporting group…their source of life, having no alternative group to join. The intense, debilitating fear of being excluded. Now who might think that that fact might be a determining issue in either a nation's foreign or domestic policies?

Chapter 7

RELIGIONS, GOD, CHURCH AND STATE

Many arguments have been presented in the past for the existence of God, arguments from philosophers, psychologists, theoretical physicists, etc. Rationale has included a First Cause, Pure Act, Unity, etc. Here we'll present three more, not from the top down but rather from the "bottom" up.

Constructing God

Every known or manufactured ideational item requires an A' set to be known since no one thing or posited thought can be known unless what it is not is also known. The A-A' principle applies to every set operative within the constituencies of human cognition. The only "thing" each of us has no A' for is "us, or "me," or my "ID"—our brain workings. We know no other mind, no other operative set, nothing to match against our individual thought factory, so we posit one. God. We now can "know" ourselves through a constructed A prime, "God," just as we can "know" an apple from a pear. We admit complete dependency thereby to an A' construct, and we are no longer alone. "God is with us!" We are made then not in "His" image but He in ours. First argument. We have two more....

Each one of us consists of a group of 206 bones, 500-1000 species of mitochondrial cells, muscles, digestive organs, brain components, neuronal circuits, organs, fingers, capillaries which, if spread out, would reach to the moon. We are each a group, a composite body, yet our linear names glide on forever. There appears to be a contradiction—our bodies disintegrate yet our names persist. If our names persist, wouldn't it be nice if our composite bodies did likewise? Let's make it so. Posit an entity which is not composite but a single unitary "being," everlasting. God. Argument number two.

Since we now have an un-changing unitary being (two arguments effected), we now must apply a name to add to our lexicon of tags which we could barter for the establishment of a group, a name to serve as a password allowing each of us entrance. Popular names chosen so far include Yahweh, Christ (God), and Allah. God now has A prime attributes directly garnered from *human* A attributes. God is One (we are composites), Pure Act (since we are passive and receive), Pure Love (since we occasionally don't), All-knowing (since we know only entries within our experiential data banks), Permanent (we are not), Without Beginning or End (not so with us), is not material (we have substance), Governance of the universe—one of Aquinas' arguments (the sun, moon, gravity, order…), etc. But problems arise. Examining closely the attributes above pinned on God, we find contradictions. Let's reason…

Commonly perceived attributes of our now-in-place God include… only *one* God. If two, then either lacks attributes of the other. If lacking an attribute, one is incomplete, deficient, and such attributes are not characteristics of God. So, for perfection read "Complete." Therefore, Yahweh, Allah, the Christian God, or any religion's God must be one and the same.

God must be *perfect*. If not perfect, then He has flaws, inadequacies. If inadequacies, then not perfect. What then is perfection? From Aristotle through Aquinas, Avicenna, Maimonides, etc., common positions are First Cause, All-knowing, Pure Act, eternal, all Love, perfect Unity, etc.

First Cause is usually considered that attribute initiating creation. Every effect has a cause. To regress to the First Cause of all causes is to identify God, since, as we know, every effect must be initiated through cause. God, First Cause (excepting Hawking, e.g.).

All-knowing realizes that un-knowing is a negative, incomplete attribute. God cannot be ignorant of any event or thing since that would imply an insufficiency ("all-knowing," an attribute made by some who could only wish).

Pure Act implies the lack of passivity. Nothing can *do* to God. Nor can God be the passive receiver of act. God is the "actor" (verb)—the Giver, the Doer, not in any capacity a passive, deficient receiver.

Are these commonly perceived attributes of God? Let's say 'yes,' and proceed a bit more…

There are religions which posit a tranquil "heaven" in which the supplicant does no work, is regaled with whatever pleases him— wine, women, song and a reclining couch. There's a problem with this, as an attribute of God may reveal.

Eternal. There's only one way to be eternal and that is to be *absent from the confines of time.* There is but one route to be so, and that is to be absent from all forms of material base since all that is physical in any form possesses intrinsic limitations, had a beginning, and is therefore subject to *time and decay.* God, therefore, must be absent from the confines of everything physical and, in consequence, absent from the constrictions of time. There comes a problem…

For God to be eternal, He must be beyond time, as mentioned. But words can be created only within the physical STEM spectra and only by physical beings *in time,* requiring as each word does, a beginning and end—*in time.* Words represent operational relations each with intrinsic limitations including exclusion and disjunction. If exclusion is used, parts result. But God has no parts nor can He know such. Disjunction involves disparate sets, non-joined. Such relations are inherent within the construction of any language. Conjunction involves the melding of atoms to form molecules. Sets, separate, join. Does God know disparate sets, non-joining or joining? If He knows sets, He knows boundaries, limits, perimeters, exclusion and inclusion. Conclusion? 1) If the words of the Koran, of the Talmud, of the Bible were created within time, God could have had no involvement, and 2) God can neither write nor "speak."

God cannot *at the same time* be both eternal and participate within the temporal. Such is a contradiction. Further, no "angel," who is eternal by definition, can depart from "heaven" to relay a message from an eternal God, *in time,* then retreat back to the eternal. If *in time,* any element must play by STEM rules and be subject to in-time laws, be physical, and be composed of limitations, boundaries and parts. Only within the temporal can words—whatever the dialect, be spoken, written, or read. How God-like then, are the holy books of the holy religions? And, if more is needed, one need only examine the historical development of any major religion, either of "prophetic revelation" or of a humanistic bent (Jainism, Buddhism, etc.) to note the developments within each of schisms, factions, interpretations, schools...*in time,* many of which countered original beliefs by espousing new. Change, in other words, was involved. Yet God, if perfect, cannot change. Therefore, no commonality. But there is commonality in the development of human religions (also political parties, adjuncts, and shopping malls).

First came Judaism. No Messiah. Then came Christianity. Now a Messiah. A'. Next came Islam, A'' (Read "A double prime"). Note another distinction, each following upon the other: no physical manifestation of God, next a physical manifestation but in terms of a Son. As both were now taken, the next intermediary had to be a Messenger. Mohammed. Then consider again: first the synagogue (A), then the Church (A'), then the Mosque (A' '). Each in time. And God plays a part in all this? In time? The conclusion has to be reached: religions are labeled constructions by man, in time, attempting to use his creative bent to create, in time, passage to an A' "eternal"—an "eternal" which overcomes the restrictions of events bound in time, an eternal which would give "substance" to the cognitive performances of man which seemingly belie time as long as man ignores it—time, with no idea as to how his brain functions. We must also not forget the *primary purpose of religion—to form a 2D bulwark upon which human groups may be formed from which individual members can extract ID food,* for if no ID, what else matters? The purpose of religion? The formation of ID acquisition through and by the formation and protection of groups. By creating groups, on whatever basis, man "saves" himself and by so doing *saves and preserves an identity* which, within the brain, apparently *might* supersede time restrictions *if* the story line supporting the religion is secure within 4D STEM verification which our bodily constitution supports. If so, he is now secure. Or is he...?

Questions...

Religions are social constrictors, history-platformed, time-less 2D scripted bodies of mores, admonitions, and dicta prescribing behaviors for the establishment of a particular people as a group. As "constrictors," any religion serves as a medical Rx to allow the construction of a prescribed "body" which could preserve and garner an ID basin for a group and to keep outsiders *out* who may, through interference, cause dogmatic conflict. Religions are artificial constructs, anti-species, limiting in behavior serving to fortify the acquisition, maintenance, and protection of ID's within a body "religious," which may, or not, cross nationalistic borders. Nor is it an accident that the goals of religions and governments coincide when similar proscriptions of behavior arise in both since both governments and religions have the same source of funding, and, since both have the same source, can we ask questions of one which could perhaps be asked of the other? Let's work religion first...

Every writer of a Gospel or of a chapter of the Old Testament, or a contributor to the Koran, or to the Upanishads, or to whatever, was a human...*in time*. Every witness to a miracle, to a heavenly vision, to a heavenly voice...was a human. Every human having witnessed "miracles" or wrote or talked or aided in the establishment of a religion, had a brain. And we know that each of our brains is different...no two the same even though the core structure is standard throughout the species (otherwise, language and communication would be impossible). The science of neurology did not exist until very recently. We know much more about the brain than was known 100 or 10,000 years ago. Today we know from Carter's *Mapping the Mind*...

- "Eyes and [area] VI: 15 per cent of people who lost part of their sight report having hallucinations.
- Left frontal lobe: reality testing area – damage to this area may reduce the brain's ability to distinguish between externally and internally generated stimuli.
- Occipito-parietal area: damage may make objects seem to appear or disappear due to simultagnosia – an inability to hold two objects in vision at the same time.

- <u>Temporal lobe</u>: stimulation in this lobe – by epilepsy or drugs – may produce intense flashbacks and feelings of a 'presence'. Objects may appear strange or change from one form to another.
- <u>Temporal/limbic system</u>: stimulation here may produce intense feelings of joy, and a feeling of being in the presence of God. Religious visions may occur.
- <u>Auditory cortex/speech areas</u>: stimulation here produces hallucinatory voices.
- <u>Visual shape area</u> (right hemisphere): 'Ghostly outlines' may be triggered by overstimulation of the visual area that detects shape.
- People with damage to the tegmentum – an area just above the reticular formation... - sometimes report having very elaborate, richly coloured hallucinations of everyday scenes.
- Migraine, epilepsy and a huge range of chemicals can create the changes in brain activity associated with hallucinations. And...

"Why does this happen? The brain evolved to keep constant watch on the outside world, sensing, sorting and shaping every stimulus in order to ensure that no danger creeps up unannounced, or opportunity pass by unnoticed. It needs to keep active so if the usual stream of clamouring external stimuli is turned off, it searches desperately for something to take its place. The slightest sound, sight or sensation is seized upon, amplified and shaped to make something meaningful, and if absolutely nothing comes in from outside, *the brain will generate its own excitement*. Hallucinations, like dreams, are part of a continuous cabaret that keeps us primed and ready for action. If the stage falls empty, the ghosts will come in to fill it."[15] (italics mine). So come questions, starting with examples first from the Quran...

"What is explicitly stated in the Koran is to be accepted 'without asking "How?"'"(bila kayf, my italics)[16] But we will ask. How?

- How is it that "Good and Evil are known only to God..." (when evil is a privation, an absence of good, and God is all-good?)[17]

- How is it that "The Koranic commands...cannot be questioned without incurring the guilt of sin...."[18] when such commands are 2D scripted, only transmutable through a 4D brain which must naturally question acceptability in order to afford accommodation within its data bank? Otherwise, comprehension is impossible!
- How is it that "All human beings stand towards God in the relation of the slave towards his master..." when Allah, in His mercy, created "the human race." But if created as "slave towards his master," man was created as a *dependent* creature, *dependency* which to God (Allah) is alien, outside His nature, and foreign to God's "understanding" since God is all-powerful, One in nature, with dependency upon any other A' an unknown relation.
- How is it that "Allah has a glorious face...two real eyes...and two generous hands," which, if physical, are subject to decay... within an eternal entity to whom decay is foreign?
- How is it that "There are allotted two angels per person; 70,000 angels pray daily in a populous House in heaven; and there are specific angels for specific purposes—Michael, who is in charge of rain and plant growth, Israfil who blows the horn at resurrection, another who questions the dead, others in charge of embryos," when the only way eternal angels could be of number is through an "understanding" of sets, set relations, parameters, limitations, absences and, if in an eternal heaven, have commerce with physicals, in time?
- How is it that "He gives...to whom He wills, females, and He gives to whom He will, males...and He makes whom He wills, barren,"[19] when, to do so, involves eternal entries into time... a contradiction, absolving thereby human responsibility for procreative act within a race created by God who knows only Act, and the "responsibility" for such?

And this could go on and on with an equal or greater number of highly questionable "possibilities" in the Bible.

So, what are we left with? In the "religious" sphere, are we absolutely certain, beyond a shadow of a doubt, that the thousands upon thousands of saints registered in the massive two-volume set of

Butler's *Lives of the Saints* sitting on one of my library shelves are legit? That each had listed in Medical Records detailed results of an MRI (Magnetic Resonance Imaging), of a fMRI (functional MRI), of a PET (Positron Emission Topography), of an MEG (Magnetoencephalography), of an NIRS (Near-Infra-red Spectroscopy), or of an EEG (Electroencephalography) so as to insure the absence of brain damage, and that in each brain all of the some fifty different neurotransmitters were working correctly, such as dopamine—overly high levels of which appear implicated in schizophrenia and the onset of hallucinations? And that there were no lesions in the brain caused by accident or injury of any sort? And that such psychic influence as group hypnosis—that mutual ID pull between individual and group, each sucking in deep waters for ID sustenance did not exist, and that children, wringing their hands, crying, and groaning deep laments in Jesus Camps were doing so only because of food poisoning? Could the same be said of Mohammed, Buddha, Bernadette at Lourdes, the three shepherd children at Fatima, and the woman who saw Mary on a croissant? Are we certain that Mohammed was not epileptic, was not on drugs (do poppies grow in the Middle East?), was not under the influence of alcohol (the prohibition of which came before or after the visit by Gabriel?) which could have led to an onset of Korsakoff's syndrome—and confabulation? All neurotransmitters were working, and normal—in every instance? Everything OK? OK. So all our beliefs are well-founded, and we have no cause for doubt? Great.

To admit to intellectual error, to admit to error in belief and thereby to admit to a faulty ID developed in vain, is to admit to a good portion of a life backed by a chimera…an admission too difficult, too awesome for most to entertain. And so we live—you, us, and the millions encircling this whirling globe, in lives based on the ID needs of others—sponsors, lobbyists, party affiliates, kings, potentates, Majority and Minority "Whips," of "leaders'" who must cling to beliefs to acquire and maintain a semblance of ID while we scrounge, care for others, and sacrifice our children to the ID needs not of the strong but of the weak—those whose ID's are built upon the pyramids of ID's encased within some "leader's" balloon. This is why the rich get richer, the poor poorer, why universal health care is touchy-touchy for those who have it, while workers bleed blood and our children fight and die to uphold the obsessive, pathological hunger of politicians to feed vacuous ID's.

"Do You Solemnly Swear…?"

"…to tell the whole truth, so help you God?" "Why in God's name…." "My God!" In God We Trust, "…one nation, under God…" as well as Islamic expressions: "God's peace be upon you," "Barakallah (May the Blessings of Allah be upon you)," "In Sha'Allah (If Allah wishes)," ""For the sake of Allah," "Jazakallahu Khayran (May Allah reward you for the good…)," "May Allah be pleased..," etc., and Jewish: "B'Ezrat HaShem (with God's help)," "Blessings in Him," with names—Elloh (God), YHWH (the personal name of the God of Israel) with titles—Elohim, Avinu (our father), El (mighty one), Shaddai (almighty), Elyon (most high), etc.

We understand that God can't speak to us, can't write us a note, can't intercede within time for us since He's eternal. Where then is the now-in-time communication link? An interesting problem… Why do we reference God in our daily transactions? It would be nice if the word *species* was, and could be, substituted for each reference to *God*, but such is and will not be the case. "In *species* we trust"…"to tell the whole truth, so help you as a *species* member," etc. No, that won't be the case, but the inclination of brain/body for communal interchange within species *is* there. Collectively, then, when we say, *In God We Trust*, we share a common A'-ID apposite…*God*, in this case, the A' source for each of our individual ID's so as to make our ID's commonly understood and known, unfortunately not as species' creations but as now-in-time commodities functioning in the court of communal commerce.

If we say, "God is watching," you and everyone else understand to what we are referring: that A' composite which provides *for each of us* an A' so as to make our individual ID's soluble for if no one else is "watching," then it's just you and me and each other of our species, and we couldn't take that for then we'd have to co-join our separate ID's and talk. The dependence would become palpable, troublesome, and worrisome particularly if you speak a different language, look different, or live over the hill within an inclusive tribe. If such were the case, then how would we get on with each other, understanding ourselves only as members of the same species? So, lacking both the means and understanding for mutual camaraderie, understanding less our species nature, we each homestead a God *for verification and validation* of an A' common link, a link safely untouchable.

For if there were no God, the loneliness of life, the loneliness of ID would come billowing down to shatter each of us with its weight… then where would we be? I'd have to go begging to you for friend-ship, for some camaraderie through which we could validate each other. You could then become my A', and I, yours! Dependence…the dependence of species parts would then rise to gorge in our throats, each of us then having to regurgitate food for the other, admitting life-dependencies and our own individual places within a spectra of dependent needs…and shake hands for survival. With *God*, however, we are spared the humility required to accept self-recognition or the need to go begging at our neighbor's tent for entrance.

Original Sin(s)

"Original sin" is a concept. "Origin" connotes a beginning. However, there must be a sufficient residue of meaning in man to make the con-cept of "sin" justifiable; otherwise we could just as well be talking about a lemon elephant. There are basically three "original sins." To the first…

Ever watch fish swim, birds fly, snakes slither or moved your body from one position to another? Ever watch the stars, the sun set, clouds move, the seas roll in, a forest of trees, or a solid cliff on the side of a road? Everything mentioned above takes up space. Where things *aren't*, is also space. We are here. If we move there, the space which we inhabited remains. We are as the birds, the bees, the elephants, the trees, and the cliff on the side of the road. We consume space… first this space, then that space…through time. We move. We are transient, not essential but transitory within a melding-to-dust exis-tence which could be filled by something other than us. My accidental existence constitutes a "sin" within this universe. But a *sin*? Let's be clear.

Human sin is that aura of impermanence which lurks beneath the surface of human existence hiding the contents beneath. *Our impermanence is our sin* as it is every man's…in all too many cases shielded by a holy book which proclaims a permanent group supporting a permanent God to which we might "permanently" belong. Religion would take our bent for species brotherhood and supplant it with an impounded doctrine, in linear script. Religion would hide our impermanence further: by attempting to meld us within a group tied to a permanence of God. The problem is…we know our impermanence, our sin, and it's a most natural thing. We do so confess. "Original sin" number one? Us. We are, and we need *not* be. We are but dollops in this pot of existence. That's our "sin." God doesn't need us.

The second "original sin" is, in a way, what you are looking at. And it is most severe. A law of thermodynamics states that for every act there is a reaction. Perhaps obvious. Not so obvious is the first *homo sapiens* who communicated via a set assemblage of phonetic sounds to stabilize even the most basic elements of communication. We have to accept the nostrum…there's no such thing as a free gift. Someone, somewhere has to pay the piper. For the gift of language, we pay, and pay to the extreme.

Man's memory banks store all sorts of things. According to Pinker, the capacity of a human brain exceeds all possible atoms in the universe, given its capacity to operationally relate this and that to everything else. And so man stores, regurgitates and creates on command, and lists what the operational brain accomplished via script, and, by so doing, wreaks havoc. We write our books and savage those who disrupt our communion with linear creations. Our brains, capable of operationally relating whatever may be scripted, do so…on command. Scripted 2D language rips from the bowels of dimensional STEM a dimension incapable of divorce, and we call it our own. We rip time from its womb and call ourselves masters thereby and kill to prove it. We form groups of "believers," of "possessors of truth," and with assembled groups, identify opponents of our ID identifying constructs and define them as A primes to verify our A-ID existence. The humanity of man is lost, communities isolated and species corrupted by surveyors drawing lines in the sand as directed by script agreed upon by men seated at a conference table thousands of miles away—each document time-stamped.

With scripted linear language, we have lost our humanity…our simple and basic understanding of what and who we are individually and as a species. Until each and every one of us is recognized and understood as brothers and sisters, we, as a species, will remain prisoners of inked scrolls, books "holy" and otherwise, documents, laws, constitutions, and be as valued as the inks thereon. The second "original sin"? Communally accepted language banks stored in vaults of exorcised time. The third…?

As we know our transience, our impermanence and potential isolation, so do we avoid with all the powers within us potential divorce from group…the impermanence, the transience, split open for all to see. We kill or repeat party mantra to affirm "belonging," for excommunication is hell whether from political party or church. The third sin? Susceptible exposure of the weakness of our fabricated ID's, natural in base, suborned to linear directives each denying STEM derivation. ID's lost to semaphores, each trying to curry votes in Iowa.

Evil

What really is "evil"? Bill O'Reilly won't discuss the subject while Ernest Becker will write a thick tome, *The Structure of Evil*.[20] A simple read of the daily paper or the 6 o'clock news on your local TV or radio stations provides examples of "evil" galore. Let's get basic…

First, there is no evil in nature. Tsunamis and earthquakes may kill by the thousands. Earthquakes ditto. Hurricanes, automobile accidents, typhoons, twisters…each and all forces of nature which may cause untold hardship and ruptures of emotional hearts. None, however, are "evil."

"Evil" is rather a man-made term for any "rational" individual or group which makes manifest against the welfare of the species—either against individuals or its groups. "Evil" is not simply "an absence of good" as the medievalists would have it (a definition which violates a major requirement of definition). If an act harms a species' brother, that act is evil *if* the intent was solely ID acquisition, maintenance, or protection. The key then? We must understand the nature of man and his operative realms if we are to develop species' peace and tranquility. He who kills, robs, thieves, or causes disruption and injury among species' members for the purpose of ID protection does not know himself and is evil. If we perpetuate this ignorance of the nature of evil, we have no reason to decry evil actions. But if we don't decry evil actions to lift species out of ignorance of evil's nature, then politicians can exhort minions to defend inauspicious and capricious acts to feed their ID's to saturation, as exemplified by G. W. Bush saying, as he did to Larry King: "I love this job. I go to bed loving this job and get up loving this job." So Bush loved his job and mothers cried and rent hearts over tens of thousands of children's deaths caused by a need for ID sustenance. But President Bush loved his job as do, at the moment, Syria's Bashar al-Assad, Yemen's Ali Abdullah Saleh, Bahrain's King Hamad bin Isa al-Khalifa, and Mitch McConnell. Does anything matter other than ID protection and acquisition?

Evil? Evil is harm upon the species or any of its parts imposed by either an individual or group disposed to ID acquisition and protection at the expense of species' members. If true, then consider political parties and their positions on benefits and concerns for species' welfare versus need for personal ID sustenance and acquisition. Evil…often subtle, vicious, insidious, but second fiddle to embossed cuff links.

Simultaneity, Homeland Security, and Prayer

Simultaneity is another of those chimeras which philosophers gnaw on to occupy time. We *assume* (we can't know!) that events are happening simultaneously to the nth degree *now*, throughout the universe. But *we don't care*! We can't. The brain wants only peace, homeostasis, and food. So why consider simultaneity? Because through its consideration we must conclude that our brains, yours and mine, are concerned only with what's going on involving operations in the *here and now in this one brain peculiar to each of us*. So, understanding this, we proceed to prayer.

We don't pray for what is in the here and now. *We pray for what isn't*, for a circumstance/event which *might* occur, but if it does, it will be *always occur in the future*. We don't pray for two feet (which we hope each of us have), for water (if we live in a rain forest), or a chair (if we're sitting in one). We see the poor, and pray for them. We see war, and pray for peace. We see illness, disabilities, discomfort and pray for cessation. Circumstances not real now, but perhaps so in the future. So we pray. Using what? Language.

We use language to make manifest, via 2D artifacts, the hidden relational operations the brain produces. Via this medium, we can relate relational operations within my brain into your brain, given its experience and understanding, which then deciphers to perhaps register an "Aha!" *Capice*. The brain also uses language for its own purposes—to acquire some degree of homeostasis.

We don't know what goes on in the world but the brain can create closure to a problem, if only temporary, through prayer. Like so… Ever rehearse a speech you were to make? Ever watch an acrobatic air pilot rehearse his gig by extending both hands in front of him and moving them…left and right, up and around, this way and that in anticipation of how he'll fly? In prayer we gather the sets (operationally speaking) of the relations and formulate them this way and that (*I pray that peace will come to the Middle East*). The brain assembled the parts, related each through its relational operations, and said in closure, *Amen*. It's the same after common prayer: *Ite, Missa est. Amen. Shalom*. Whatever. And with the *Amen*, comes closure. Homeostasis…*in the face of the unknown*. But we don't even know what's going on in the house next door! How can we effect respite by talking to ourselves? Solution? Create an entity which can both hear us and possess the power to effect change. If no "deity," we're paranoid, talking to ourselves. So, we create, as we must, an *A', apposite in every way to our A, in time, to match our specific requests*. The brain cannot continually cope with anxiety, with the unknown, with the plausible, only, always. There must be surcease. So, from ancient tribes to modern day assemblies, individuals pray to an *A'* for closure to this problem or that and in each and every instance, *to protect and nurture the ID*. In effect, we use language, through prayer, to effect the first Homeland Security system, to protect the ID, and to do this we will invoke, we will importune an A' deity through an A' recognition and a ritualistic symbol via 2D language to reach homeostatic closure. The brain can then rest.

And in our sleep what dreams may come, for indeed dreams come! We dream, and, with eyes open, dream again. And pray, then to commit closure. The brain becomes incestuous—self-feeding, realizing that it can reach respite, and rejoice silently, imperious in its own power. Hundreds of thousands of years old these brains of ours. Each knows how to work, in species tandem, if allowed to, *sans* roadside bombs. No respite, contradictions that won't go away? Just strap on a C4 pack and press the button…or pray. Respite. Yes, we pray. We pray that someone hears us.

Church and State

"So, Jenny. I hear you're pregnant. A lot or just a little bit?"

The problem here is the "either or" of inclusion, not the "no…no" of mathematical disjunction. And what does this all have to do with "church and state"?

In the '08 campaign Barak Obama urged the Democratic party to "court the Evangelicals." What's involved here? Well, first, Obama admitted to a deficiency in the Democratic Party. It "needed" the Evangelicals, apparently. If so, any Democrat voting either for Democratic candidates or along party lines would be admittedly voting for a deficient political party. Was Obama saying that quantity (the number of assenting voters) equaled quality (the platform and execution thereof by the Democratic party)? Apparently so.

The church, generically, offers a time-*less* steroid for human organisms engrossed in time-*full* 4D commerce. The two are disparate in both kind and degree. Why then curry the favor of one, by the other? Answer? Because the constituents of both occupy the same 4D space. For both, votes count. The state (political party) doesn't care who votes along its chosen lines, nor does the religious group care as long as it acquires 4D members to its group, since from where else could it garner members except from a 4D source? The fulcrum of any religious group lies within its linear platform. With no linear script, no religion. The object of any religion is to both retain and to accrue new members and to supply its constituents with sustaining ID food, its goal. The target of a political party? Mobile hands to either check off a name or to touch-screen a candidate. Both are after group adherents. Leaders of both groups want to be in the position of controlling ID's and such desire leads to the potential merging of bodies. So, in effect, it's the communal thrust of the leaders of both factions to further, support, maintain, and acquire their own ID's *through group acquisition*. And what can't be sacrificed to achieve those ends?

A "little bit" pregnant? If a religious group merges with a political group, how "deep" is the merger? A merger is a merger. Pregnant is pregnant. There's no *coitus interruptus* here. Conclusion? Upon merger, the political party *becomes* the religious party and the religious party *becomes* the political party. Conjunctivity, and a Santorum need no longer "throw up" at disjunction.

Chapter 8

EXTREMISM—DOMESTIC

Sticks and Stones...

"And names will never hurt me." But they will, if you don't understand what's going on.

Ellen Goodman, in an article written for the *Boston Globe* ("Absolute Demonizing") listed at least a dozen "name callers," including Bush I and II, Rumsfeld, Byrd, Reagan, Santorum, Byrd, Bob Jones, Khomeini, Chavez, Falwell, etc., who applied such names as "Hitler," "Devil," Great Satan," Lucifer," "evil," to describe their "enemies," "enemies" which included Republicans, Democrats, the U.S., the U.S.S.R., Hillary Clinton, Bush, and on and on. Stupid.

Let's make it simple, really, since such episodes as mentioned above cause wars...by operational incompetents.

Y ("them") calls X (us—you or me) "evil," (or *dense*, or the *devil*, or *Hitler*, or *soft on crime*, or *liberal*, or whatever. Your choice).

RULE: Every attempt at "name calling" is an attempt to elicit a response *if* emanating from a lower level ID source.

Goal? ID verification. Otherwise, why bother? "Name calling" is the first step in a primitive request for in-group affirmation or an ID request for conjunctive communication. If X, for example, after being called "stupid," simply walks away leaving Y standing there, how does Y look? Even if standing before the UN General Assembly, and Chavez calls Bush a "devil," he doesn't want to talk with Bush and be thereby associated? Of course he does. Otherwise, why bother? But what if Bush ID'd an "Evil Triumvirate" or an "axis of evil," did he, Bush, want to talk to the "evil three" or get from them a response? Clue: It's all

A-A' and the need to preserve, protect, and serve the ID...by accruing group-ID affirmation.

The genetic/evolutionary thread (g/e) "dictates" expansion, growth, and "moving-up." If Y is a level below X, Y would want to move up. However, if X is above Y, X wants to stay there. Universal, g/e rule. Bush, as X—above Y in status, can use Y as an A', doesn't have to talk, and acquires an automatic boost in ID status since any attempt at refutation by Y (the "axis of evil") will be met by, in Bush's case, force, a retreat unto silence, or an "I won!" with plaudits from his close-knit peers. The "Bully" pulpit, in other words, gives out to get in-put. But Y...what does he get if he initiates a name-calling communication attempt? Chavez gets inclusion into an "association with" manipulated, created set—"Bush and Chavez," force-fed by effusive worldwide media. He couldn't lose! Or could he...?

RULE: Every "name caller," as source and as A, reveals a deficient weakness inversely proportional to the derogation leveled at A'. Always.

Example: If Al calls me a particular epithet ("You're stupid!"), Al—by "putting" me (*including* me) within a manipulated set ("stupid" which only he could define!), defines himself as supposedly within an opposing set—"not-stupid," or "smart." So I ask Al, "Al, could you please tell me, convincingly, why you are smart?" Al asked for a conversation, he got it, and now has to justify the A he used to initiate the A' attack. If he can, he wins. If he can't, he loses. But *he did the initiation*, and thereby expressed a deficient need. Otherwise, why did he bother? Remember that in each of these A-A' confrontations, the initiator, A, knows only his own ID-data bank, not mine, nor that of any prospective A'. It's from his ID-data bank that the name-throwing began, not mine. Of me he knows only the remnants of the 2D detritus I've left behind (words, speeches...) which he incorporated into *his* data bank. Everything else is his. Let's put all this into practice, pinch the screen and go local for a bit...

In 2010 Florida, we received probably twice a week, a flyer—usually one thick sheet with pictures and printed verbals ranting against a Kendrick Meek, running for Senator against a Jeff Greene, flyer put out by "Jeff Greene for Florida" campaign. Picture upon picture of Meek, but few of Greene. "Why would Kendrick Meek want to deny health care to 616,000 Florida kids?" ran one caption. Really, does that make sense? Greene, a billionaire who made his money betting on a bursting housing bubble using derivatives, and Meek, a quiet black from Miami. During a debate Greene said, "Those are personal attacks against me!" Really? The hypocrisy stunk. Rarely, if ever, had I seen such blatant, vitriolic attacks…continual, never ending, and this guy wanted me to vote for him? Do we understand the A-A' involvement here, the name-calling? Why such intent, long-lasting, never-ending rants unless…unless Greene had nothing else to run on but the hope that people wouldn't vote for Meek and were thereby left with Greene, the "honest" candidate who cared so much for you and me and our children? And we have no Political Candidate Review Board by state? Of course not (See "Campaign Finance Reform?" below). Money talks and pays the bills…for all those coalescing to put out scam and scab flyers. Then consider Rick Scott, Florida, Republican who ran for Governor and won after spending millions of his own money (money trumps ability, if made to)!

For ten years Scott was CEO of Columbia/HCA, a health care company, was forced to resign after a 10 year FBI probe found the company guilty of 10 different kinds of fraud and which was forced to pay $1.7 billion in both criminal and civil fines for Medicare fraud, authorities finding Scott guilty of business practices violating federal laws. He runs for Governor? And no Political Candidate Review Board, by state? No testing mechanism for honesty and integrity? So on and on it goes…and on and on… (But XCAT the kids!)

Or, try voodoo! Really…?

There's really no difference! In the one case, take a 4D STEM doll and stick 4D STEM pins into it. In the other case, take a 2D set (e.g., "evil") and stick (include) any other 2D set (e.g., "empire") into it. Result? *Evil empire.* Or, construct the double inclusive relation "green pig." Next, construct the relation "Great Satan." Same relational operations in each. Different toppings. One causes a stretch in the imagination; one could cause a war. Difference? Place your ID in the relation *green pig.* Next, include your ID in the relation *Great Satan* (a term used by Khomeini with reference to the U.S.). Feel a difference?

Infidels! Apostates! Non-believers! So what do you do when the only game in town which would allow a concept of "permanence" to a Heraclitian universe is your religion, a religion which *requires* that you work under an A-A' relationship with others of your species...a species which, through genetic and evolutionary protocol works naturally within a disjunctive/conjunctive order far above the primitive A-A' protocols of stone throwers? The g/e thread will proclaim dominance no matter how strenuous the effort made to suppress it—which is exactly what i/e religions do. Religions—founded on 2D time-*less* histories transacted via 2D time-*less* script "structured" to constrict a 4D *time-full* species to A-A' groups! For what? For the protection, acquisition, sustenance, and maintenance of *group ID's*—the *only* game in town! It's not the religion. It's the cognitive repression, the suppression of g/e demands which compel the g/e thread in those so affected to commit, to admit to a "universe" out of order, "out of joint," but who will refuse to admit that they are it—out of joint!

The issue is one of dissonance. Y—the name caller, must be structured to either admit to, or admit to hiding, dissonance. Stone throwing has become name calling. Unless the stone thrower felt dissonance, he would never have tossed a stone. Same with name callers. No need...no stones. The need is always in the thrower. But what he throws *can be redirected* (a skill the best parents and public school teachers understand and master). You are thinking politicians...? *Politicians require votes to affirm unrequited ID's.* It's not any country which comes first. It's the need to validate un-confirmed ID's! Poorly based politicians require A-A' relationships and to do this will deny opportunities for either disjunctive or conjunctive behaviors (leaving only hostile action available), and will call foreign acts *or domestic*, "provocative" to maintain the A-A' status, never apologize, and throw stones.

We understand. Reasoned discourse is not name-calling. Throwing "stones"—epithets, is. So witness the next "stone thrower." If he/she isn't tossing bricks to substantiate and maintain a deficiently formatted ID, we're a duplicate of Brad Pitt.

A Workable Two-party Congress?

Political parties are not mentioned in the U.S. Constitution. Parties came into being with the Jackson and Van Buren administrations, not

that long ago in ice age time. But they came into being for a purpose—to allow alignments of arguments for this as opposed to that,
effecting the separation of governmental operations from the actions
of everyday man who in time, became proscribed to voting chits. We,
in our operational ignorance, allowed such to happen not having the
vocabulary, the terms, or the understanding to prohibit the theft of
our rights as belly-button voters, unable to protest our transforma-
tion into tokens on a Monopoly board. In any case…

Our two party system of government offers an example of an
operational mishmash otherwise hard to come by. Only through an
understanding of operational relations can we reveal the problems. A
couple of analogies…

The Green Bay Packers are playing the Minnesota Vikings…two
disjunctive sets on one playing field just as the Republicans and
Democrats sit "playing" on the house floor. In the stands are the
fans—Cheeseheads for the Packers, horned Vikings for the Vikings.
The two teams barter, scam, scramble for advantage, one to win.
The scrimmage (the execution of plays) lies within conjunctive regulation mode, in time, the two teams/sets retreating after each play
into huddles to set up the next sequence. No member of either team
joins his respective fans in the stands, for if he did…everyone would
know his name! (Think a Republican or Democrat breaking ranks with
party and receiving name exposure. Not better to remain hidden,
ID shielded by group?) For if a team member did join his fans during game…if he did, his team ID would falter losing an element of
its composition with its ID thereby changing, diminishing in quality
since quality, in both cases, is dependent on quantity. With a football team, quality loss lies in a lack of depth. With a political party,
quality lies with its number of votes and membership adherence to
leader's dictate of platform. Therefore, the team must retain its composite integrity to retain its group-ID. No argument. But what if a
team member did enter the stands to sit with his team's fans? Would
the fans push him back onto the field to continue play, to contribute
to the in-time action? Of course. So what have we…?

We have two disjunctive sets which, by definition, must remain
such. After all, that's why they are "teams," each separate, each with a
linear disposition and distinctive tag, each with one goal—to defeat

the other team to attain "victory." If no "teams," there would be no contest, no football, no Super Bowl, and no tailgate bashes proffering high-cal burgers. On the other hand, witnessing—and vicariously participating in the combat on the field, are the i/e sets of fans, one set sub-divided into Cheeseheads and the other into horned Nordics.

Composite disjunctive sets can have no now-in-time conjunctive commerce with singular member ID sets. A disjunctive set has but two options: to merge with another disjunctive set in conjunctivity, or to re-integrate into its inclusive-ID subsets and thereby lose in-time disjunctive status. Only by relinquishing inclusion within a composite disjunctive set can a one-on-one relationship with "fans" exist, singular set to singular set. Disjunctive and singular ID sets are therefore in distinct and operationally separate modes, in kind and degree. We must probe a bit further the intrinsic nature of disjunctive sets (considered as composite)…

Each member of a human disjunctive set *must "know"* that his ID within the set is essentially dependent upon the existence of a counter A prime to his composite disjunctive set (A Republican disjunctive set is totally dependent upon a Democratic disjunctive set for ID reciprocity). No A′, no A. The rivalry, the combative stance, is *intrinsic* to the disjunctive ID. No combat, no rivalry. No disjunctive set, no ID. We understand then that there must be, simply, rivalry for a disjunctive set to exist.

Operative disjunction must be *sporadic, tempered in time*, here and then, but not with continual engagement for disjunction would then cease to exist, conjunctivity taking over, purely disjunctive ID's lost in the shuffle reverting to i/e inclusiveness in mother's breast for surcease. The obvious question comes home to roost: if your ID is dependent upon membership within a disjunctive set, would you relinquish same…would you allow alteration to your ID, to switch membership to and within a *conjunctive* set, negating disjunctive membership? Now pick any politician of your choice and pose to him, or her, that question. We begin to see the problem. *Disjunctive sets, to survive, must avoid conjunctivity!* If the ID's of disjunctive members are fragile, un-developed, conjunctivity will be shunned like the plague…for the ID survival of the weak!

Place on the gridiron of Lambeau Field both teams—the Packers and the Vikings. 11 vs. 11 on the field, respective teams on either side of the line of scrimmage…and halt play. Allow both teams to stand, or in stance, but no play…no contact. And feel the temperature, the angst rise…and rise…and rise…until phallic fireworks explode in frustration, each team denied the opportunity to exercise its disjunctive ID's, fans in the stands reaching for, demanding tea bags to toss as palliatives. I think we're getting the picture…

The issue becomes, as always, the continued acquisition and protection of ID's. There are priorities. Both the Packers and Vikings get their ID's quenched not from the fans in the stands *primarily*, but by combat with their respective A primes—the opposing teams. Can it be otherwise? Could either the Packers or Vikings acquire salving ID's *primarily* by catering to and "winning" over the crowd without taking on their respective opponents on the field? The obvious question no longer lurks: Is our two party Congress any different composed as it is of members of two disjunctive "teams," so named and so identified and therefore so engaged—or not? *Disjunctivity compels protective action*. To engage in conjunctivity *requires loss* of disjunctive-dependent ID's. The vital issue then rears its head: what compels ID's so group-dependent that so many will lie, retract, cheat, or retreat unto hypocrisy so as to remain lodged under mother's *party* skirt? Is it a fear unto death of the possible loss of contrived, steel-dependent ID's, no other source for ID food available? Yes.

Rebuttals and Political Parties

It is not that Democrats choose planks in a Democratic platform which influence their joining, or that Republicans choose planks in a platform which might dictate their choice of party affiliation; it is that a party platform must match itself with the thinking styles and ID needs of individuals, the constituent food of groups. The degree of match to thinking styles determines party affiliations (No one will join a party with a plank advocating the abolition of water). In other words, party platforms do not dictate party affiliations; it is thinking styles which determine platforms, but with only two parties from which to choose, a woefully deficient education system (purposely!) with citizenry to match and with the A-A' operational mechanism in full swing, politicians are boxed in, as are we.

It used to be said that men are either people oriented or "thing" oriented. Obviously, there are degrees. One cannot be totally people oriented absent degrees of "thing" orientation as well. There are MD's who are totally "doctor" minus good bedside manners. Then there are the opposites: good bedside manners but you wouldn't want this one to take out your appendix. Most, thankfully, are in the middle. With one political set, a large measure of group-pull exacerbates the "thing" orientation.

There is, however, a greater difference between doctors and politicians. Doctors (MD's) have referents for almost all of the terms they invoke—bodies, books, chemicals, tools, etc. No guesswork unless they say so. With politicians, the only things they have going are words/terms and the relational operations which can be used to string them together. A doctor might say, "Your wound is infected," with proof. A politician (Ron Paul) might say to Santorum, "You're a fake!" offering no substantiating argument. So, the point? Anyone can string words together to employ relational effects: *Blue kangaroos play ping pong while sky-diving.* We can imagine this, but not very well. No referents, yet the words/terms are strung together in such a manner that the brain is provoked to find some semblance of meaning. No objective STEM referents. So where's the fault with the spume from politicians' lips? *Rules...*

Any attribution must identity its target in terms of its exact extension [a logical term] and no more. Example: If one is talking about Rome apples and *only* Rome apples, a rebutting argument cannot bring in Granny Smith or Gala apples. Illegitimate extension. In other words, unless the target for the term "fake" is *identified exactly* with neither more nor less "extension" than that contained within the target, the attribution "You're a fake!" is a scam (agree with it or not. We'll get to the *why* below). Further...

Any rebuttal necessarily involves an analysis [a *division*, in logical terms]. Rules for analysis:

1. All parts taken together must equal the whole.
   a. No part may be omitted (Otherwise incomplete and faulty).
   b. No member of the analysis must equal or exceed the whole (*Animals* can not be divided into *sentient* and *living*, since *living* has wider extension, *e.g.,* tulips).
   c. No member can include another (Immigrants into the U.S. an not be divided into Europeans, Englishmen, Germans, etc. since the latter two are Europeans).
2. The analysis must be clear (Animals cannot be divided only into men, mammals, birds, reptiles, etc. Mammals include men. Not clear.)

How many of our politicians have been schooled in the techniques of straight thinking? Well, very few since such a curriculum is prohibited within our schools. Prohibited? Well yes, since other curricula are mandatory so as to afford a platform for testing—caste division in effect, to keep citizens uninformed as to logical analysis, this to allow politicians to proceed apace *unencumbered by rules*…logical, behavioral, or operational. But another…

Two groups, generically constructed…

Group A: Medicare, Medicaid, education, Head Start, Pell grants, Planned Parenthood, health care, care for developmentally disabled, the EPA, national infrastructure…

Group B: Financial institutions, defense spending, opening National Parks for oil exploration, opening 3,000,000 acres of North Woods (Maine) for development (Gov. Paul LePage); reducing from $50 million to $17 million budget for restoration of faltering Everglades and 1B from education (Rick Scott); or calling the Highlands Water Protection and Planning Act which preserves more than 800,000 acres of open land which supplies drinking water to more than half of NJ's residents, an infringement on property rights (Gov. Chris Christie)[22] and additional programs nationwide calling for deregulation…

Two Groups, two questions: 1) which of our two national political parties pushes for an *increase in deregulation* of policies across-the-board affecting the welfare of U.S. citizens (Group B), and a *decrease in funding* for programs beneficial to species in Group A? 2) Which political party pushes for an *increase in funding* for programs in Group A, and an *increase in regulation* of programs affecting the health and welfare of U.S. citizens?

Question: How many positions "supporting" Group B employed foisted, illegitimate arguments simply to promote A-A' political backwash, species welfare a distant incidental? Is it possible that recognition of fallacies in thinking might separate political hucksterism from legal argumentation?

Fallacies in Thinking

Material errors are errors of fact or faulty use of ideas and words, and if used to deceptively resemble truth with the purpose of misleading, are called *sophisms*. If unintentional through ignorance of matter, they are *fallacies*. Fallacies fall into two categories: *Fallacies in Language* and *Fallacies in Matter*.

Fallacies in Language (specious use of words):

Equivocation—using a word with meaning different from that intended

Amphiboly—using phrases/sentences ambiguously

Composition—taking co-jointly what should be taken separately

Division—taking separately what should be taken co-jointly

Accent/Prosody—using emphasis to construct ambiguous meaning

Figure of Speech—using similar construction to forge false meaning

Fallacies in Matter (confusion of ideas and things):

Accident—equating a non-essential attribute with the entirety ("Obama is black. He must therefore be African.")

Absolute and Qualified—making what is generally true, absolute (Generalizations and snap judgments. "Children must obey their parents." Not always.)

Ignoring the Issue (AKA 'mistaking the question,' 'evading the issue,' 'irrelevant conclusion,' 'beside the point')—does not prove what is supposed to be proved, proves what is not in question, or disproves what has not been asserted.

Appeal to the People—appeals to passions/prejudices of people lacking solid reasons for act or measure ('We must prohibit collective bargaining which drains money from our coffers.").

Appeal to Might—threatens loss of jobs if employees form labor unions…

Appeal to Shame/Modesty—"Huckabee, a minister, must know the workings of a secular government."

Appeal to Pity—"Madoff must receive a light sentence due to his age and two children."

Appeal to Ignorance—sways uneducated audience with enthusiastic fire, fear, or specious interpretations (radio/TV talk show hosts or, "The National Security Level is at orange.").

Appeal to the Individual—ridicules opponent but avoids nature of argument ("Obama needs to be a one term President," reiterates Addison, Romney, etc.).

Emotional Phrasing (propaganda)—'Birthers,''Right wingers,''Leftists,' ignoring specifics of argument.

Invalid extension—'Advocating state control of public utilities or federal oversee of universal health care equates with socialism and totalitarianism,' or, 'Advocating mandated pro-life enforcement extends beyond the purview of governmental control and infringes upon the natural rights of person.'

Diversion—sidesteps original argument and substitutes a different question in its place. Too common.

Tabloid Thinking—using slogans, epithets, labels to incite to action absent proof of correctness of reasoning ("Take Back our Government,""Obama is a Nazi,""Universal Health Care will increase our national deficit and cost jobs," denying need for proof of slogan).

Reiteration—Repeat something often enough and people might believe it (ever watch repetitive commercials or listen to Limbaugh?).

Unsupported Conclusion—"Everyone admits that government spending is plunging the country into bankruptcy." Who is 'everyone'? Paying for electricity? Proof of "government"

spending line by line is required to prove unwarranted conclusion.

Fallacy of the Consequent—"If Hispanics in Arizona are allowed to
vote, Obama will win in '12." He loses. Therefore Arizona was
correct in its immigration policies.

Fallacy of False Cause—"Patriotism caused me to commit adul-
tery," might say a Gingrich, or "Because Y entered the Iowa caucus, he allowed Z the Republican candidacy."

If one political party regularly practices the use of fallacies such
as described above, and citizen Z has no education into such but
carries a Bible as proxy brain in his pocket wherever he goes, and
hears an Appeal to the People, which party will he join? Which party
demonstrates the greater use of 'straight thinking' with justifiable
proof for positions taken? If citizen A can make such an informed
decision armed with an education allowing for such, which party will
he choose? If an un-educated citizen, B, lives via schooled bias and
insular exposure to reasoned debate, which party will he choose?
Do we see why funding for education receives short shrift but 'testing' is mandated so as to imply an understanding of the process?
(Do we also appreciate the on-going interplay of A and A prime in
all this?)

We see then why political parties are like the sirens of lore, calling
gullible sailors into port with welcoming arms. It is not the party *per
se* which does the 'calling,' but the need of the sailor to find a compatible wharf to which he might attach his dinghy, understanding that
the wharf commandant will exact his toll, but to those rendered wor-
thy, acceptance into fold.

If we understand a bit more about political processes, listen to
your next "rebuttal." If everyone in this country understood the above,
would we be exposed to the shameful demonstrations of illogic so
many of our national leaders or Presidential candidates present to us?
Would they not be a bit afraid of naked exposure, of recognition of
intellectual, reasoning, and behavioral deficiencies? We must remember: House, Senate, State, and committee 'leaders' in-house determine
whether you and I drink contaminated water, build caskets, watch 10
developmentally disabled adults struggle to live with only one atten-

dant, cry with seniors who lost their homes forced to eat handouts while GE paid no taxes in 2010. The rich are the totem pole one political party wraps its arms around for safe haven lest their intellectual nakedness appears visible to a Stevie Wonder.

Campaign Finance Reform? Easy!

Campaign finance reform? Well, it's a choice, isn't it? If a political candidate cannot present his *bona fides* of character and behavioral stability backed by legitimate, verifiable, proven authority, he then has no recourse but to spend…spend… spend to "prove" authority within position by every trick and method used by hucksters over the millennia. But your children have no money to spend for ID verifiability after being tested…tested…tested in all levels of schools with millions of our children subject to social trauma and lives forecast by age eight!

Campaign finance reform can be achieved by simply asking candidates to provide results from a Political Qualifications Assessment Test (PQAT) as proof of qualifications. Then, pay for what? Once qualified, post it with categorical results stamped by an imprimatur, either as sponsored by "party" or by self. Clients (potential voters) can then rest assured that, compared with the populace (themselves), candidate Y has proven both qualified and representative. Then, save your money, candidates, except for that required for personal introductions.

If, however, a candidate runs not having verifiably proven qualifications across the board, that candidate can be so declared by one who *has* been professionally assessed, and such basic differences can be so specified as to potential clients who would so sponsor, by vote, either. Further, if one candidate is proven professionally qualified, so should all voters for that individual deem the assessment as vital to community integrity and growth and settle for nothing less. So, if one candidate represents the best position for species beneficence yet *loses* the vote for political position having been assessed with highly favorable marks as to both professional or personal qualifications, we think it quite feasible for all parents who *voted for this losing can-*

didate to refuse to allow their children to submit to *any* high-stakes test in school, anywhere, any time, the fallacy of voter fraud (Citizens United?) having been evidenced. Further, we think it not unreasonable to ask each and every politician to pass at least one XCAT at tenth grade level in whatever area felt most comfortable. What is good for the goose is good for the gander, we think it said. If a Tea Party stood on such a platform, we would join in an instant. Will No Taxation Without Assessed Representation ever come to pass?

Name a few politicians of your choice. What if we could have assessed their qualifications before voting? What if political candidates were assessed before spending a dime on a campaign? What if political candidates were capable of being assessed according to…

I.   Self-Assurance, Interpersonal Proficiency, Poise, Ambition… within such areas as *Dominance, Capacity for Status, Sociability, Social Presence, Self-acceptance, Sense of Well-being*… or,

II. Maturity, Responsibility, Structuring of Values, Degrees of Socialization…with such areas as *Responsibility, Self-control, Tolerance, Communality, Good Impression*… or,

III. *Intellectual Efficiency*, Achievement Potential…with the areas of *Achievement Goals Attainable via Conformance, Achievement Goals Attainable via Independence*… or,

IV. Intellectual Behaviors and Interests…with such areas as *Flexibility, Behavioral Weaknesses, Psychological Competence*…

Would the reader be interested in knowing how a candidate ranked among thousands upon thousands of peers in any or all of the above areas before voting? Personally, we have a problem capable of being posed within one very simple question: How dare national and state political leaders spend millions upon millions enforcing the testing of our children while refusing to submit to a professional assessment of *their own* intellectual capacities, behavioral maturities, or suitability for office? Parents, by school or state, should demand proof of their elected politicians' qualifications for office as certified by standardized assessment protocols *or* refuse to allow their children to submit to tests ordered by those same politicians who refuse to submit to an analogous equality of assessment.

Maybe two or more people agree. Somewhere, some hamlet, some party will demand that prospective political candidates be assessed as to qualifications for office before permission is granted for names to be put on a ballot. Somewhere, some time…and millions of dollars saved along with lives placed under the mallet hands of extremists who care naught for others but for ID food and the sating of validation need.

The areas of assessment mentioned above? Each and more will be found on the California Psychological Inventory (CPI), an assessment instrument which, with language translatable into local custom, has been used as an effective predictor of behaviors in Italy, Japan, India and elsewhere. But there's more, much more…

Normal people are deathly afraid of arbitrary or irrational political behaviors (re species good). Politicians are who they are because we put them there. Are we to tell our prospective governors that they need to be "assessed" prior to vote? Well, yes. But who has the wherewithal to tell them so, or to effect execution? Well, we do, to both. And we want them assessed prior to assuming office…any office. So, let's get into a few particulars…

To assess the working guts of an adult brain, we need to have the applicant submit to a measurement protocol, an instrument devised by professional, licensed psychometricians to "measure" this or that times ten. (Here, we invite the reader to visit www.bridgew.edu/library/testlist/cfm to view a good sample of testing protocols available.) Involved in the calibration of results are such vital factors, understood well by any psychometrist (clinical psychologists are often so licensed), as *factor analysis, multidimensional scaling, data clustering, sampling, structural equation modeling, path analysis, Pearson-product-moment correlation coefficient, Spearman-Brown prediction formula, Chronbach's index of reliability, validity (construct, predictive, content, concurrent, internal, external, diagnostic…), criterion key, reliability coefficient of measurement, standard errors, bivariate distributions, error variance, item sampling/analysis, scales, statistical significance,* etc.

Psychometry is both a science and an art. Psychometry measures equate highly with any protocol which measures any factor within the physical sciences, and two, a representative sample (people population) must be processed within any protocol before any individual can be so assessed relative to the general population of the sample. Therefore, any testee can be considered representative of a *species* sample. Conclusion: Assessing a political candidate measures him/her against that sample population of which he is a member. We really can't then consider that a viable assessing protocol will "pass" an extremist unless the entire sample is so categorized! These first types of assessing protocols are thus devised for a population. Given a targeted population, or individuals within such population, any one protocol/measurement device can be used for many applications. How would Bachmann's, Palin's, Boehner's, Santorum's, Romney's, Obama's, or McConnell's responses sit with the responses of thousands upon thousands of others who took the same assessment protocol?

Crash test dummies are tested. PVC pipes are tested as is your drinking water, Behr paint, and Ben and Jerry's ice creams. Potential college roommates get assessed as do marriage candidates by suitors. Which are more important to assess: the competence of a potential postal worker or politicians who would engage in war, or surrender to oil companies the rights to rape our earth, refuse sustenance to our citizens most in need, abolish the EPA, remove all state and federal funding from education, object to then approve of the Detroit bailout (Romney), aspire to the office of President as the office of Emperor of Narcissism (Gingrich), believe in a religion which baptized thousands posthumously including Hitler and Stalin (Romney), lobby for the Keystone XL pipeline (McConnell), or proved anti-authority in disposition to legally imposed pro-species authority figures even if the authority was God Himself (Limbaugh, McConnell, etc.), or....?

Or, might a province, a county, a city, a school district want candidates assessed as to qualifications for office prior to running for political position or school board? "Want to run? Take this assessment protocol, then we'll see." Or, "Want to sell mortgages, run the financial end of our company, head our bank, run a nursery school, direct a hedge fund? Take this assessment protocol for integrity, honesty, conservative concerns for safety, etc. (just name it). Then we'll see."

The major obstacle to the implementation of appraising protocols? *Fear* of exposure. Nothing less. *Fear* of the exposure of group submissive money-bound ID's absent character, integrity, intelligence, and honesty...*Fear* of exposure of ID's submerged with umbilical dependence upon "anonymous" SuperPacs...*Fear* of ID recesses, convoluted with hidden aspirations for ID acquisition dominating any accidental interest in species welfare...*Fear* of the exposure of a life spent wrapped around a 2D darkened maypole, to disintegrate at the first exposure to light...*Fear* of releasing children from assessment protocols, "proof" that chronological "adults" have no need for such... *Fear*. *The* infra-red *Guiding Light*. The CPI shall remain locked in chamber, politicians loath to disclose bogeymen in the basement.

Chapter 9

ANATOMY OF WAR

The Five "Reasons" for (Mass) Killing

We act at any time *only* to meet a need. Killing others may satisfy one or more of five needs (excluding pure un-premeditated self-defense).

First, to *fortify the status of one's own group* (and heighten one's ID thereby) by eliminating the ID's of A primers (other groups) lessening the impact of potential ID threat… *Examples:* counterinsurgencies, Navy Seals, snipers, US Army, LA gangs, Mafia…

Second, to *heighten the status of an A's ID through A prime absorption. Examples:* ritual killings, eating the hearts or brains of slain enemies to "absorb" qualities held in envy by the A-home group; conquests (Alexander the Great, Genghis Khan, Bobby Fisher…); Sunnis blowing up Shiite mosques (If the Shiites were not important, why would the Sunnis bother [and vice versa]?), This stage establishes "total" conjunction, ignoring the fact that the A prime's ID was used to "justify" A's response. Incestuous.

Third, *to remove 2D-strictures of an A prime group which could expose A-ID inadequacies.* Envy of A prime groups, feelings of gross inferiority and the like will promote a "retreat" for ID safety but will also promote hatred toward A prime groups which would reveal, simply by being what they are, flaws and lack of development within the A-ID group. *Examples:* any act of genocide; enacting voting restrictions (photo ID required) to "kill" the right to vote which otherwise could lead to subsequent exposure of fragile, in-House ID, i/e weaknesses; defeating any initiative by Obama liable to succeed which would reveal the impotence of an A' Republican party unable to do likewise; Bashir al-Assad and inability to govern "democratically;" "Killing" a Simpson-Bowles Bill which would otherwise reveal an i/e House body (Paul Ryan) developmentally *capable* of *conjunctive* governance...

Fourth, *to cut off A* prime's *means of survival.* Two results: 1) the A prime still lives but with diminished ID caused by A's ID which becomes "elevated" as consequence, usually by saying "No!" and 2) A's ID is elevated simply by demonstrating *capacity to diminish* A prime's ID. *Examples:* (attempting to) blockade the Strait of Hormuz; universal taxing of the poor to keep them poor (elevating the ID's of the rich as consequence); "killing" the Simpson-Bowles Bill (as category) to elevate both ID capacity and to stifle A's ID (Democrats') growth/survival if otherwise passed (filibusters, Nay votes, delays...deaths inconsequential byproducts); casting children as "failures" through testing, ensuring the ID stability of those privileged "adults" already "passed;" exercising acquired "power" by curtailing social security, Medicaid, Medicare, the right to vote, etc.; causing starvation of citizens through land use deprivation "proving" A-ID's non-dependence on "low level" survival techniques (Examples: Kim Jong IL and Un— notice immense statues and wall images)...

Fifth, *to join a group!* If the only group available to join for the acquisition of ID food, a group forged through restrictive, anti-species dogma, the natural evolutionary consistency of any isolated, hungry man will, in every case, *rise to the surface and overcome* any consistently anti-species platform even if by suicide. Inevitable. The g/e thread. The natural evolutionary history of man supersedes, surpasses, overcomes then and now, any and all rigmarole of 2D dogma supporting anti-species group formation. *Example:* If the potential suicide bomber or Virginia Tech assassin could find no natural, personal satisfaction through membership within a welcoming group and concludes that *he will never find such* situated as who he is or what he is, he may reach a point wherein he chooses simply to kill, make his own group, and *join them!*

So he kills, and finally belongs within a group which can neither excise him nor direct him to shun his fellow man. He rose above it all and so provided the evidentiary proof that his cultural underpinnings were woefully short. (Think the "Times Square bomber," Timothy McVeigh, or suicide bombers, the killer-zealot understanding that families will glorify his meeting with Allah or that media will solidify his new "group membership" through pictures, victim-members included, spread across the covers of *Time, Newsweek,* and CNN.)

Basically, we can reduce the five needs to two…

1. Mass killers belong to a group whose Articles of Incorporation are incompatible with the g/e STEM thread underlying the nature of the species, whose Articles offer incompatible support for the individual development of natural g/e-based ID's, or…
2. Killers don't belong to a viable group, but want into one.

Typical serial killers or mass murderers are outside a viable, naturally healthy ID supporting group and, since they need a group in which to belong (to acquire ID food), yet "outside," they make their own through force! So the other members are dead. So what? So will he be, all then together. The killer can, with psychotic calm, imagine each "victim" portrayed on his bracelet chain, he the master controller making a group *by his design*, as only he could. "Alone no more," each mutters, giving eyeball proof to the camera.

RULE: No one kills save for a means to form and elevate meaning for one's i/e ID.

Killer Groups

Is a group an organism? If I prod a paramecium with a needle, will its compatriots join in a group-defending attack? Probably not. How about a bee? I squash a bee in a strawberry patch. Retribution? No. No responsive bee attack. But I'll move closer…closer to the hive. Fifty feel away, and kill a bee. No attack still. Twenty feet…I'm still safe. Five feet…three…two…bingo! They attack! *Why?*

RULE: A group becomes an organism when its living members coalesce in common cause.

The point here is simple: As a group behaves only with those actions available from its members—whether they be good or bad, that group must be considered an organism…a living, vibrant organism suffering those constants defining both the nature of its members and itself. As an organism, it must be treated as such. If you attack it, it will respond with a counter-attack. A given. But if you ignore it…? If you slight it…? If you derail or cheat it…? *Any group-organism with which we may have dealings, of whatever nature, must be treated consonant with the level of operational capacity achieved.* Why? (Think i/e level Afghanistan) Based initially within identity, any group has access to the same operational relations as any other organism. How then should a governmental administration treat, or interact with, a group-organism with goals counter to those agreed to be beneficial to the A STEM-based home-group? Secondly, *as organism*, is it beyond comprehension both to understand and to appreciate the fact that, as organism, the group craves—as does its members, *union with others of its kind?* If one operational group is extant *as is another* within the same or proximal class, a disjunctive relationship is formed, good or bad, of whatever nature, but a relationship nevertheless and incapable of being ignored.

Try living in an group which exercises behaviors contrary and therefore non-supportive of those of your given STEM nature without the possibility of another "natural" ID supportive group within reach. Do you finally reach a frustration point and kill those of your own group who could have satisfied your g/e ID needs, but didn't, or, do you kill those of the outside g/e group because they have what was needed to provide surcease to frustration? Maybe both?

Dissatisfied, unfilled individuals kill *potential* members of a *potential group* to which they *could have belonged if that* group proved closed to conjunctive meld and *they wanted in*. Too, they would kill in desperation and frustration those of their own who failed to afford some support to a natural ID whether they be strangers, travelers, children, mothers…what would it matter? Any group which does not afford fulfilling, sustaining ID food becomes useless, painful through recognition and of no value.

The problem becomes one of identification…*who, what, and why is this or that group?* Every group must have a platform, a reason for being whether it be simply of tribal origin (basic) or contrived for purpose. In either case, the group mandates linear tagging. Nature, the properties of this 4D universe, the myriad species this body hosts, the neurotransmitters, hormones, propensities of brain components to perform this way or that due to chemicals, minerals, gravity and a mosquito's bite, all matter not a whit. Every contrived death becomes but the result of linear composition, hypnotic belief and arrogant self-indulgence which places personal quests for ID sanctification above the obligations of species membership and rights thereof. We have elected Presidents, congressmen, Secretaries of this and that who know and understand little of the constituents of the human presence or its nature, yet watch icebergs melt and totems in cemeteries spread across hillsides.

Governments/factions/tribes *must remain ignorant* of the operational nature of their enemies. That is why *extremist factions refuse to talk* with "enemies." To do so would imperil those 2D linear bases/biases upon which such ID-feeding groups were founded and would force exposure of the artificial platforms upon which they were built. Think of those of our national politicians who vehemently refuse to talk with "enemies," yet would so easily vote "Aye" to send our children off to war…to validate their position, glossing over their ignorance of this species' operational nature.

RULE: Wars are fought to support ID protection and for no other purpose.

In 4D time, 2D linearity becomes the bulwark for not only national commerce but for wars. As linear artifact, man's language turns and poisons, as a scorpion's tail, its creator. That's why we drive children to be language proficient, not necessarily for cultural assimilation but to take as *4D in-time* gospel *any* script upon which a faction may be founded so as to stand as potential sentinels to, if necessary, preserve or acquire for that social/cultural group its ID. For if a child is trained to accept a 2D script *as equivalent to 4D reality*, he must perforce accept such script as an adequate source upon which to pin his life's ID and as a source to potentially die for.

No one wantonly kills who possesses an ID stable unto death. And how to acquire such? Try education…education unto stable families, education minus concern for medical bills; education relevant unto individual lives, not life-stealing high stakes tests (you won't find one in Finland, tops world-wide!); universal, species-specific education relevant unto an appreciation of the natural sublimity of the individual man—begun in elementary school! That could do it. And the winning group?

The winning group will provide testimony to the world that it is the most species friendly *by caring for its own and others not its own*, for those who sit waiting for the means to offer themselves as testimony—to the handicapped, the disabled, the mentally retarded, the abject poor, the thirsty, the hungry…any of those of our species who can so powerfully provide that sanction. For who so cares for the least of our brethren can do nothing other than provide a beacon to all those subjected to anti-species, debilitating, political controls. And what else? True leaders *talk*. They move to conjunctivity. For if conjunctivity becomes a goal, then perhaps the writings of Emma Lazarus can shine…at home and in the ghettos of those waiting… and still waiting.

The Terrorist—Top Down

The formation of a terrorist begins from the top down, generically within a culture defined as "state." Since man uses artificial languages for communication as opposed to non-language species which may group according to swarm instinct (flocks of birds, dingoes, fish…), man, using language, defines for himself leaders who in turn determine the uses to which language will be put for the purpose of group control—defense, ID acquisition, group maintenance, etc. Such is the case with a preacher who will adapt a language for the institution of religious practice, of a Drill Instructor (DI) who will adapt a language for the purpose of instilling discipline and instruction within troops, of a patrol officer when instructing a driver concerning traffic regulations, of a teacher adapting language for the purpose of Latin instruction, of a parent engaged in child guidance, or of a Dictator or generic tyrant for the purpose of regulating group behavior. So is it within any group, caucus, or town hall. Language is adapted for use by…whomever. In order to be a part of the group—the native inclination of any of us, we must also adapt to the language of that group of which we chose to be a member (dialects!). The language used then forces us to adapt or we exit and choose another venue. However, those with little choice due to bias, ignorance, force, or repression can assent to acceptance and remain within a non-species-relevant group but form ID tumors as a result *in every case*, and will construct defenses for simple ID protection. Agita may result. However, if others react and bond in collective ID defense against the existing regime, perturbations may bubble to surface, perhaps initiating protestations in a Tahrir Square (Remember the dominance of the g/e thread and the A-A' protocol).

Any human group must have a leader to dictate the use of language coordinating behaviors. If the language use and directions are in accordance with individual men's natural g/e thrust, all is fine. If the language use directs behaviors to un-natural thrusts, the natural ID within each of us will *naturally* rebel even if only in the form of cancerous suppressions. We understand that individuals anchored in bias, ignorance, or a need for tribal protection cannot enter into a generic *species-beneficent* group. Enclaves arise to meet the insular needs of insular-led groups, incestuously xenophobic (Birthers, Tea Partiers, Ku Kluxers, skinheads, Taliban, etc.). So we set the stage with the leader's language and the uses to which he/she puts them.

Within any political state will be found a culture, whether it be laissez-faire, democratic, socialistic, tyrannic, communistic, or based on arts and crafts. Whatever the culture, the means to acquire g/e needs must be available. In the main, of course, without the proper and complete understanding of the nature of man, recourse must nevertheless be had to acquire g/e satisfaction if for no other reason than to satisfy the autocratic needs of the singular brain. Isn't this the case with any gang member, any political protestor who operates absent any understanding of man's nature? Simply run through the names which run across your TV screens on the political channels. Donald Trump…a Birther? If he doesn't understand or appreciate the basic nature of man, to join a group entrenched in a group-adapted language soliciting group adhesion, no matter the validity of grounds, doesn't he substitute for basic g/e needs, *personal* ID needs in an attempt to equate the two? One we listen to; the other bellows from deep within bowels for recognition…but nothing comes. "No birth certificate" becomes the substitute for the recognition of species-bent commonality disallowing any g/e recognition that would destroy the group. We understand then that people, ID disenfranchised, will invent A primes when recognition of specious ID's would be ego-catastrophic, not conducive to garnering votes from those equally like- (but absent-) minded. To the terrorist...

No one can escape the g/e thread. We each strive, at some point, to reproduce, to eat, to breathe, to expand ourselves beyond the breaches of confinement...to grow, but when stifled by a lexicon of compacted language, stifled by leaders who derive sustenance from such use absent concern for commonality, stifled by cultures which are confined by pockets of language designed to both proscribe and inscribe, stifled by groups which derive ID maintenance from adherence to anti-species protocols, we hit dissonance, and dissonance causes all sorts of problems.

Dissonance makes action immobile, yes, but the brain will struggle its way out one way or another. If it doesn't, catatonia results. Absent catatonia, we find every way imaginable used by the ID hungry for escape, by people who, deep down under the covers, "realize" that something is amiss: primarily, they fear "living a lie," and even more so, of being exposed with veneers removed. Examples: 1) Franklin Graham, preacher's son, saying that Obama carries within him the "seeds of Islam." (What if neither religion "worked"?) Purpose: to percolate his ID while destroying another. 2) "The American people take part in all their government's crimes," said Al Awlaki, "justifying al-Quaeda's attempts to kill U.S. civilians."[23] 3) Then, your choice: pick any "way out there" proposition by anyone you might consider an extremist... any proposition un-verified, un-validated, with no supporting logical argumentation. Object for the extremist in any and all cases: the maintenance of ID, in time, while the proposition is locked in, linear, like a rolling carry-on trundled through an airport terminal, rolling until someone forces it to stop or the puller realizes the inefficacy of the attempt.

From the top is the dictator/tyrant (DT). Any DT is the cheerleader for the team, and he must have a "team." Otherwise no base. Is the team the military, religious clerics, linear financiers, political parties in Congress, disjunctive tribes, nepotics, or the heart-achingly poor in an Indian sweatshop? Any DT must have a base, and now to it...

Any "base" for DT occupancy is a culture. If the culture is linear, *i.e.*, banks, Goldman-Saks, etc., DT's can only be dethroned through linear attack. If, on the other hand, the culture is human, 4D, the only way to disenfranchise DT's is to emphasize the practiced distance of the DT from the g/e base within each of his "subjects." Such, of course, involves education, now the occupant in a hot air balloon floating… somewhere. However, no matter the distance removed from hallowed ground, if distance, dissonance. Inescapable. And there is an easy way to detect dissonance within "outside" politicians…our concern. Listen and count the words (e.g., Limbaugh). The more words used, the greater the dissonance from operational sets voiced to g/e species base. Otherwise, why mouth off? The wisest man will sit on a park bench and simply smile at the "players within a play." The dissonant, the false warriors struggling with scimitars to preserve shaky, founded-in-sand ID's, grasp and use any and all means available to pontificate the most specious of arguments. But, we're getting smarter. To the terrorist…

If the terrorist is lodged within a repressing, restrictive culture with no way out, consider him repressed. Neurotic if you wish. No access to g/e commerce…no opportunity to create, to appreciate his g/e nature…no opportunity to choose this group or that…no opportunity to forge a world-education to buttress a shaky, insular ID. Locked-in with no viable passport. What if a state was a courier for Islam, Islam forming that state's primary culture, or a national repressive culture via a Kim Jong Un, could g/e dissonance result?

What if man possessed no autonomy whatsoever for the execution of individual act? *Depend on Allah when doing any action because both the cause and effect are the result of Allah's decree* [and] *there are allotted two angels per person* (Quran) [to oversee. For each new birth are two angels created?]

What if man had no control whatsoever over events, manmade or not? *We believe in fate, whether good or bad.* (Quran)

What if man had no control whatsoever over the gender of his children or the fertility of either himself or spouse? *He gives…to whom He will, females, and He gives to whom He will, males…and He makes whom He wills, barren* (42:49-50) and *others* [angels] in *charge of embryos.* (Quran)

155

What if man had no control whatsoever over weather or the productivity of agricultural products? *Michael* [angel], *who is in charge of rain and plant growth…* (Quran)

What if threats of hell befell any disbelievers? *They who disbelieve and deny our Revelations, such are the rightful owners of Hell.* (5:11)

What if threats of sin befell all disbelievers? *The Koranic commands and prohibitions are of course absolute, and cannot be questioned without incurring the guilt of sin…*[24]

What if belief in Koranic commands inherently resulted in the creation of slaves with no rights? *All human beings stand towards God in the relation of the slave towards his master. Slaves as such have no rights…*and on and on…[25]

We get the message: inhibition, suppression, relegation, all movements, acts, inclinations toward individual initiative submerged into script (any affinity with lock-step, follow-my-way-or-the-highway congressmen?). So why do anything? Why grow food? Why educate children? Why turn to a neighbor in reconciliation if discord of some nature? Just obey, obey, and obey and fulfill the Koranic definition of yourself. And no repression, suppression, or angina? There is no greater enemy of a Muslim man than…Islam. And we come to a rule…

RULE: The greater the repression of man's g/e nature, the greater the inclination toward extremism.

It's the same as the escape valve on a pressure cooker. Heat up the insides enough and the valve pops. So is it with any man in Yemen, Libya, Iran, Syria, Pocatello, or Washington D.C.

In any repressive culture/state controlled by military, religion, or whatever, our nascent terrorist (NT) can't create, can't innovate, can't independently think, can't question, can't grow crops independently (if Michael is the overseer), can't access alternative groups (there will be none since more than two require different Articles of Confederation…not consonant within a singular articled repressive society), will have repressed educational opportunities (which might otherwise lead to independent behaviors), will be bound by the physical perimeters imposed by the repressive regime so as to ease and monitor control (the borders of Iran, North Korea…), and will have to abide by the mores prevalent within the society.

Nascent Terrorists have shackled minds. Of all types of abuse prevalent in this world, one type often overlooked is mind control (often through starvation). Without access to alternative modes of behavior or paths to correct thinking perhaps involving set theory, human biology, neurology or equivalents, NT's are stuck in quick sand with no ladder to aid escape. Entrenched. No passports or ticket on an Amtrak, kept in a tribal "crib" *with nothing to do* except pass the time in whatever mundane, group-okayed ways found acceptable.

To "reach" these shackled minds, should, could we as a g/e species offer to introduce secular, wide-ranging educational institutions as opposed to the bandwidths prescribed by Islamic/cultural Madrassas, Texas school boards, or a Rick Perry or Santorum who would disband any Department of Education? But that would insult any regime opposed to free/alternative thinking and would reveal consequent in-bred needs for social control. Not acceptable to Conservatives and hold-the-fort evangelicals. Could a g/e species, us, introduce agricultural know-how with offers to dig wells for water or to promote irrigation? But that would also insult regimes which operate only under "fate" (or rights of the state) to guide the day or who lack the know-how themselves to improve a citizenry when independence might lead to further…independence (North Korea, Syria, Somalia, Sudan… not examples?). So we can't do that. We can't counter a repressive culture with a counter-culture. "Sovereignty" prevents that. *What then could we do* to light the fire of action, to arouse NTs' natural, most base instincts to do something, to break out of shells of stagnation, of cultural resignation, of subservience to detrimental cultural mores? One simple answer: *Invade*…invade and arouse the medullas and amygdales of primate man who will then leave his repressive culture behind to protect the ID that he has (Iraq, Afghanistan…). Or, give Christmas gifts of military materiel to a nation's neighbors, and slight those living next door (airplanes and armament to Egypt) and commit invasion via insult. Or invade via media…throw barbs, ridicule, taunt like a Florida pastor or a Billy Graham, Jr. Arouse the A-A' rift. Invasions don't have to be physical…the mental/behavioral work just as well as those tossed out by degreed men like an occasional U.S. President…but stupid. But we invade, and NT drops the N and becomes a full-fledged T. Then…then *he will have something to do, to break the monotony of repressive, slavish servitude demanded by a demeaning, thoroughly i/e culture, and he will say "Thank You" for giving him a new life, *a new time*, perhaps a *new name*…and he will play the A-A' game full tilt, stuck as he is in i/e behaviors. *There's no better way?*

"What" Does a Killer Kill?

Everything we do…*everything*, is done with purpose. Nothing is done without need whether forced, "willed," or entered into through chance. Let's go basic…

Think of a killer in the act…Taliban, al Quaeda, suicide bomber, Virginia Tech, it doesn't matter. For whatever reason, the killer (good guy, bad guy… no difference) has ID'd his target either with a pre-meditated fix or on-the-spot. In any case, his victim (or victims) is ID'd…and he kills him. Nothing is done without need. Now, what if the victim was not ID'd? Would he have been killed? *Only having been ID'd by the killer* was he, the victim, killed. *From whom* did the attribution come? From the killer. The victim died because he was the recipient of an ID proffered, extended, ascribed by the killer. As a result, the killer kills…the victim. Why? Because the victim received his ID from the killer! In other words, the killer constructed an A prime-ID, applied it to the victim resulting in the victim's death. Major question then follows: *What other than the victim did the killer kill?*

Any ID-brain holds, subliminally or otherwise, an operational "set" prescribed for species *membership*. "On the ready," each brain holds open entrance by other species members, *the set of which he is a set.* Inclusive. When the front door bell rings, aren't we prepared to meet a fellow species member, perhaps with a pizza? So is it with any man, any time, anywhere. There's a place reserved in the brain⇒set⇒species for the "entrance" of any member of fellow species, any time, anywhere. Now, ID a "victim," kill him, and…what else gets killed? Consider: part of the brain⇒set⇒species comprised the "killer's" ID! Of course! If in the brain, it's in the ID. So what else was killed? Answer: part of the killer's ID!

Why did Moses, Joshua, and followers institute a seven-day rehab for their soldiers after killing orgies? Answer: to let the brain scars heal. Why are so many (if not all!) of our returning soldiers suffering from PTSD—post-traumatic stress disorder? Why do 18 veterans kill themselves each day? From cooking marshmallows? When anyone kills another, it is for a reason, for a need, and the "victim" *was* because of an ascribed ID implanted on that victim *by the killer*. Want to paint a blue sky? Take out the blue paint. Want a drink? Raise water from the well. Want to kill an "enemy"? Ascribe to him an ID constructed from an operable brain and from an ID repertoire. The killer gives, kills, and goes home wondering why he's troubled. It's insane that one or two men can send thousands of our own out to kill *parts of themselves*, parts of their most precious ID's, offer no remedy, and then vacation home on a ranch with never an apology for none is expected when the nature of the sin is beyond operational grasp. In sum...

The killer traumatizes that part of himself which is species-bred, vitally connected to that part of himself which is species-dependent, linked-to from birth, and by killing he isolates and removes himself from species-bond, from that most integral part of self. So why does he kill? The killer, who so engages, kills to *surrender his inbred species-ID to insular group*, a group within tangible reach, within touch, within earshot, within an ID storehouse of ID food. In effect, he sub-sets himself below and separate from *species set*. Major, major conflict inasmuch as all visible peers *belong to the total-species set*. He can't escape. He locates himself, ultimately alone, with a feed-group on the other side of the glass. And the result? Incurred schizophrenia wrapped within the cocoon of group-meld. And no one recognizes the cause. Any wanton killer fractures his species bond by removing, distancing himself from that species of which he is an integral part and isolates himself, willingly reducing his font of ID succor to his commanding clan, he now a committed slave. Inclusive/exclusive at beginning...and at end. No change. Behavioral level—early adolescent at most. Food for the sixth commandment.

War as Proxy

Not all men require war. Some men are beyond the need—a Gandhi, a Mother Theresa, a Martin Luther King and others who fall within this set. But because we think ourselves far unique, above the plain of other species, we separate ourselves from truth. Gorillas, lions, wolves, penguins…all abide by Robert Ardrey's *territorial imperative*. We call it "my space." Species below us don't have language but we understand—for family and tribe to advance, a territorial imperative is a must, not attended to by blue jays. We however, possessing language, can arbitrarily define a territory be it academic, physical, religiously based, defined by a political bias, municipal plats, surveyors lines, or as dictated by any group of choice. With such territories (plats) defined, we can go to war to defend or to attack encroachments.

Animals beneath us fight for physical territories defined either by piss, fur rubbed onto trees, an aggressive, defending beak… We define territories to defend a group's belief platform, a platform which need not be founded in STEM-truth nor in experiential evidence. Witness eight or ten presidential candidates, all in a row, each defending a belief platform. The Christian Right defends a belief platform in opposition to a Liberal platform, each to defend the ID platforms of the individuals comprised. Romney defends, Gingrich defends, Hussein defends, Khomeini defends, as does Maddow, Obama, Haggarty, O'Reilly, or a Limbaugh. But notice that any defense of a belief platform requires *offense*, an attack upon threat to the belief system, the platform upon which each particular ID rests. Given that our brain structures are all alike, any neurologist searching for the caudate nucleus or the angular gyrus in any one of us will find either in the same locations, given each as species member. How then to differentiate one from the other, me from you, or Ahmadinejad from Brad Pitt? Construct a belief system, ink it, and proceed apace with scroll held upright in raised hand. Territory struck. War may now commence since any A demands an A prime, such scrolls providing invitations for opposition from anyone, any group desirous of up-building its ID as our forces in Iraq and Afghanistan help to up-build terrorist groups… our troops equating with A primes and most welcome to derelict, i/e ID's. But there's a flip side…

The species-bent, inbred impulse of each of us within this species is to propagate...the species. Prime directive. Wars do not assume inbred status inasmuch as wars demand belief-system protocols inked in cuneiform, bannered and stuck on car bumpers. Our species, however, provides necessarily the implements for procreation inbred—male and female, hormones, epididymis and ovum (+ accouterments). Some most natural, some contrived—via language. So male rams butt heads during mating season, male walruses fight for harem dominance, male gorillas the same... So is it with species upon species upon species. It's not difficult to locate the males, physical inspection in most cases not required. Are human males an exception to the rule? Hardly.

The human male, as almost all males within all species, needs to dominate...to fluff plumage, to puff chest, to bare abs, to use Old Spice deodorant, to drink Dos Equis... Why? To fulfill nature's need... to have males, dominant males, visibly on the shelf ready to inseminate. And if no females around and the possibilities for perpetual, daily insemination out of reach, the drive for dominance nevertheless persists and is kept active if only by proxy, not to be purloined through distraction. Wars provide the answer. Fights, caucuses, debates, protests, filibusters, whatever...all because of purloined belief system protocols. And how do language-bearing males make known, absent growls and radiant plumage, their availability and dominance at-the-ready for impregnation of mind or body? We define four ways...

Bunting. Think Khadaffy. Robes of all variegated colors, stripes, swirls, all radiant to eye, which covered a most precious commodity guarded by female Amazons, each professing obeisance to a well-plumed peacock so distinguished. Then, think locally...of $500 haircuts, thousand dollar suits, each with a red, white, and blue USA pin attached to lapel, or the reduction of such to open collared sport shirt and Levis in deference to population courted...("He's so like one of us, and so caring to dress just like us!").

Staging. Add staging and eager puppets who, grasping needs for grouping, mount stages, tables, pulpits of all description surrounded by more bunting—flags draped and flags flaccid on poles as beacons calling to action...colors, attendees, CNN interviewers, each puppet to his own cause standing *erect*, bunted for occasion, spewing spume as required to defend belief platform, spume as from camels who froth at mouth attracting females yet forecasting ferocity to rivals…puppets thieving time and space from independent minds perhaps more suitable, adept, and promising in lineage…like that guy watching at home, chugging popcorn. Staging like the bowerbird, throwing trinkets and things shiny to attract the gullible to tinsel.

Banking. Females attend not only to the attractive but to those who give promise of strong genes…the burly, the protective leaders, to those who give promise to a stable future and strong offspring. With language, letters, and numbers developed for assorted usage, we can hype futures by holding up bankbooks. Instead of female gorillas depending on future gene input from the strongest in battle, we answer to such questions as, What job do you have? Are you independently wealthy? Will our future be financially secure? With bankbooks offered as collateral to future and to quality of gene bank, females attend and too often surrender, as we to the ministrations of Wall Street and ilk who brandish numbers, obscene, certain of security behind cement moats protected by directives prohibiting interference while blooded genes tote bales onto river boats moving downstream to river's mouth, disgorging life and floating caskets.

Marching. Whip bunting, staging, and banking into a froth, emerging with ID-satellites to imitate the cause and call of the head male…acolytes used as surrogates to leader's intent—to fend off rivals, to indicate *readiness to penetrate*…whatever, whomever as needed, acolytes goose-stepping down boulevards, alternating legs in front, each *stiff, erect, pulsating in rhythm*, each acolyte armed with a steel barreled *epididymis*, man-made, able to shoot *sperm-shells* repeatedly, cannon barrels *more fertile* still, rockets, missiles…*sperm banks* on the ready.

Then people say that we need more female heads-of-state, females who might frustrate penetration through use of IUD's, sponges, patches, vaginal rings, spermicides…all forms of glues which both attract and make males impotent. Impotence. Is it any accident that, in early 2012, women have become the target of congress*men* giving such fruitful evidence of shaky, quaking ID's fearful of their impotence discovered by…females, refusing to pay for contraception lest the impregnating "power" of males becomes forfeit?

Glues…the power of which in all its forms, varieties, and usages, if implemented, could frustrate war machines, put thousands of soldiers out of work, yet save thousands of numbered lives. Glue…power in a spray can or out the belly doors of a fire-fighting C47. Contra-ception. And people suggest that women assume the mantles of heads-of-state, women who don't even have a political party dedicated solely to them, such as The Women's Party? What's the emoticon for *You've got to be kidding!*

PART II

Results

Chapter 10

ANATOMY OF A DYSFUNCTIONAL GOVERNMENT

War Paint and Orgies

Extremists require confrontations. Dictators and tyrants conspire to confront weaker numbers. "Civilized" politicians confront "opponents" through disjunctive barter. Leaders of any extremist group are of course required—leaders who coalesce bondings impenetrable by outsiders—incestuous coiti among Members Only, extremist leaders dedicated to locating A prime groups living STEM based protocols for species advantage. Food sources. Nationally, tribal leaders taunt to confrontation using such linear tags (war paint) as *Debt Ceiling, Taxing the Wealthy, No New Taxes, Pro-choice, Immigration, Corruption, A One Term President, Take Back our Government, Invaders, Mau Mau,* …each and all catalysts to promote flash groupings or Twitter tweets…brain excitations leading to orgiastic explosions among followers each with a Thank You for the invitation to party.

For the Constitution was evolved by men in such "leadership" positions—slave owners and landed gentry who, abstracted from huddled masses, acquired position to repeat self-empowerment through a Constitution which deprives men of "one-man, one-vote" protocol through Senate stacking, an Electoral College added for backup, making the cause of individual citizens moot. So it is with a two party system which inherently demands an A-A prime disjunctive constituency…two tribes, "leaders" of one as the 'wealthy" they emulate, flourishing on the backs of disenfranchised *who must be kept in servitude* yet intact so as to make evident those who "have" species dominance and those who don't…two tribes—one the more closely identifying with species' needs, the other feeding off every such reference possible to so construct antagonistic postures. Any time a STEM President might then open his mouth, provided is an *ala carte* menu for A primes to commit to orgy—to coalesce and put on war paint, utter war cries, and march…each welded together with tenured security to orgiastic war. For *it doesn't matter* if the poor starve. *It doesn't matter* if Latinos, blacks, seniors, or college students without picture IDs' are disenfranchised and denied entry into a "one-man, one-vote" society. *It doesn't matter* if government must allocate funds to create jobs for those without. *It doesn't matter* that children, the poor, or seniors are denied health care. *The only thing that matters* is the establishment of cauldrons of visceral A prime soup from which politicians most needy, hungry, and thirsty can feed, pitching rants as *Demagogue, No new Taxes, Liar, Kenyan, Anti-American, Pro-Life*…all war paint, each of different color but sufficient to rally zombies to a cause, to confrontation—to perpetuate specious groups. Only occasionally do we wonder why.

When an Addison says No to an Obama (budget debate), it's not the people of the U.S. speaking. It's McConnell, his ID struggling most purposely to garner food from confrontation for the establishment of ID station. But…what is real, *truly real,* based in 4D STEM concrete? Is either the debt ceiling or the budget based in STEM reality? Are the dates on a Calendar, reformed by Pope Gregory XIII in 1582, STEM based? The language used for communication…not artificial? The only "thing" *real* in political confrontation *is the confrontation*, however devised, between 4D STEM men—people breathing, hunting till death food to keep ID neurons firing at optimum, ensuring a gratuitous life in the moment. But operationally, why?

Latinos, blacks, seniors, children, teachers, laborers, college students, immigrants…all can be *seen* and are by social status inferior to elected governors, communication between the two sets tenuous at best. But the wealthy? How can you "attack wealth" when wealth is but a 2D, time-absent construct? Confrontation with a bank balance is impossible. "Wealth" is digitized, recorded in bankbooks and found on-line when screening portfolios via password. ID's can't be fed via confrontations with paper, numbers, or an accountant's say-so. So how can extremists confront a digitized script? They can't, but they can *adopt and adapt!* If they did not, their anti-species, specious ID platform would be exposed, for if confrontation with the inequalities of social "wealth" *is on the agenda*, then the quest for substantive individual ID food *cannot be,* the issues different in kind. A moral, ethical, and STEM-based platform does not advance confrontation usually, but for famished, phantom ID's, it will serve. But such species beneficence is obviously not the case here. So, to prevent the exposure of ID-conducive platforms, extremists choose not to appear as barriers to species' equity but rather assume the warrior's mantle of Protectors… Protectors not of you or me but of the Wealthy hoping that no one notices the reptilian shift. To keep the charade intact, "justification" is promoted: "No new taxes!" cry the Protectors, and the issue is neutralized. We understand. "Trickle down economics." Protectionism. Of course.

Dictators and tyrants use force *to acquire* confrontations: guns, naked cavalry, tanks, persecutions based on printed sheets and rounded minarets of assorted shapes or declarations of territory printed on makeshift maps, all *to establish* A prime "opponents" with whom the game for domination could be played. "Civilized" politicians throw dishonest, deceptive, confronting barbs unlike the honest war paint of a Cochise.

And they don't mean to kill? Orgies feed, as in the Roman coliseum, never mind the artificial words, artificial language, and makeshift cause used to satisfy crowds, all ignorant of the nature of an in-time dimensional man. Two political parties fake legality to make confrontation "legal," never mind the deaths and negligence to families or human rights abandoned by the wayside. Spawn of the epididymis, each swimming through its own *vas deferens*…in time, the extremists elected by those with ID's just as hungry, fighting for high-cal, high-protein, ID steroids, tumors kept hidden behind "the wishes of the American people."

RULE: The stronger the disjunctive set built through confrontation, the greater the food supply required for upkeep.

The greater the number of confrontations, the greater the opportunities for ID obesity—for self and political party. So, *Confront!* Confront with "No's," with filibusters and never bend; never support with full, unbiased empirical information; "stand firm" (Tea Party platform); keep students stupid and confront from a distance the disenfranchised, each the product of petrified, specious schooling. Purposely.

Domestic Policy Replicates Foreign Policy

Or, foreign policy replicates domestic policy. This rule is inviolate, twist it any way you wish. Let's start with invasions…

Of how many invasions are we aware? Germany, of course, into Poland, Hungary, the low-lying countries, Russia into Afghanistan, Mongolia, Hungary, Germany, etc.; The Mongol Hordes into… Japan into… Serbs into…Hutus into… and so many others we will purposely leave out. How about the United States into Iraq? What laws (taken in the most general sense possible) were imposed *upon its own people* by the invading leaders as described in histories? From heightened security at a nation's linear borders to violations of Article Four of the Constitution (unreasonable search and seizure minus Warrants), to violations of Amendment Eight (no cruel or unusual punishments inflicted) to… Sound familiar?

It has long been understood that people in the same walk of life—the same or similar professions across boundaries, are closer in bond than to citizens within their own countries. Briefly put: What was done to the citizens of Iraq must, in varying degrees, have been done to the citizens of the United States, with alterations, in equivalent degree. Why? To insure compatibility and "authorized" justification within ID set—both out and in, for after all, nothing can go "out" absent the same "in." Simple. Then, simply equate partitions of law foisted upon the U.S. citizenry during the Bush 43 administration and compare those set upon the Iraq nation, and the world. Isn't it the same the world over, with every dictator and every "leader" who would fortify his ID with food stolen from an A' "enemy" even if the "enemy" must be manufactured? First, *start at home.* Once the exercise of controls needed to impact an "enemy" has been established then, perforce, those same controls (or lack of, *i.e.,* Wall Street) can be unleashed against a *home* "enemy," such action *naturally* required to maintain ID position if anti-species and unnatural through initial cause. Institute Shock and Awe in Iraq, then institute a Fear Index at home—Red, Orange, or Yellow as directed by your Homeland Security division. Citizens, enmeshed in contrivance, have no recourse but to submit.

What is the 2012 Republican platform? Does the platform consider in any way taxing the middle class while protecting the rich, restricting rights of our citizens to vote, gerrymandering for further ID protection, restricting funds for Pell grants, Medicare, Social Security, education, infrastructure, research, and on and on? What then might be the nature of this country's governing body regarding foreign policy...regarding China, Brazil, India, Germany, Iraq, Iran...[see below]?

National governance has but one head, twist it this way or that. Consider Israel. Does Israel's foreign policy replicate its domestic policy, or vice versa? Let's consider the main thrust of Israel's foreign policy as protectionism. Protect what? Land, yes. What else? People...Jewish people, immigrants, natives...whether through religion or ethnicity. "Jewish." Are the ID's of the Jewish natives sufficiently evident as to be unquestioned? Yes. And so is Israel's foreign policy. Without the one, absent the other. ID's unquestioned and protected. Want to change Israel's foreign policy (or anyone else's?)? Change the ID's of its citizens.

Iran. Are there homosexuals in Iran? Do stonings occur under state mandate? Are hikers who wander into Iran's territory sequestered for two years for trespass? Do UN delegates from around the world walk out on Ahmadinejad's rantings? Are Iran's citizens under the continual watch of Big Khamenei? Does Khamenei attempt to reconcile his self-imposed status with the rest of the world either through force or threat? Whose ID's are the ones which need protection come hell or high water? Politicians, we think they're called, no matter the cloth of cover.

Zombies in Congress

The ID status of any individual is dependent for validation upon group membership *no matter* the caliber of morality, ethics, social position, or relevance to species advancement. These plastic ID's of ours abide in time and need not be subject to encrypted glyphs of a culture, group, or even species since such are "accidentals" to a conscious ID existing in 4D time, time which cannot be erased, altered, or entered into via either a Constitution or group platform. Khadafi, Assad, Addison, or Pope Benedict…all have ID's and none is prescriptively dependent for support upon the platforms of any of the others. It therefore follows that the primary directive of man—to secure his ID within the culture in which it finds itself, is core. Absent an enfolding culture, the *isolated* ID is amoral, has no concern for society, for ethics, or for any aspect of species beneficence. Embedded within a culture, within a group or with a political party, the ID assumes the dress of its host. If within a religious group, the ID will assume its platform so as to have an embedded and protected ID. If within a political party, the ID will follow leader-led dictates to sustain the party's disjunctive separateness *as determined* by the platform of the party's A prime counterpart. If Republican, anti-Democratic regarding issue Y. If Democratic, anti-Republican regarding issue X. Conjunctivity weakens the disjunctive ID and, for stability and the sustenance of group-dependent ID, must be denied. Disjunctivity reigns, as it must, for all group-dependent ID's which, by nature, *are absent concern for species membership or welfare* since ID sustenance, group-dependent, remains the priority. Raise the debt ceiling no matter if raised 60 times previously since the 60's? And weaken fractious ID's dependent upon party membership, or deny soul-surrender to a Norquist via pledge? Impossible. Nation be damned, country be damned, everyone damned…except the necessary dominance of the ID…the only thing, to any politician or to any of us, that counts. And pledges…?

234 House Republicans (out of 240) and 41 Senate Republicans (out of 47) signed Grover Norquist's "No New Taxes" pledge (2011). Addison's primary goal in life is to make Obama a one term President. Does species welfare, the stability of government, the welfare of the poor, children, handicapped or unemployed merit consideration when it is *only individual ID validation which counts*? Such is sufficient to cause not only loathing but full disgust at a dysfunctional government. To bring down a black President because he's black, or intelligent vs. a Bush 43, one party of a two party system need only blackmail, extort, or hold hostage…collective political behavior not an entry in our Constitution.

Men can be both intelligent and ignorant…intelligent relating to the manipulation of operational relations (depending on operational maturity), ignorant as to the physics of our natural realm. These moving, breathing, pulsating bodies of ours live in time and occupy space. 4D. Alphabetic letters are artificially contrived as are the words in any language. The ink used to inscribe these contrivances onto man-made paper or keyboard taps unto a digital hard drive are also man-made. Inscribe a word…inscribe a compendium of words onto whatever… onto a pledge sheet, onto a love note, onto a Post-It note. Contrary to our 4D STEM existence, any such inscription *is absent* Space, absent Time, absent any Electro-Magnetic impulse, absent all that is necessary in this universe for our individual existence. Sign a pledge "stating" that you will never vote to raise taxes, never OK gay marriage, never agree to federal funding of abortion clinics, that you will never vote to tax corporations or hedge fund managers, that you will never do this or do that…and on and on or Norquist and ilk will withhold voter support and with it, your group-sponsored ID.

We give names to pet dogs, to racehorses, to gorillas (if on friendly terms). We tag fish, call an elephant Jumbo, and categorize birds. We give names to children, to each other, and ranks to servicemen and women. In no instance do either names or numbers relate to or identify the inner essence of whomever or whatever named. There are several John Johnsons in existence, we are sure, as there are Mary Smiths, yet the developed essence of each is markedly different from all others. There is no difference between a man assuming that his signature on a piece of paper captures his total essence and a Voodoo priestess sticking a pin in a doll to promote paralysis. Any signature consisting of artificial letters within artificial words within artificial nomenclature is but a culturally concocted contrivance designed to differentiate one individual from another for the purposes of historical tabulation and communication.

There is one reason and one reason only that men would surrender, via signature, the responsibility for future act, and that is *to keep secret a tremulous, facile ID lacking the maturity of full development*…injecting an ID, a persona, into a dimensional vacuum… a pledge sheet *absent time*, perpetual, ever-lasting…a signature, devoid of time-dependence but sculpted as on a restaurant receipt to indicate *subservience to dimensionless demand*—a poseur surrendering life-blood for artificial recognizance to artificial groups, to Constitutions, to political parties and their controllers, the STEM signer left to fend for water at the nearest fountain to remain hydrated, occupying space and time while each Mephistopheles, each anti-species, pro-wealth lobbyist or puppet master saunters about bandying on high the signature of each Congressional Faustus captured, grouped souls in hands, ensnared, bought and sold.

Violence against innocent man is a sure sign of an extremist. The theft of men's "souls" belongs in the realm of fiction…until executed in fact. If souls stolen belong to U.S. Congressmen, we enter the realm of terrorism, treason at best, for we are culturally taught that signing a document is a legal act, that forgery is illegal, signature authentic if certified by a notary public. We "learn" that our signatures, embossed and petrified unto script, are perpetual unto life in prison if sanctity forsworn. Yet such belies the nature of this Einsteinian universe encompassing, demanding adherence to the immutable laws of physics. Sign your name on the blackboard 100 times and each example is but lines of chalk, but reduce your existence to ink on a pledge and bring a government, "yours," to its knees while a Mephistopheles laughs as his name and picture is spread across whorish Media, the "souls" of Senators and Representatives gathered in both hands as he gloats at his catch. Only a Devil himself would ask a soul to give up his *life in time* to live in absentia. A drop of blood, an oath for glory, fame, of fealty…a signature only He asks, then each Faustus frees himself from responsibility, from choice and free will, life surrendered to a Devil master…each Faustus deaf, blind, and soul-less, each as lost as his manhood.

This is our Congress…zombies entombed in script, souls clinging to "leaders" who lead souls to decay, through self-ignorance, blind to the honesty of human needs, or nature.

The Urohidrosis Effect

There is a reason Evangelical Christians, conservatives, and right wingers oppose any theory (or scientific proof) of evolution. They don't wish to "let the dogs out." No peeking under the petticoat or behind the mirror in the bathroom. The problem with anti-evolutionists is that they take the T out of STEM...SEM minus T, time. Considered is only the knife edge of now...now...now... No past, no passage of time. After all, is there any "past" right now? Of course not. Clouds don't roll, hair doesn't grow, stomachs don't rumble...not in the immediate now of instant. But was an anti-evolutionist ever a child? Did a hair grow, ever, here or there? Did a cut ever mend? Dismiss time and nothing changes. Parmenides wins.

Anti-evolutionists are very confused people. Timeless words can make people that way. Even so, they have to protect their self-ignorance in some manner. Banding together provides some sort of solace...an ice floe in a melting ocean. Protectionism arises...of ID's, the dominant position of those most weak and deprived of species understanding, deprived of any willingness to accept natural humanity or themselves related in any way to...apes, gorillas, chimpanzees, baboons, giraffes, lions, cats, dogs, frogs, mice, chickens, or vultures, yet we share elements of DNA with each, and all.

Gill Bejerano, U.C. Santa Cruz, using high speed computers, located 481 unchanged DNA segments common to fugu-fish, mice, men and to all vertebrates, segments up to 400 million years old (each segment 200 base pairs long). Chromosomes, mitochondrial DNA sequences, genomes...elements in a highly complex science (visit www.dna-rainbow.org for a look at excellent research). We are coming to a point: vultures.

All men share DNA and genomes with each animal, bird, or fish mentioned above. *This includes vultures.* While vultures have become pets to a few, we know of them as high flyers with abnormally high vision. With wide wingspans, tensile-strength claws and tearing beaks to match, they prey on carrion—dead flesh. Turkey vultures (there are varieties) initiate the unique practice of *urohidrosis*—pissing on their own legs. This practice causes a cooling of the legs through evaporation, allowing accelerated movement. While not linguistically adept at describing their own action, sufficient to say that they are pissing on their legs, their supports, to inspire, increase, and make further adept the total function of bird—to sate ravenous appetites on dead carrion. Do we see the link?

There is no guilt involved. Vultures act for one purpose—to satisfy appetites keeping the ID's intact. No ethics, no morals, no alignments other than to peers for mutual ingestations. (Was Rick Perry far off when he referred to Bain Capitol as "vulture capitalism" in the 2012 debates?) Supports (individuals or groups, no difference) are pissed upon with equanimity if, by doing so, advancement and survival of ID's result. Analogy, of course, but anti-evolutionary positioning cannot remove Republicans in House and Senate from *urohidrosis* behaviors—refusing to fund FEMA in its death throes, refusing to raise the debt ceiling, refusing to pass a jobs bill to get people back to work, pissing on unions and right to bargain, pissing on education from low to high, pissing on whatever legs it may have (support groups, *used* for ID acceleration) to piss on, for this is exactly what vulture-politicians do. This is what they want, what they "run" for, and what they use for food—dead carrion, and if alive...to either make dead or to hasten *extremis*. And the cruelest cut of all? My friends, extremists will piss on us and our children. Literally. How?

"I want Obama to fail," says Limbaugh. "Our goal is to make Obama a one term President," repeats Addison, cohorts nodding in forced assent. Then ask, how often do you hear a parent say to his/her children, "I want you to fail!"? Ever hear a teacher say to a student, "I want you to fail"? Yet we hear the major, major leaders of our country say to all of us, "We want this President to fail." When parents talk over the dinner table and recount these aspirations of "leaders," what might the children think? Might not the children think that they are in a different universe, that to the leaders of this entire country, *It is OK to fail?* "For if the leaders of that party of which my parents are members want the President of the United States to fail, *it must be OK for me to fail!*" Certainly the ranking of a President supersedes any ranking of a lowly student! And so kids fail, with no remorse, no guilt, no nothing. Gangs form from dropouts. Education suffers from bottom to top, blood in a body in which it's OK to fail because the leaders of the country say it is. Desirous. So why not comply?

"Failing" is not necessarily the term. Rather, *vulture-politicians want to kill*. They need carrion. They want a dead Obama so as to reap from the carcass. They want a dead certified Leader so as to claim equal "legitimacy" to throne. They want a dead President hoping, wishing to the core for his speedy death. Vulture-politicians feed on no accomplishment of their own, do not build, create, construct, or innovate. They simply circle overhead waiting, waiting for life to cease, then gorge on death... death of a nation through downgrading by a Standard and Poor's, death of the right to bargain, death of workers' families through starvation and unemployment, death of choice through gerrymandering, death of right to vote through intemperate restrictions...death to whatever confronts in life form. Death...to prolong life. Theirs.

Dysfunctional? Of Course!

If anyone was searching for a method to make a government dysfunctional, he need look no further than a two-party system. The two-party system embodies the principles of the *most basic* of cognitive acts—the A - A prime split. (We know the Principle: anything known can only be defined in terms of what it is not. We know also that the *Prime Directive of man is the acquisition, maintenance, and protection of his ID*.) Look at fields of cemetery plots. Each gravesite has the name of the deceased. Each deceased is so named due to membership in groups. No membership—family, armed service, social service, government...no name. No one has ever looked across fields of crosses, Stars of David, or Star and Crescents to see instead, *Species Specimen, Species Specimen, Species Specimen*...specimens absent group involvement.

The two-party system provides all: for acquisition of ID, group/party provides. For maintenance of ID, group/party provides. For protection of ID, group/party provides, but it is the nature of any group member to want to evolve, to acquire, to develop into the highest evolutionary level attainable within species.

If there are no obstacles, sated homeostasis rides in like lead-encrusted lethargy. No hunger, no need to look for food. No thirst, no need to dig a well. But if man has language, the capacity to relationally operate (think) with words to implant upon conquests, he will activate such capacity to procure ID food sources. And he does, to the extreme. Groups.

As any one group can define itself only in terms of what it is not, a group must either locate or construct an A prime counter—an anti-group by means of which it can *define itself*. Don't we do this all day long? What was Bobby Fischer absent a Boris Spassky? What is a man, absent a woman? What are the Mets absent the Yankees, or equivalent? What are the Republicans absent the Democrats? To protect, fortify, build, and strengthen the ID, an anti-group must be developed from which an A group can define its ID in terms of the characteristics (platform) of *that anti-group of which the A group is not!* The A group *must go contrary* if it wishes to develop, prolong, and strengthen its own ID. This it can only do by bartering the attributes of a constructed prime party/group into its own ID. The characteristics of the A prime group then become those upon which the A group is totally dependent! *The scenario most conducive to a dysfunctional government is a two party system by behavioral, developmental, and operational definition.* An applied example of petrified, undeveloped, i/e behavior restricted to i/e level, pre-adolescent…

The Bush 43 Presidency irreparably damaged the standing of both the Republican Party and the United States as well as by exposing the weaknesses in our electoral system. The goal of the current Republican Party: to recoup status and nothing less. One way to do that is to ensure that the Democratic President following would be allowed one term only, *no matter the reason* for termination. However, such would not equate with moral, ethical, or professional competence. Such only would equate with a childish tit for tat, a child smashing a dish because Mother wouldn't let him go to a sleep-in.

A "leader" would be needed to step into the fray, a foil to effect retribution, to bleed infusion of a back-at-you, scapegoating platform… a point guard shielding the effusions of hate and resentment coursing through the veins of the rebuffed, children who live only under the color of gown. Perhaps a leader could be found with the following attributions: estimated worth—$34M; backed by large financial institutions—USB, Fidelity Investments, Citigroup, Bank of New York, and by lawyers and securities firms; anti-finance reform, anti-health care, anti-government spending, etc.; pro-big oil and corporations (financial and otherwise, presumably board-membered by predominant "whites"); albeit divorced, 4F due to optic neuritis (a form of MS), called by the Citizens for Responsibility and Ethics in Washington one of the 15 most corrupt members of Congress (2009)…qualifications most acceptable, and "elected" as Senate Majority Leader, most "fit" to attack…

…this newly elected President, black, a lowly community organizer, married to one-and-only wife subsequently producing thereby two black daughters, non-divorced, athletic, young, good-looking, honest without taint of corruption or heavily doused with financial backing and certainly less than a millionaire when elected…who acquired fame, notoriety, a welcome presence and a dominant number of votes and who stood in the Senate Majority leader's presence face to face? Would not this fault-riven Senate majority Leader not want, most naturally, this President hidden from view so as not to see himself through a mirror, backwards? Who would want to see an individual of personal success, independent of thought, lacking financial grease, free of taint, lapping up approvals day after day, elected to the office of *President* when the SML could only acquire a facet of the attention by greasing media and a crew to follow? Wouldn't this SML want such a President as far out of sight as possible, a one-term President? Of course, and 300,000,000 U.S. citizens need suffer because of the impact of the behavioral desires of this one, deficient man? Of course. It's a two-party system, members un-tested, glued to ship to prevent desertion. It's the Constitution, after all, which protects like an insurance policy, a copy of which is stuck inside the SML's coat pocket for inked security (and the Founding Fathers envisioned a Congress held hostage by an Imperial Guard?).

In addition to the natural, operational, dysfunctional nature of a two-party Congress, there must also exist contributing dysfunctional members since every group functions only upon the composite of ID's therein comprised. In addition…

If one *really really really wants* to ensure a purely disjunctive, dysfunctional congress (in addition to supplying two mutually parasitic political parties with their consenting dysfunctional membership, each un-tested, un-assayed for competence), *Elect lawyers!* Lawyers are by bent, nature, and profession *adversarial*. What is any lawyer absent a contentious issue? Lawyers are script dependent. Enter any lawyer's office to notice the rows upon rows of indelible tomes of pro- and anti-confrontations. Such adversarial encounters are the lifeblood of lawyers and upon such they thrive. Blood pumps, temperatures rise, ID's and bank accounts swell.

50% of the Senate (2011) are lawyers, 38% in the House; 244 in all, millionaires. Notice the lack of educators, scientists, mathematicians…and notice the same failings by category in our public schools. Not an affinity of ID? Lawyers run for positions in Congress as dogs for Purina Dog Chow. Confrontations are built in, easy food for the ID hungry. No solicitations, no need to advertise, just a galleria, a coliseum wherein ID's expand as balloons gassed from a helium tank. And the beauty of it all? No judges to render final decisions.

Lawyers without judges? Heaven on earth. The only judge becomes the outcome of the case…won or lost, and who is there to curtail an extension…after extension…after extension, or to limit filibusters…pleas before the court? Lawyers above the law. Just crises, hostage taking, and while the lawyers float on slavered egos, the country waits and wails for word on how, and when, repair or replacement of dilapidated bridges, weakened dams, slipshod roads, decaying schools can occur…none of which find reference in a lawyer's library or mind unless as food for the contentious, most welcome by ID's voracious for self-recognition under a purloined cloak, colored by party…for these are the hollow men, species bound, who nevertheless hunker to the cloak room to grab gowns—protection against the cold of isolation, gowns of the two colors available—red *or* blue, species proxies each, substitutes for the seven billion of us threshing wheat, thinking that, robed, humanity lies underfoot. The sham of man entire condensed onto the dissonant leather chairs of a House or Senate. A dysfunctional Congress surely, with but the exceptional member rooted in the ground of species recognition and concern.

Sedition—All Day Long

We, our "Founding Fathers," constructed a Constitution, an A prime to an oppressive Europe's A. Within this Constitution, however, are holes wider than the Grand Canyon and into these holes creep worms, corruptive, greedy to the core…worms which gorge on you and me and our entire societal body. How did this come about, and why?

It is impossible to institute behavior onto paper. Inscripted nota become, in every instance, out-of-time, 2D, never in sync with a 4D STEM universe. The holes in the Constitution? *Term limits* as the epitome for content. For another? The Constitution is written.

Is the reader a parent, a teacher in any capacity, a mentor to one younger? What happens when a child does something wrong… steals, swears, tries to cross the street without looking both ways? Do you wait a prescribed amount of time before reacting? Do you have a manual which details the time-lapse, given the circumstance, before response? The Constitution is such a manual, a guide to response times…term limits. Further, the Constitution equates with a union contract protecting those "on the job" as elected by those so determined as fit and qualified voters. Try to fire an incompetent teacher under a UFT contract. Try to fire an incompetent, self-serving, antispecies governor, Senator, Representative, or President…each under union contract as specified by a ratified Constitution. You can't? Behavior thwarted, competence of the voter thwarted, democratic participation thwarted… Frustration to the core. Rejected, impotent, of no apparent value…each of us who would be so inclined to effect a personnel change (elimination and replacement). We become "outsiders," beyond contact…members of a disparate tribe.

If we are each members of a participatory democracy, we want our voices heard. Now. Not later. But if we have no sounding board within this government, if no one heeds our calls, what to do? Redial? Can we replace recalcitrant incompetents? No. Can we recall them, now, or is there a manual which dictates when, where, and how we can attempt their ejection? No, and yes. Thwarted again.

What to do?

Behaviors are immediate, in each and all of us, and if Teacher, or Mommie, or the Constitution of the U.S. says "No!" or "Don't" or "Wait" or whatever to impede reaction time, wish, or need…we get antsy to the extreme. Communication goes by the wayside. Cut off. A hole in the firmament. So, *what has to happen? Natura vacuum abhorret* (Nature abhors a vacuum). The vacuum gets filled, naturally, for if we can't get "leaders" to minister to our needs, immediate or pending future, we "elect" others equally hungry for ID sustenance and follow them, they *geared precisely* to our wants and our wants to them…they the fishermen, we the bait balls. But…but, what if an even more invidious method could be found *to infiltrate government itself,* to insert "worms" into the governmental fabric using the same food sustaining a chartered contract—obeisance instead to a "Party Constitution" and parlay that into a patriotic-defend-the-constitution gambit to frustrate delayed reaction time, to thwart that very institution which, in and of itself, thwarts us, its "constituents" by nature of its construction whether petrified on paper, carved onto granite or copied into American history text-books for all to see, like the Rosetta Stone, language for a chosen few and beyond change.

Our Founding Fathers realized the danger, the danger of artifice which was the Constitution. Jeff Jacoby (*Boston Globe*) quoted John Adams (1780): "There is nothing I dread so much as a division of the Republic into two great parties, each arranged under its leader and converting measures in opposition to each other." Adams may not have had the language we have today, but he "felt" the A - A prime split redundant in our daily commerce. He "knew" that the petri-faction of laws, directions, guides, platforms, and statutes inherent within the Constitution were holding patterns, inked and subject to infestation by worms… out of time, out of "touch," the Constitution but a guide for those capable. He knew. And today…?

Today we have the products, the innovators…threadworms, seat-worms, tapeworms…infestations devouring the human, constituted body…worms which eat at the body politic to render it ill, struggling with half-life, the "Protectors" sailing under the banner of "Party," "loy-alists to the core," copies of the Constitution in lapel pockets for proof, eating…eating…whatever is alive with future hope…killing, driving to death so as to feast. And *there is no cure.*

An Addison, Republican Party leader, Senate Majority head, can mount a federally constituted rostrum within a federally constituted building and commit sedition as easily as breathing foul air: "Our goal is to make him a one term President," said even *before* Obama assumed office. Filibusters, Nay's, delays, No's, "refusals to hear," riders to defeat, "Dead on Arrivals" and on and on… Is this not prescribed, directed, doctrinaire conduct devised to insurrect, to resist lawful authority, to prevent persons with lawful authority from executing their (his) trust and duty?

> **Sedition:** In law, **sedition** is overt conduct, such as speech and organization, that is deemed by the legal authority to tend toward insurrection against the established order. Sedition often includes *subversion of a constitution* and *incitement of discontent (or resistance) to lawful authority.* [Wikipedia]

> [1798] *That if any persons shall unlawfully combine or conspire together, with intent to oppose any measure or measures of the government of the United States, which are or shall be directed by proper authority, or to impede the operation of any law of the United States, or to intimidate or prevent any person holding a place or office in or under the government of the United States, from undertaking, performing or executing his trust or duty; and if any person or persons, with intent as aforesaid, shall counsel, advise or attempt to procure any insurrection, riot, unlawful assembly, or combination, whether such conspiracy, threatening, counsel, advice, or attempt shall have the proposed effect or not, he or they shall be deemed guilty of a high misdemeanor.* (And the recognition of such by…? Penalty imposed? Enforced by…?)

A government which cannot police itself cannot police institutions over which it may have nominal control, i.e., banking. Such a "government," having demonstrated an inability to self-discipline is a papier-mâché pretender leaving open hatches for invading "worms"…and the worms come. Any un-disciplined child *knows* how far he can go and in which circumstances. He knows how to feed, if improperly, upon the weaknesses of others. Enter a gang into the halls of Congress intent on wreaking havoc, always for personal gain. Who is to stop them? Under the guise of "Senators" or "Representatives" or "Governors," duly elected mountebanks practice, in the main, two major defense mechanisms: *sublimation and displacement.* We should understand something of each…

Harry Stack Sullivan, the pioneer of interpersonal psycho-analysis, defined **sublimation** as the unwitting substitution of a partial satisfaction with social approval for the pursuit of a direct satisfaction which would be contrary to one's ideals or to the judgment of social censors and other important people who surround one. The substitution might not be quite what we want, but it is the only way that we can get part of our satisfaction and feel secure. [Wikipedia]

Displacement operates in the mind unconsciously and involves emotions, ideas, or wishes being transferred from their original object to a more acceptable substitute. It is most often used to allay anxiety; and can lead to the displacement of aggressive impulses or to the displacement of sexual impulses. [Wikipedia]

There are scads of defense mechanisms, some of which we use daily just to keep the ship on an even keel. Every fallacy used in argumentative discourse is, in effect, a defense mechanism (barriers to honesty, truth, or ID exposure). So do defense mechanisms hide the truth of emotions, prejudices, hatreds, etc. If we understand a bit as to their use, we might then understand a McConnell *displacing* a hatred (racial?) from Obama the man to Obama the President—"a more acceptable substitute," *sublimating* his personal prejudices and hatreds under the cloth of Senate Majority Head to obtain "a partial satisfaction with social approval." Isn't this what Norquist's terra cotta figurines do...*displacing* their faux responsibilities to him, *sublimating* their fears of personal identification to a pledge sheet in order to get partial satisfaction with some sense of anonymous security? But we don't elect psychologists. We elect lawyers, blind to creepy crawlers and to seditionists who spin webs of deceit, calumny, and bitterness each fearing a social recognition of distorted and inadequate minds, seditionists who huddle together as worms, eating away at the warp and woof of this republic.

The Alien and Sedition Act has been modified, adulterated and adopted innumerable times and rarely enforced. Meaningless. Why? When sedition can be exercised with impunity, we know that two-party anarchy reigns, chosen members lavishing the ID income and that there is no controlling authority within this "constituted" government. *There is no cure!* The Constitution has developed multiple cancers, organs shot to hell, yet it shuffles along with plaintive cries of pity from past and passive well-wishers, its immune system on "malfunction." We see, we feel, we know. And there is no cure.

We can think of no source, no body capable of effecting change in this imbued system of "government" to which we have, through tradition and lack of will, surrendered ourselves. The reader might think, the Supreme Court? It seems quite unlikely that a Supreme Court which has proven itself incapable of differentiating an ExxonMobil from a fish monger, has here the capacity of differentiating other disparate classes. The classes? Constitutionally empowered representatives elected by free-rights citizens for them to so represent, vs. these same representatives, Janus-faced, ID's wrapped within political party, subject to group control by nature of party membership *superseding any obligation to represent citizenry.* As such, any political party extant within Congress through embodiment within elected representatives is, by nature, seditious. And the reader thinks that our Supreme Court will recognize such? C'mon, man.

How to End Our Two-Party system...

1. Find the Two-Party system un-constitutional (find adequate grounds—there are many. A dichotomous two-party system is antithetical to any advancement toward a more perfect *union*).
2. As voter, refuse to vote for any candidate aligned with a political party. If not declared as "Independent," don't cast a vote.
3. As a voter, *cast no vote for a lawyer, attorney, or professional litigator.* Such derive life and livelihood from *confrontation.*
4. As voter, vote only for candidates thoroughly vetted for competence, social adherence, ethics, intelligence, and inclinations for bias by independent political assessment boards comprised of psychologists, social anthropologists, psychiatrists (ortho- or homeopathic), experts in specific fields (economics, math, developmental psychology, intelligence. If

politicians are not good teachers, they should not be elected…and teachers—each and every one, is tested. (Politicians are above such?)

5. Do not vote for any candidate who either financed his campaign himself, or received more than $1,000,000 (?) in contributions from *identifiable* citizens.

6. Do not vote if the physical means to vote (logistics, machines, etc.) is not equally available to all qualified voters (through computers, Ipads, smart phones...coded citizenry, etc.,).

7. Do not vote if the right to vote is proscribed in any manner through discrimination (picture ID's, e.g.) instead of simple citizenry identification.

Slowly…slowly, the two-party system might be cast out like a kidney stone, excised like a tumor, expunged like stomach bile…properly, perhaps through the largest assemblies of protestors ever to assemble at governmental centers which confiscate the rights of its citizens for purposes morally, ethically, and perversely self-advancing for the species-aberrant few…nationwide.

SCOTUS

Extremists always operate outside species' norm either for personal ID acquisition or ID protection. Always. Even suicide bombers. We learned above ("Logic Reason and the ID") that formal, reasoned, academic logic has no place within the operational nexi of extremists, yet we would think that well-educated members of the Supreme Court might be practitioners of such—disciplined logic. We might even think that, as Catholics, the most conservative members of SCOTUS might have had some affiliation with a Jesuit institution in which refined Aristotelian logic held a key place in academic curricula. Apparently not. When the ID is at stake, logic goes by the wayside.

Logic, as Euclidean geometry, has rules, rules apparently oblivious to occasional members of SCOTUS, rules involving the three classes of terms—univocal, equivocal, and analogous…that if you use an equivocal term in a required three proposition syllogism, you must have an invalid conclusion; the distinction between universal, particular, and negative with implications upon validation of a conclusion; illegitimate extension; major and minor terms; undistributed middles, etc. Then *Citizens United*...

Vital to any relationship of *person* and *corporation* is a univocal determination of *class* (as discussed above). However, Dole Pineapple Corp. and Terry Bradshaw are of two *disparate* classes, the former forged on a 2D base enlivened through signature, the latter an ex-football star. Could a natural mind equate the two, one a STEM citizen, the other a product of structured Articles of Incorporation via a concocted relationship, *unnatural in kind*? Not the natural mind, no, but if unnatural to species yet sponsored by litigants demanding ID preservation, yes. *Citizens United*—a most severe violation of even the most basic logical substrata, provable as a multi-tiered logical *insequitur,* the decision forced through the sole decipherable cause... the acquisition and protection of ID.

Try SCOTUS' pre-decision arguments regarding the legality of the Health Care Act...

"I don't see the difference," (between burial insurance and health insurance) said Justice Alito. "Most people are going to need health care. Everybody is going to be buried or cremated at some point. What's the difference?" Chief Justice Roberts argued that if Congress mandated health care insurance for everyone, could not Congress also mandate that every one purchase cell phones? Newsweek's Paul Bagala ("Supreme Arrogance") labels such arguments as *reductio ad absurdum.* Go deeper, Paul. The real fallacy should be labeled *redutio ad me* (ego, mei, mihi, me, me). Let's see why...

Group the Supreme Court Justices. Lawyers. One job—the dispensing of "law." Required: not a law degree but appointment by politicians with similar disposition toward ID enhancement. Not required: workable familiarity with structured logic. The Issue? *Illegitimate extension.*

SCJ's (Supreme Court Justices) "know" that the class *burial Insurance* for the dead does not equate with *health insurance* for the living. There's no "health" for the former, and if dead, bye-bye. For the living, possibilities of illness and the need for care. Living. Roberts "knows" that mandated health care is of a disparate class from a mandated use of an electronic medium to GPS a local restaurant. They "know" this. So what are they really after?

Consider a man who spreads peanut butter (PB) on his bagel each and every morning whether at home, on a cruise or wherever. Everyone knows this guy—"He spreads PB on his bagel each morning that the sun comes up." *Everybody knows him*, and doesn't he get ID fed, from everybody, simply by using PB on his bagels? Now ask him to change...to switch to cream cheese. Will he switch and lose the central focus of hundreds, thousands, who know him for PB on his bagels, he to sink back down into the Epididymis awaiting speculative ejaculation once again? Hardly. Now ask a "conservative" ID-promoting SCJ to do the same...to switch from an ultra conservative stance fruitful solely for the acquisition, preservation, maintenance, and protection of his singular black-robed ID to a stance beneficial to that species of which he is a member. Ask him to forsake pacemaker-dependent ID allegiance upon particles of a Constitution's fading black ink and a political party which bestowed his SCJ's ID, forsaking ID glut for the benefit of the lesser, the weaker, those not health-insured (as is he) for these are the generic tyrants...the Assad's, the Koni's, the Hussein's, the Bashir's, the Khomeini's, the Pol Pot's...not a one of whom we would expect to divest himself of an ID entombed within protective garb of chain mail to then trod streets to help the homeless, feed the poor, or to assume the mantle of a Saint Francis or a Mother Theresa (all fellow Catholics to several SCJ's, just like Paul Ryan, Budget Master), for when fools come lapping at a petrefacted SCJ's door for sustenance, expect only a armored warrior mounted on black steed, lance locked in place until curtain drop.

Such are the products of our national educational system within university or grade school, curricula absent the human/species' constant. Such is the reason our children are shunted from species study and hijacked into "high stakes" testing of curricula void of any rationale of disciplined relational operations common to the nature of man as is found in logic, for *every SCOTUS decision can and must be reduced to syllogistic form and be subject to syllogistic review to verify validity*. The safety of "judicial" ID's (including those of House and Senate) resides in a populace *incapable* of recognizing illogic, bias, prejudice, and an inability to think in rational form as man's operative nature so inclines.

Even so, might we dare venture into causatives...behavioral and experiential, realizing that politicians rule the packaging not only of a Supreme Court but also of history within textbooks, whether or not children learn of their species roots, or the components of the brain and the physics of supporting operations common among all men? We might. Let's do...

For one member of SCOTUS, might it be possible that "the Word was made Flesh" was taken quite literally...that the "Word" (God) was made flesh and that the *words* found in any tome of jurisprudence should likewise equate with physical STEM reality and be considered therefore sacrosanct unto perpetuity? Could this member be considered a "strict constructionist" and most avid supplicant to constitutional liturgy?

Nor is it a great stretch to theorize that one SCOTUS member who entered a seminary as a youth is after something—perhaps a standard, a linchpin around which one could center a life having sprung from un-centered beginnings. Transfer the search to jurisprudence also embodied in timeless script and perhaps found might be a keel around which life may bend and twist, but always with words afoot to direct movement of the unsure, and then *hold on*, as one must when riding a San Francisco cable car, but silently. Maintain and persevere, for the creaking Constitution must be upheld in intent, meaning, and interpretation by those most in need of protection for a naked but appointed ID.

As for the Chief Justice, is it not unusual for anyone raised within a sliver slipper, from private elementary school through Harvard, to be prone to an adoration of money, prestige, and to what both can bring? Some raised in well-to-do families shun all, divest artificial gain, gird in hair shirts to help the poor, the forgotten and become saints. Others unfurl full sail, tack with the wind, and set off to seek El Dorado invited to sit in well-appointed captain's chairs on someone else's boat, unmindful of those who caulked the planks. So...

Is it possible that a Manchurian candidate, a SCOTUS member, could so direct interpretation of law as to extract from those decision-affected, attention and after-effect focus *upon himself*, the decision maker, garnering through behavioral alchemy the alteration of quantity (those affected) into quality—an explosion of personal ID into the nooks and crannies of this nation's social fabric even unto effects entombed within a National Cemetery? Could a Mother then be made more proud? *Citizens United* is off the edge, as are the black robes, who, with a linguistic *fiat*, violate those natural laws to which we are all subject, so that El Dorado, for a self-chosen few, can become reality.

So to retain a Republican sponsored ID and to make Mother proud, *Citizens United* could allow a candidate for President to buy his way into office, all because ID petrified Justices required ID attention and preservation of ID's standing on the ink of ancient script. And the *behavioral and dependency protocols* required to be assigned, assessed, and passed by any justice before deployment to office? Nowhere. Not for President with a Father complex, Senator, Representative, or Mayor. But for children? Control exercised. We can then ask, with deeper understanding…

Is it true, as Gabler writes (Neal Gabler, "Supremely partisan," *Boston Globe*, May 8, 2012)…

that "since Bush v. Gore, a case which the court could have easily remanded to Florida without adjudicating, the conservative majority has been brazenly partisan—voting not just for conservative interpretations of law but for Republican electoral success"?

that "This court…gladly took on Obamacare, and you don't have to be a genius to guess why. The majority wants to damage Obama's reelection chances."?

that "judicial partisanship…is the most potent and pernicious form of judicial activism—one that seriously threatens the separation of powers."?

that "The court has already determined one presidential election; it is about to determine another. In banana republics we call this judicial usurpation. What do we call it here?"?

that "The Roberts court will likely do everything in its power to elect Mitt Romney, including overturning the D.C. appellate court on Citizens United, which has given corporations virtually unfettered license to contribute to the Republican Party or upholding state laws that result in voter suppression."?

Do we understand that extremists, of whatever stripe or calling, abide to the death man's primary directive—to acquire and protect the ID? *It matters not* that the usurpation of Bush v. Gore allowed the election of Bush 43 and, in consequence, the deaths and mutilations of thousands of American soldiers (children to all) and the uprooting of hundreds of thousands of Iraqi families in a thieved war, as long as the beholding source of ID, the Republican party and its loggerheads, were given obeisance for bestowed ID's otherwise unobtainable? No extremist will acquire an exalted, Brahmin-enclosed ID to then discount the bestower *even if* species deaths result in the thousands, for these are T.S. Eliot's Hollow men…pledges to a Norquist's sedition, slaves to an Articles of Confederation, slaves to ink-buttressed ID's, minions to a Mephistopheles under glass.

RULE: It is impossible for an extremist to alter his petrified, group sponsored ID even if knowingly harmful to species' needs.

NOTE: Four alabaster Catholics, all in a row, stuck in the Douay dimension. Bush v. Gore, *Citizens United*, and anti-Affordable Health Care. Extremists who would complain if the soup was too cold but not if millions suffered, and died, as long as each ID remained intact unto *extremis*. Peanut butter on bagels. To prove the above rule invalid requires the display of an inward foundation of character, integrity, and an awareness of the obligations of men to men. Justice Roberts proved his possession of such attributes in writing the majority opinion supporting the Affordable Health Care Act. Such men are few and far between. Roberts' decision did something else. He did what pleases this writer to the core. In this case he proved me wrong. "Congratulations!" is too weak a word…for a man.

PART III

Combat

Chapter 11

TRANSACTION FUNDAMENTALS

One of the problems arising when taking aim at problems with a new cannon is terminology. Two sections follow, sections most important for which reliance and the obligatory thanks are due to Ernest Becker (*The Structure of Evil, The Denial of Death, The Birth and Death of Meaning, etc.*) and to the many works of Gregory Bateson (husband to Margaret Mead. For a background, check out *Wikipedia*). We will first discuss within these sections *transference* which may be considered *the key of keys* required to unlock an understanding of man's behavioral inclinations, then wind up with newly processed "double binders."

Transference

Within a few pages, Becker (*The Structure of Evil*) summarizes the term as used by a series of writers. Understanding that relational operations work with every human and that *no behavioral transaction whatsoever is absent the operational interplay of transference*, the terms will be presented, followed each in turn by a translation into *relational operations* (RO).

Becker: "[transference] refers to man's tendency to seek stable meanings in others, instead of himself."[26]

RO: Individual man, a unitary set—consciousness and all, acquires ID only through a group-meld with ID stability dependent upon the "stability" of the group.

Erich Fromm: "This mechanism [transference], idolatric worship of an object, based on the fact of the individual's alienation, is the central dynamism of transference, that which gives transference its strength and intensity."[27]

RO: "Idolatric worship of an object" is precisely that need of an individual to ingest into ID those properties of a group which assume 2D linearity and, as such, transcend now-time to assume permanence and adulation precisely to the degree that the individual is socially/culturally alienated.

Jung: "…always trying to deliver us into the power of a partner who seems compounded of all the qualities we have failed to realize in ourselves."[28]

RO: The "partner," whether individual or group, equates with group. If the group had no other "powers" than the individual possessed, why then would he join the group? There must be a "payoff," and that payoff is acquired, ingested ID food.

Adler: "[transference] is basically a maneuver or tactic by which the patient seeks to perpetuate his familiar mode of existence that depends on a continuing attempt to divest himself of power and place it in the hands of the 'Other.'"[29]

RO: When the individual ID is weak unto emptiness, "power" is both inscribed and acquired through conjunctive entry into the accepting "power" exercised by a group. These are the goose-steppers, the cliques, the "empties," those with no ID's other than as members of an accepting group.

Becker: "…transference is a form of fetishism, a form of narrow control that anchors our own problems…a taming of terror."[30]

RO: Like a treatment for autism—wrapping the patient tightly within an enclosing wrap, the individual fearful for well-being of whatever type will seek surcease to anxieties through tight adherence within an enfolding group, particularly one with life-controlling, life-directing protocols.

Becker: "The transference object always looms larger than life size because it represents all of life and hence all of one's fate."[31]

RO: Total investiture, total conjunctivity, total dependency. Without it, ID chaos. The only shop in town. If another, dependency may be weakened. That's why anti-species groups are so anti-competition. Weakness is not to be revealed.

Freud: "[transference is] 'a universal phenomenon of the human mind' that 'dominates the whole of each person's relation to his human environment.'"[32]

RO: *"Transference"—the need for group membership so as to acquire ID is indeed universal and does dominate each person's relation to his human environment. This "transference," however, is the operational need for a conjunctive relation within an ID food source. Set into set.*

Becker: "...the less ego power one has and the more fear, the stronger the transference."[33]

RO: We've said this often. *The weaker the ID, the greater the need for ID support accrued through group/individual idolatry.*

And so we get the picture. Transference has traditionally been viewed as a "fetish," a literal transference of one's "innards" to someone else, and notice the singular intent as to object. To a "one." Becker bends transference to an "object" designed to "save" one from death, or at least to mitigate the inevitable outcome. Fromm and others, rightfully, view transference as a somewhat universal phenomenon, a tendency, a gross inclination in us all to "inject" our wishes, desires, fears, terrors, needs...upon an other caused by our individual weaknesses and needs. Each of the above touch on the problem, each view with a somewhat specialized intent, but let's keep it simple: *transference is the amalgamation of behavioral relations instituted through species interaction—the consequential structuring of ID. Considered simply, transference is the basic lynchpin of ID acquisition* and takes place even when asking your waitress for a cup of coffee.

Transference is universal, a commodity resident in each of us. Use of the term is OK as long as we understand the mutuality. The patient transferring a father image to his psychiatrist is "transferring" a need to a potential source for possible fulfillment. The psychiatrist is, however, "transferring" *his need* for both source of income and verification of training (ID need) to patient. Transference is mutual, a two-way street. *None of us acquires ID absent others, but neither do others acquire ID's absent us!* If you join a group, the group changes. And so do you. In-time. A group supplicant affords that group whatever ID food he can supply (like the home-generating electric output supplied to a community grid), and receives in turn. The individual, a singular ID set, remains individually disjunctive while entertaining a group-conjunctive relationship with an ID food source (This fact will be seen as vitally important when we encounter Double Binders). However...

Before transference can take place, an "object" (person, group, etc.) must be ID'd. The operative relation here is the identification of an A prime—the initial operation. No overt action yet. For transference to take place, *in-time* communion must occur, a communal thrust from the g/e thread. To myths and an introduction to Gregory Bateson for a few implications...

Myths

Once we posit a belief in linear form, we can transfer to it whatever emotional constituency is needed to keep it in place, for we need to localize "beliefs" in order to function as a society—that money is real; that c's, a's, and t's are real; that the God is real to whom millions of my peers devote their lives in worship is real; that tomorrow will come with each hair on my head still in place. We require a steadfastness of beliefs or cultures will literally fall apart. And so do we believe in power and transfer to objects and people beliefs as we would amulets to a bracelet.

So what's the difference between a belief and a myth? Probably, just the spelling. Neither one posits a referential object in STEM reality. But, because an important myth is approaching, we need to broach the subject by steps and consider numbers and letters.

There are no letters or numbers, physically located, anywhere. We can't go to our supermarket and buy a pound of either, nor dig in the back yard for a bucket or two...of either. So, let's ask the correct question: *upon what foundation does either sit?* This question is so vitally important since, not understanding the answer, the option is left open for aggregations of deceit and proxy answers. As long as this question remains out of sight, out of touch, the shortest route to homeostatic relief is to...believe, to believe that numbers are real, that alphabetic letters are real, and that everything comprised of such must be real as consequence. But, delusions let us live the day. And so to Bateson and the myth of power...

The Myth of Power

"What is true is that power corrupts. Power corrupts most rapidly those who believe in it, and it is they who will want it most. Obviously, our democratic system tends to give power to those who hunger for it and gives every opportunity to those who don't want power to avoid getting it. Not a very satisfactory arrangement if power corrupts those who believe in it and want it."

And...

"Perhaps there is no such thing as unilateral power. After all, the man 'in power' depends on receiving information all the time from outside. He responds to that information just as much as he 'causes' things to happen...it is an interaction, and not a lineal situation. But the myth of power is, of course, a very powerful myth, and probably most people in this world more or less believe in it. It is a myth, which, if everybody believes in it, becomes to that extent self-validating. But it is still epistemological lunacy and leads inevitably to various sorts of disaster."[34]

The themes covered by Bateson recur throughout this book. Perhaps a few have been recognized. But we have a problem on our hands, and the problem is not necessarily one of transference.

Is "power" a myth? Perhaps, but a few questions: Does "power" accrue to candidates running for office? Do flanks of Secret Service personnel either denote or imbue power to those candidates qualifying for such service? Do the millions and millions of dollars spent campaigning endow candidates—singularly or collectively, with "power"? Does the time spent by TV political analysts and TV stations endow candidates running for office with "power"? Do candidates accrue "power" incrementally as months/years pass in campaigning? Do candidates running for political office exercise any station of cause-and-effect regarding any aspect of any of our daily lives? Is there "power" inherently within the Supreme Court? No? Then what's going on?

Epistemologically of course, Bateson is right. "Power" is a myth… or is it? What is needed, of course, is a definition of power.

No man has "power" (read "authority") unless "given it" by members of that group over which such "power" is to be assumed. With the issue of campaigning candidates, the issue is *transference* shifted to the need for ID acquisition and verification, avoiding anxiety through fear in the process. If I align my sympathies, feelings, desires with candidate X, I will not particularly want candidate Y to "win" and thereby disavow, disassemble, or prove mistaken my ID-identifiable projected inclinations toward X. Who wants his favorite team to lose? Loss engenders disappointment, not necessarily in the team's loss but in the loss of time-accrued ID verification. The team's loss diminishes me. Fear of such loss of ID verification equates with anxiety. A winning team equates with positive ID verification. Same with political candidates.

But power a myth? Absolutely, and we propagate the myth. How? By investing truckloads of money, months/years of time; quantities of TV, radio, and print media to warrant governmental subsidies for trees cut for pulp and electric generating stations for output. Certainly, *certainly*, only a society bereft of its senses would endow such political pursuits with in-time, 2D and 4D physical, emotional, and operational acts unless such prolonged acquisition of "power" were an absolute! We strive for ID verification through the degree of commitment which we surrender/transfer to any candidate, group, or golden cow. If our accrued, past-built ID gets verified via the "wisdom" of our choice even if we have to put money into the kitty, then what else is there?

What is the difference between promoting a "democratic" system of government with all its rituals of timed tenure, campaigning for office pledging with life-giving blood to "preserve, protect, and defend" the Constitution of the United States—a 2D, out-of-time decaying document, *and* a political "religion" (voting) which even George Wills refers to as part of a civic "liturgy"? Both embody belief to the edge of the plateau. And the return? There isn't any. Any beach consists of an infinite number of grains of sand. I am one, you are another. And if you want your ID verified, challenge yourself with a jigsaw puzzle, and complete it. If you accept the "myth" of "power," of one man or men over others, yet dismiss the operational dimensions of ID verification and acquisition through groups, you deserve to do the jigsaw only to find a piece missing. "Power" corrupts, as does continued schizophrenia. There are those who hunger for it like the Three Christs of Ypsilanti and those who choose to work in an orange orchard.

So we find that "transference" isn't really transference after all (but we will continue to refer to it as such). Instead, we find transference to consist of sequential relational operations entailing the ID of an A' with a tentative formation of disjunctive states prior to tentative conjunctive gropings in hopes of acquiring A-ID satisfaction—ID verification, protection, and sustenance to some degree or other. In these sequential operations so do we each and all participate—daily. It's *what* we are, attempting to prove *who* we are. To the brain…

The brain directs us…what to do, when to do it, how to do it, and can retreat into subservience if so forced, still, however, with a never-ending quest for homeostasis. So, if our brains, our ID's, strive for dominance, don't all other epididyan brains and ID's do likewise? And dependence still reigns? Absolutely, and, as such, rise is given to transference again, that domineering interactive behavior which treads those unfortunately unknown paths throughout every sulcus, every synapse and co-joint cell within every brain on earth. For we live through transference. We talk, eat, move, swear, and behave in every instance due to transference. To what? To whatever provides dictate to our behaviors. It isn't pigeons, Mr. Skinner. It's my wife cooking dinner; it's Stupak changing a vote and getting called "Baby killer." It's a black President, a Republican, a Democrat, an Assad or McConnell or an opposing linebacker. It's whatever becomes an in-time target of the ID's attention and to which, therefore, the ID must respond. Transference. In-time…now. Respond and react through incorporated recognition of source—inside. Otherwise, we're dead. And so…?

Who out there in this cloud of humanity understands his nature to such an extent as to be able to stand and say that his ID was built totally upon dependencies…dependencies of transference to parents, to teachers, to car mechanics, to every little pinprick of reality within which he sat, sits, creates, and abides? I am nothing without you, nothing without my species mates, nothing without all endured from my moment of conception to my now with balding crown. We understand this. But do we? If basic to core, if true to core, then any who understand should be able to stand and admit to such dependencies…upon any A'which at any instant of now can arouse the A-ID response which *is*…at that moment. To the issue…

There is no tyrant who would admit to dependency upon any issue affecting his ID status of the moment. For to admit to dependency would be to reveal a lack of autonomy, to a lack of "position" upon which his status actually rests. The only dependency a tyrant would admit to is the dependence of others *upon his* autocratic status/position which such other-dependence-upon-me supports and defines. This inability to recognize species-interdependence defines the most flagrant of tyrants as it does the individual who decries the "positions" of others as meaningless, harmful, or "out-of-step" with the demands of the moment when such positions are of ID-nature-bent, produced by species members in hopes of ID advancement even if perverted and anti-species. Otherwise, why are such "positions" produced? And where does all this take us regarding politics, government, genocide, murder, leadership behaviors and the de-fanging of extremists? Right into their garage!

Priming the Peace Pump

Life is like the MasterCard[r] logo…two circles inter-joined. The astute reader will recognize that the intersecting circles represent *every relation possible* in this 4D STEM universe: identity, negation (exclusion), inclusion, conjunction, and its converse, disjunction. But within time, and within the human experience, these relations are forever bouncing this way and that…enlarging, shifting, excluding…and in so doing, they define for us the operational stability of groups, of us as individuals, and any politician. So…

With the circles connected only by a wisp of connectivity, you may find the mystic, the seer, the wise pundit. With the circles almost on top of one another, you will find the undeveloped, the immature…

the individual so bound within the group as to have no visible ID apart. So, what determinations can be made?

If, as a species, some of us are so mature as to be relatively independent of group domination, of an involving membership, and others are so stricken by membership as to have no workable ID apart from group membership, then an operative disparity could be roughly measured. Example: if the level of cognitive (operational) stability of a particular group could only be defined through the defined dicta of membership requirements, then the latter membership equates precisely to an inclusive-bound level of development. As we know, inclusivity, in the scheme of time, excludes the higher levels of cognitive operations, namely, the conjunctive/disjunctive (c/d). Any group and its members which therefore operate only and exclusively upon the defined 2D dictates of *group* membership forgo any release of group dicta so as to allow *individual independence* within the scheme of species-defined behavior. In other words, to the degree that individual members of a group act *en toto* in accordance with the defined dicta of the group, to that extent are both the individual and that group immature, operationally delayed, and behaviorally restricted…to the i/e level. Knowing this, can there be instruments of behavior modification exercised toward an immature, ID-demanding inclusive group? Yes, but there's a rub!

The rub? The "rub" lies in finding people in leadership positions with sufficient smarts to know approaches, strategies for ID manipulation. With ID the issue, we have three MUST rules regarding i/e "enemies"—nations with leaders seemingly beyond touch whose barbs, enmity, and intransigence we would wish to remove, from neighbors and from political leaders at home, ID's petrified unto group:

RULE 1: To acquire peace with particular i/e nations and groups, the collective ID's of each social level must be promoted from inclusive to disjunctive.

Wars occur between i/e nations/groups which have lost both the ability and opportunity to reach concurrence among issues. Ever have a child who wanted to "go his own way" or do his "own thing" when you fully understood that "his way" was wrong, damaging, and an absolute road to failure for either himself or others, and you needed to stop it? What did you do…talk, which due to his behavioral set perhaps led to further estrangement (He needed to develop his A-ID using you for his A'), punish (sanction, which further increased his A-ID shell), or…ignored? If congenial, reasoned talk failed with a "closed mind" ("closed" to the purpose of discovering ID independently), then the best course (I'm certain you found) was to ignore, which is often the best route to behavior modification. However, after a hiatus in behavior, how did you win him back? Well, ever sit a platter of Mom's spinach lasagna right in the center of the dining table, junior sulking in his room? Does junior come out, sit at the table, and perhaps enter into a bit of un-pressured dialogue to "pay for" the lasagna? From an i/e recalcitrant, you brought him to disjunctive. Dialogue is now possible if within mutually acceptable boundaries.

RULE 2: Dialogue is impossible between two i/e sets. Dialogue *is* possible between two disjunctive sets.

With nations and groups, the same route must be followed. There must be a reason for Y to come out of his shell to desire talk. Threats are out. Punishments are out. Sanctions are out. Exclusions of whatever nature are out since they do nothing but force Y to thicken his A-ID shell against his potential A' ("us" in this instance) which *could* help him define his ID within an accepting world community. If we, X, refuse to enter into an A-ID fortifying relationship when such is possible, there may be hell to pay. An example and Fareed Zakaria: "Imagine if we had kicked Russia out of the G8 and broken most ties with Moscow—as the Republican nominee, John McCain, and many neoconservatives have long wanted to do. Then, when the Russians attacked Georgia, we would have had only two options—appeasement or war."[35]

Let's understand…*i/e politicians need A primes for ID sustenance, if not outside our borders, then within.* So where does that leave us?

RULE 3: Always congratulate, if possible, the ID'd leader of the offensive group for an action committed, no matter the act and no matter the perhaps odiousness of the group and act.

If any approach other than the congratulatory—which is conjunctive promoting—is used (if used), exclusion/negation results. *This rule is absolute.* To reproach is to exclude. To label with epithets is to exclude. To criticize group-enforcing and defining dogma of whatever sort is to exclude. The reigning question then becomes, of course, why not? Why not label as exclusionary, groups or leaders as "evil," "thieves," "hostile," "inimical" with "Western" or "our" interests, "Anti-American," "Kenyan," "socialist," "Cultist," or...? Well, because...

Every act committed by anyone, any time, is done for the purpose, even if forced and species-negative, of acquiring, sustaining, or developing ID. The "leader" acts; he is responsible for acts committed within his reign and he wants ID recognition. Give it to him. If you don't, *he will do the same thing again until he gets the ID recognition he's after!* Again, *exclusion never works* (and that includes sanctions).

If Y isn't congratulated (when feasible to do so), animosity, estrangement, and deep i/e behaviors may result—war, in other words, since you were given the opportunity to provide ID food but abstained. Absence of ID opportunity is as noted as is its presence and the key vehicle at work here is again, *transference*.

If any leader "congratulates" correctly a nemesis for a correctly identified act, *he who was congratulated has no choice* but to admit to *an equal identification of response* and therefore to mutual recognition of himself as having been ID-fed *by the congratulating leader!* (Transference cannot be denied!) And, if he doesn't want X's congratulations so as to appear as a bedfellow in X's camp, what must he do? Right. *He must stop the inimical action.* A given. So, deny the act and the ID of the egregious leader is denied. Peace becomes impossible. To get "fed," he'll simply try again, and he needs food! Therefore, *the act must be ID'd*. Then, with the act and actor ID'd, transference becomes overt and that's what we're after.

Transference is the chink in the armor of the inclusive (exclusionary) ID.

Inclusive/exclusive thinking involves a single subset within a mother set—one apple in a bushel of other apples. No room for an orange, kumquat, or peach. To allow the insertion of an orange, the conscious apples, each with an ID, must want it! If force is used, the opportunity for d/c (disjunctive/conjunctive) thinking is lost. "If I can't choose to have it, then I don't want it. Destroy my ability and facility to chose, and you destroy my autonomous ID. Do that, and

I'll do whatever I can to destroy you in turn." Sound familiar? It's the cause of every war. Lack of understanding of the behavioral impact of operational relations. Iraq, Korea, Vietnam, World War I, II, Iran...*ad infinitum*. So we congratulate to open the doors for communication.

To be a devoted inclusive member of an inclusive group is to be operationally immature with highly diminished capacity to expand operational thinking to countenance the conjunctive. Because of that operational immaturity people die, are dying at this moment, and will die in the future. We must pry open closed minds. With an understanding of humiliation, we have a starting point, an appreciation of the fragility of the human ego—an ego, an ID, which we must learn to play.

The Roots of Humiliation

> Diplomats and intelligence professionals must acknowledge that honor and *humiliation* often weigh as heavily in the minds of statesmen and citizens as do economic and security interests...perceived humiliation—one of the most prevalent, least explored factors behind global violence. Samantha Power[36]

wounded pride, impaired security, forced to swallow, lost grandeur, emasculation, neutered, honor and humiliation, running tallies of slights, invading a country out of humiliation, humiliating Russia, lost status, Georgian aggression, brewing rage, how far Russia will go...all phrases used by Power. "The time of humiliation is over," says Putin. *Russia's simmering fury, alarming sense of victimhood,* and also from Putin, the "stick" that Western countries had employed "will come back to knock them on the head."

It is no accident that synonyms for humiliation are *debasement, abasement, and mortify*. We all understand what the root *mor* or *mors* stands for, and that *bassus* and *base* leads to "basement," *humus* to ground or soil.

The limbic system of a nation's leader(s) is, by notice of office, incorporated within the operative policies of that nation. A man in

Russia is equipped with the identical emotional repertoire as a man in the U.S., Guinea, Pakistan, Kazakhstan, Libya, or Syria. Humiliate the man in titular office and humiliate a nation. The reverse also holds true. One acquires ID through the other. Intertwined, conjunctive, inseparable.

When cultures co-join, either through mutually accepted assimilation or as a result of time-elapsed conjugation following an invasion or some such, the humiliation initially encountered by those "invaded" often renders itself into forced acceptance—to survive. History is replete with such—the influences of Alexander the Great, the Roman Empire, the Greeks, the English "Commonwealth"…simply look at Sicily or Afghanistan as microcosms invaded countless times, or European and African countries (minus imposed borders). At one time or another tribes, factions, groups, nations…all suffered humiliation. However, the problem today is, none of us have the time for it and we have to save ourselves from those who are so abysmally ignorant of the impact and effects of humiliation. These are the ones—the ignorant, who would kill us and untold numbers outside our borders, innocent, caught in the crossfires.

Humiliation is the mildest form of genocide, leaving bodies intact but with riven minds. ID's asunder, and not in the best interests of either the U.S. or our species. But humiliation feeds the pernicious hungry.

RULE: Whoever humiliates either individual or group (nation) creates two *exclusionary* sets: one, the humiliated target, and two, the causative instrument.

RULE: Promote exclusionary sets to advance war or to bolster A prime's importance as an ID food source (e.g., "Hell No, You Can't!" [And I'm so important I can stop you!] "We must constrain Russia." [Romney]).

Any ID-hungry national leader, to accrue ID input—even if negative, has, does, and will create i/e status within one or more separate nations (or political parties). The conclusion follows: *Weak ID'd leaders draw nations into war or political parties into combat to guarantee income of ID food.* The same operational structures are used by extremists in any of our home-grown political parties—one continuously feeding, symbiotically, through the other. Witness Cantor walking out of a "bipartisan" debt-ceiling conference in June, '11. Or visit an interview with Rudy Giuliani in *Newsweek*, May 20, '11 in which he expressly stated, "they [Republicans] *better start dividing* over things [in preparation of the'12 elections]," or a McConnell who said to TV audience, "As long as *this President* is in office, there will be no solution to problems." In democratic nations we "elect" such "leaders" to so perform as their emotive ID needs and operative capacities dictate, and we are the poorer for it.

The purpose of humiliation, to flaccid A-A' politicians or media mouths, is to fortify A-ID's *through division*. If success is achieved in one instance, the process becomes addictive (witness continual attempts by a Beck, Limbaugh, McConnell, Coulter, Gingrich, *et. alia.*), each instance an attempt to curry leader-needing minions, through divisive attacks. We must note…

RULE: The possibility for humiliation cannot exist outside group affiliations.

Try to humiliate a hermit in an Alaskan outback. He'll laugh at you. However, humiliate any singular member of any established i/e group and you've attacked a beehive.

Any attempt at humiliation in any arena is an exercise in futility. The "put-downed" is the "put-downer" also, in-separable species members. Too, every humiliation *requires* a "get-back" to retain ID stability. Those brothers, those sisters living within another nation could be us were it not for the accidents of birth. And where do politicians—nations' leaders, acquire the "food source" to implement humiliations upon other nations? Why, at home, of course. The impetus to humiliate comes not from nowhere. Consider *any* national leader who would attempt to humiliate—through any means, and you will find that *first, he is a prime subject for humiliation himself* (and he knows it!). He would implement humiliation on others to hide his own vulnerability (Did the ineptitude of a Palin ever result in her humiliation, or a Bachmann, now moving to Switzerland? Does either rant against anyone…or any thing, ever, or does a Gingrich, McConnell, Limbaugh, or ___?). Humiliat*ing* becomes a practice and a bounce-back identifier of ID weakness. But then…

Isn't the base form of politics the art of who can humiliate the greatest number with the greatest effect? Consider our politicians who would humiliate *us* through insipid behaviors, who would attempt to prevent legal immigrants from voting ("They'll become Democrats!"), who would attempt to restrict potential votes unfavorable to "party" through "photo ID's" and the like; who purposely restrict funding to schools, nurses, mental health, public radio, planned parenthood, etc.—groups intrinsically dependent upon federal and state funding (but very weak in political support); who gerrymander local political districts as easily as splitting continents, drawing lines through tribes, factions, cultural groups with the ease of a French curve and pen, and when disruptions occur, collectively bond and feed upon the A prime food sources, the "carrion" which *they created*! These aren't attempts at social, cultural humiliation, "circling the wagons" efforts to prevent invasions of "germs" which would expose extremely weak ID-immune systems? For the issue is and will continue to be, finding adequate ID food. Isn't this what fish, meerkats, and vultures do all day long? All of the above instances of act involve attempts at *humiliation*—of you, me, and the deprived of our neighbors. And the easiest way to establish ID hegemony of one group over another, for those so weak and absent species concern ("I don't care for the poor…"), to proclaim power over another as superior is to inferior is to do…what? Species be damned. Humiliate and be fed.

So what does a Y *need to do* if humiliated? Y has two choices: 1) he incorporates the humiliation, accepts it, acquiesces because he has no profitable outlet and moves on, or, 2) he ingests the humiliation within his ID-body-apparatus and strikes back hoping to kill the vehicle which recognized his ID deficiency and destroy it! So, from 2D to 4D to WW I, Pearl Harbor, to 9-11, to genocides, world wars and "He needs to be a one term President." Mission accomplished! (Ring a bell?). Name your poison. Exposure of the inept.

Political humiliating is usually done behind either closed doors or at a rostrum and only under the cover of group support. Rarely, if ever, is it done individually, face-to-face. This little fact reveals the customary cowardice involved in the humiliating act. Would a Limbaugh or McConnell ever stand toe-to-toe with an Obama on a public stage? Would a Beck ever "debate" a Biden? Would a Bush 43 ever have shared dual rostra with an Ahmadinejad, a Kim Jong, a Chavez? Attempts at humiliation couched in sarcasm, non-verifiable criticism, or tags on bumper stickers simply identify the ID needs of dangerous, hollow men.

The Apology

The true leader will be open to all varieties of human attributes, indeed welcome the differences, indicative of a well-developed conjunctive countenance. While the entrenched –A-ID (Minus A-ID) "leader" can never "apologize" and thereby reveal weakness in ID—a shell incapable of withstanding criticism (Gingrich), the d/c (disjunctive/conjunctive) leader *can* easily apologize, out of strength. The difference is clear. For a strictly hard-core –A-ID politician to admit to ID-shell fractures is to wither in felt stature, to admit to false construction. He therefore admits nothing, stays blind, doesn't apologize, and stays firm within the confines of a carefully constructed web of 2D deceit, his imaginable time-less world remaining out of commerce with 4D STEM. Conversely...

A politician who can admit to a "crack in the wall"—an imperfection in his ID shell, reveals that, even with the "crack," both he and his group can withstand any onslaught which may arise. Such a politician gives evidence of membership within *two* groups, not just one: his species-stalwart personal ID group and the larger human group— his species. For only people sensitive to the imperfection of species' behaviors can recognize the need for apology. The -A-ID politician, by refusing to bend to apology, admits to an ID shell *incapable of behavioral (i/e) alteration*. The g/e thread again proves dominant. It doesn't take a class in Behavior 101 to recognize admiration for an apologizer, who in the same instance is "man enough" to admit to a weakness, a flaw, an imperfection. No one of us is perfect and the public recognition of such cannot be faulted.

We understand that -A-ID politicians are *anti-species*. Their heads are in lock-up, in a closed i/e set incapable of penetration either from the inside out or the outside in. So what's the difference between a tightly closed –A-ID i/e set and a bunkered Khadafy or a Mafia-protected Assad? Answer: nothing. Nothing in, nothing out. And guess what gives rise to war in each and every instance?

Locked-up, frozen i/e behavioral sets incapable, unwilling of penetration.

Any apology gives rise to disjunctive behavior—the precursor to conjunction and peace, the intermingling of species' members. The g/e thread in each of us gives rise to the recognition of such. No apology = no movement behind a structured wall, either in or out. Apology = the Door to Peace, open if attendant to species' behaviors and good manners. So...

What if a national leader stood before a world pulpit and apologized...for whatever? Hmmm... If such were ever done, and his supporting group remained intact if not stronger, what might any citizen of any tyrannized country feel about *his own* leadership group? Hmmm... "Why can't my leader ever apologize? Does he think he's perfect...that we're perfect? Oh, that's it. He thinks that we are perfect, his cause is just, and that he is the reflection of truth, justice, and the ___ way." But, does our tyrannized citizen ever note imperfection in anything? Was the soup too cold? He then notices that the leader who apologized remains in power but that, after the apology, *his* political group and military exert more social control than ever...his leader's group encased, rigid in plasticene, unmovable, unable to... and he's suddenly very, very afraid...of a pinprick, and to prevent any upsurge of natural bile at the revelation of his, the leader's ID lock-up, the dictator clamps down and drowns the citizenry in the fear of an imposed Armageddon (Assad, Khadafy, Hussein...)

Coupled with the arsenal of combat techniques presented herein, the effective apology must *automatically* initiate a crack in *any* tyrannized group's ID wall or expand an extant crack unto collapse. Sequence: Apology to reception, reception to comprehension (if operationally capable); from comprehension to assimilation (if capable of grounds for understanding); from assimilation to recognition of a schizophrenic split within the very inability to give evidence of species-bred grounds for conjunctive act! An in-escapable bind. And the number of potential lives saved...at home and abroad? Locate a good calculator.

The apology. The unused double bind—anathema to dictators of all stripes and just capable of instigating revolutions, stopping wars, or making functional, dysfunctional governments. But who is so capable...?

Listening—First Course

The road to peace goes along two canals and into the inner ear. If world leaders listen, *really listen,* there will be no wars. Two participants are needed, both in disjunctive states with the potentials to enter conjunctives. This means freedom for both from restricting, dogma/doctrine bound i/e sets. Double Binders (below) can break the perimeters of petrified i/e sets but unless parties are capable of listening, no progress is possible. Let's be optimistic for, as we will see, good listening can shatter the walls of the most hardened, entrenched tyrant or trained zealot.

There are three types of listeners—the Good, the Bad, and the Ugly. In sequence...

The Good (X)

Sticks on topic initiated by Y

Switches topic only with Y's consent

Stays silent when necessary to allow Y to explain his position fully

Does not interrupt

Does not insist on presenting his own position without Y's consent

If incontrovertible conflict arises, states "acceptance" of Y's position and reiterates* Y's position to indicate full understanding

Asks for clarification of Y's position to clear any possibility of misunderstanding (thereby reducing the A-A' operational structure in Y)

Searches for any route to an conjunctive bond superseding Y's need to operate from an A-A' status

Meets Y on his terms, whether by means of garb, food, locale or whatever

*"Reiterates"—mirrors Y's position (most probably absent tiers [below]) from an A' peer perspective, requiring Y to present rational support for his position or appear foolish, irrational, or out-of-touch. Such mirroring *demands* identification of mode of support—historical, protection, vengeance, ideological,

group constraints or whatever, ID'ing for X the mode to resolution.

X makes the powerful point of apologizing at the slightest indication of an affront to Y or to any aspect of his country, group, or party revealing thereby a crucial ID independence from any group-bond which would coerce submissive behavior (a dissonance-causing petard!)—a state impossible to maintain by a group-sponsored ID.

By every act detailed above, X reveals a constrained, quiet strength *which demands matching by* Y, and if not matched, reveals Y's discordant operational structure and weaker, emotionally submissive ID.

NOTE: We understand that this prelude to an end-game could only be achieved by parties *submitting* to a talk-and-listen, *face-to-face* meeting. Any rejection of such meeting identifies those factions (politicians under whatever guise) whose need for ID food supersedes any and all needs for conjunctive, species' peace.

The Bad (Y)

In defensive mode, switches frequently from topic on hand due to inadequacy of understanding, ignorance, operational development, or fear of ID attack

Attempts repeatedly to put topic on familiar ground he can handle

Overtalks X to impede X's full disclosure of position thereby showing lack of respect for both X and X's position without clarification of reason

Insists on presenting his own position with or without X's consent

Never reiterates X's position for fear of inadequacy revealed, but readily accepts the status of conflicting positions as indicative of an A-A' gulf

Discourages any attempt to locate a middle ground and his readiness to leave his A' bunker

Insists that X conduct the interview on Y's terms—locale, time, etc., indicating ID intransigence buttressing the A-A' gulf

Never apologizes for any act no matter the severity or injury in any manner to X's ID or to that of his group.

The Ugly

Refuses recognition of commonality of species affiliation

Remains group-bound in ID-lock and at i/e operational level

Refuses to question, refuses to reveal factual support of positions, refuses to answer questions directly, evades issues, refuses to examine supporting arguments of opponent in any regard due to fear of exposure of his own fractured supports fearing that his own platform would be revealed in its deficiencies

Generally speaks *absent the potential of rebuttals* which could wipe away his façade exposing faulty facts and poorly founded ID (Ahmadinejad at the UN, Presidential candidates campaigning...)

Refuses to listen to challenges however directed to protect tenuous defense system

Let's examine...

Every UL (Ugly Listener) *has an agenda,* closely guarded. If the normal g/e-species impulse is toward conjunctivity—the joining of members, and the UL as his group leader refuses to attempt an offered chance to bond at whatever level with his A', it must be for particular reasons. One, we easily understand: *fear* which will counter the g/e impulse to bond if A-A' bonding, to any degree, might dissipate an "insoluble" bond to i/e group. Will Hamas talk with Netanyahu? Will Netanyahu talk with Hamas? Would a McConnell ever wish for the President to succeed for the benefit of country and children watching, achieving success, not failure? Consider the Hawks who would choke if Obama countenanced talks with the Taliban. Consider a Ryan who might go apoplectic if the need to raise revenue would involve tax increases to his surrogate support group, the rich. The issue: ID protection at all costs. The second reason for refusal to commit to conjunctive bonding is a bit more subtle...

UL (our Ugly Listener) *needs to go fishing...*for ID support, support peculiar to him/her since he forsakes that natural communal bent in which both he and X ply life. A joining in species-bond with a g/e based group would short-circuit that bond he has within his closed i/e group, species absent. UL knows of only one source of ID support, that same source from which he derives 100% of his ID, that source upon which he is totally dependent—his group, his food source which needs to be continually replenished.

To fish, one needs bait. Bait, particularly as used in the context here, flies under false colors. Example: if a fish "knew" that a barbed hook was embedded in offered bait, would he bite it? Well, of course most humans do just that. They go to movies (they "ate" the promo), they use Cialis (having been "baited" to consider a twenty minute erection indicative of impotence), they buy Double Whoppers ("Everyone's eating 'em!"), and they bond in groups to protest anything from A to Z if, by bonding with a group, they get fed. So...

UL must *not* get at the truth (if "truth" it is). The process is simple. UL must first extract just that part of an improvised proposition (X initiated) which could mesh within his operational structure so as to become ID bait. This he does by acquiring a fishing pole—an instrument with which to reach out to "fish"—for you and me and anyone else who could offer him food. The fishing pole could be any microphone in any town hall, any speaker's box, any media receptive to op-ed pieces, any media which needs servicing and which would spill UL's spleen to an equally needy audience...*absent X's presence!* So, UL dissembles, hides, obfuscates, and invokes voices from other rooms, X never in sight (it couldn't be otherwise! Bait ceases to be bait with the hook in sight!).

So our UL drops his line...doesn't have long to wait, and gets bite after bite...little fish ignorant of the brain's operational prowess, little fish who band together under UL's song and sing Hallelujah to UL's sermon. UL reels them in...and feeds...becoming what he eats, rising in stature equal to X *because of X*...with X never "listened" to, never directly resourced or questioned, for UL needed his food and slave to X he refuses to be (but became so, dependency of ID buried under operational suppression). Dependence repressed, submerged, within souls kindred in kind, tingled into cramps causing tumors marked by strapped-on-guns brought to town hall meetings, Hitler signs, Obama with mustache and swastika...with a UL on *Time's* cover with his tongue stuck out. Mormon. Sanctifying all.

But media needed food also, as does any AIG, insurance company, Wall Street behemoth...having filled baleens with masses of plankton—you, me, and money, assumed into ID for sustenance.

Never mind the needs of species-like hunkered in bunkers with hands out adrift in time seeking only water, food, salvation for body's shell within which reside the awake, aware, conscious residue of species' spawn. Never mind. "There are priorities and our isolated-ID-world reigns supreme," say the brokers. That's why your terrorist, party leader, insurance head, banker, or political extremist will never allow open dialogue, compelled thereby to listen to species' cries (How often is it that one sees a Boehner or Cantor or McConnell or ____ questioned while standing behind a podium?). As unresponsive to species' needs, they require sequestering, quarantine from open space, a rostrum usually with bodyguards standing behind. "Refrain from solicitation."

RULE: Extremists will sequester themselves to avoid face-to-face talk-listen confrontations for fear of revelations of faulty, aberrant ID's out of-step with species' needs. Those desirous of peace will demand the opposite, recognizing that…

RULE: The greatest fear of any man with an operationally immature ID is that his ID will be challenged in cause and forcefully changed due to disclosure of faulty construction by a group of which he is not a member.

For indeed, each fragile ID must be protected, most often within the bulwark of group. In response to ID attack, straw men regroup, form an A' and fight within an immune system operationally constructed for defense. The "home group" is sacrosanct—the one primary source of ID food no matter the man or the group. So is it any wonder that groups would fight, scream, kill, rape, maim, bludgeon, lie, or hold an entire country hostage (debt ceiling, Jobs Bill…) whenever…to retain the lie, and the group, intact? No wonder.

Listening—Second Course

To understand further the effect of listening, we have to go rather deep and perhaps change our way of thinking. Listening is the Rorschach test of operational competence, the tell-all as to whether or not a man is in control of his operational capacities or is simply a marionette dancing on the end of controllers' strings.

RULE: To acquire an ID (A), one must first identify a determinant A prime (A').

This rule states that *what we know must first come from an out-side source.* Simply stated. But what are the repercussions? We need two contenders. Pick any two you wish: Hamas's Khaled Meshal and Netanyahu, Limbaugh and Maddow, or… For simplicity, let's pick a Y (him) and an X (us). A scenario…

If Y refuses to talk with X but X wants talk with Y, there's a problem. X uses words to sustain and acquire his ID. Y uses the same arsenal. But no contact! Result? Y maintains his A' bulwark using X as his A' foil. X wants discourse, to have Y admit membership within a common bond. Y doesn't. Result? The U.S. gets a poor credit rating. A bit further, with a switch…

If J (Ahmadinejad) consents to "listen" to an N (Netanyahu, or vice versa) face to face, meeting agreed upon, what happens? The tools which J uses to acquire ID throughout his lifetime have been used to build N as an A prime counter to substantiate his, J's, A-ID. Now how-ever, this same array of circuits is not substantiating an A' (Netanyahu) at a distance but is communicating with it, face to face! So, accord-ing to the rule above, it is not now J's A-ID at work, but the A prime's (Netanyahu's) since one's ID is acquired *only through the ingestion of an A'*—and Netanyahu is it! If, therefore, Ahmadinejad talked with Netan-yahu, it would be Netanyahu, simply as a conversant A-prime who, by the very act of conversing, could disrupt Ahmad's entire communica-tive network simply by listening! And, if an A prime is ingested, what does it become? A *worm*, part of the A-ID! Do we then see that it is not primarily the A-ID (Ahmadinejad) and his targeted A' in the network that counts—*it's the network itself!* For if the commonly used com-municative network falters, *so must the operative means whereby any A' sustains his ID!* Then too, consider any J's (Ahmad's) minions who derive their ID's also from J's! We understand why recalcitrant politi-cians refuse to face-to-face with those very A primes upon which they are dependent for ID substantiation. Bachmann at a distance, Gin-grich at a distance, Limbaugh in a shuttered kiosk, or, as a Cantor, simply walk out if the threat to ID becomes too great. The ID opera-tive network is manifold, cumbersome, and complex. But unravel the fasteners and you'll find those most fearful, those most afraid of

ID exposure, hunkered in bunkers, addicted to saying "Hell No, You Can't!" Food passed through the door's hatch.

RULE: Listening breaks the network by which Y affords X, A prime status. Take away the A' status and the ID of A (Y) deteriorates.

Corollary: Don't listen to Y and both the "power" and influence of Y's ID and his relational operative network *increase* as might his followers, army, tanks, and military complex.

RULE: The party who refuses to talk most likely has a greater need for a supportive A' counter to sustain ID than the party who wishes to talk.

Understand what's going on here, dear politicians, and peace might be in the offing. *It doesn't matter what the issue is* which Y might harbor. He is a species member and has cause for his need, whatever its nature. Break his ID need for you and he might retreat to becoming a simple in-tune citizen. If you feel that out-of-time 2D scripted religion or a tax code or defeat of a Jobs Bill is the basis for his need for you as an opponent through which he can play his ID-need game, provide the methods outlined above and below (Chapter 12): establish transference, insert dissonance through face-to-face listening, apply a Double Binder (see below), and pump up his ID—as a welcome species member! Apply any or all of these approaches and a few mothers, fathers, and children might bless you! Otherwise, you are as one with them.

Listening With the Third Ear

One doesn't have to "talk" to listen. We understand that the A-A' relationship rules human behavior. Use this principle to "listen," to understand what individuals or groups *really* need to locate cracks in their ID walls.

The procedure is rather simple but precision is required. Rules: 1) Use precise language. 2) Distinguish carefully between "need" and "want" (I *want* a hot fudge sundae but I *need* a liver transplant. If necessary, decide on the difference depending on the "code" the speaker uses.) 3) Realize that one "needs" *only what one doesn't have.*

4) Implant the above three rules, then reverse engineer. Three examples (each paraphrased)…

Palin: "We don't need a professor standing behind a rostrum telling us…." Pinpoint the words: professor, standing behind rostrum, telling… Reverse engineer. Obama was a professor. Palin not. Standing behind rostrum. Palin is OK with a shotgun. Telling us… Palin…no need to "tell." What are we getting here? Palin's degree was in journalism, was not a professor, had no need to stand behind a rostrum… *We only need what we don't have!* Palin gives recognition to the facts that she understands herself to be lesser degreed, less well educated, hasn't taught, and…what? Does a politician need to be well educated, stand behind a rostrum, and "tell" people…? Usually, yes. Can we reach a conclusion? Here's one: Palin wasn't running for political office; she was running to reap the bounty of ID feed from followers with no answers to questions unknown! No need for full education, no need to "tell," no need to stand behind a rostrum. But talent? Such talent beats attempting music on a washboard. Anything correct here? Try…

Limbaugh: "I hope that Obama fails." Ever done an examination of Limbaugh's résumé? Is it true that RL married four times but has no children? That he dropped out of college after two semesters and a summer school, and failed a dance class (causing him to call Rahm Emanuel a "ballet dancer")? That he was proclaimed 4F due to a pilonidal cyst on his backside? That he was fired from two radio stations? That he was arrested for "doctor shopping" and pill addiction? That he was arrested for soliciting a gay man in Pittsburgh? That…? No attestations here regarding each or all. But…this man is the ex-officio head of the Republican Party with members cowtowing if found in disagreement? And he wants Obama to fail…a well-degreed family man with children, straight, athletic, good build but black, who never got fired but who won a national election through voter affirmation? Is Limbaugh green?

Limbaugh, like the puffer fish, has one defensive organ which works: his tongue, which, like the tetrodotoxin in the fugu (puffer fish) is deadly to humans. So, why would Limbaugh want (need) Obama to fail? As we know, loneliness is hell. By wanting (needing) Obama to fail, Limbaugh accedes to Obama's success and in so doing, to his own failures which a $400M salary and a $24M mansion can't hide. Painful. Limbaugh's need? If Obama fails, Limbaugh will lack the need to look at himself. Kill the A prime, the A remains. Lonely, but *dependence* upon an A', Obama, extinguished. Question: who listens…*really listens* to Limbaugh? Only those with like needs. Try…

McConnell: "I want (need) Obama to be a one term President." Why? We can surmise. McConnell (Wikipedia) ran for office five times, winning with good majority only once. Obama/Biden won the '10 Presidential election, 365 electoral college votes to 173. Obama is a black man, father from Kenya. McConnell is a white man, roots in Alabama and Kentucky. Obama has solid family, McConnell divorced. McConnell polio at very young age; Obama, healthy and athletic. McConnell is considered a master tactician in *stymying* procedural action in congress (read *killing*). Obama was an effective community organizer working for species advance, voted President as a newbie Senator. Barack is a strong masculine name, never changed. Addison is a feminine name, altered to "Mitch." Obama is younger by 19 years and rather good-looking. Has the Republican Party ever been tainted with the term *racial bias*? Is there any possibility that McConnell would like Obama, a man in every sense, independent of political party in many areas, to fail while McConnell's ID is dependent on party backing from foot to mouth? Does anyone listen…*really listen* to McConnell? Refuse to listen, pay totems to your masters and get re-elected…but never tested beforehand.

Hopefully, against all the tidbits of hate, hypocrisy, and illogic thrown at progressive legislation, answers may be found. Just locate the arrows in mid-flight, engineer their reversals to points of origin, *and listen.*

RULE: ID the cause for an A' ID choice and you'll identify the need of the A ID.

Automatic. This is *listening*!

This principle works anywhere, with any individual or group. What do the Israelis *have* which the Palestinians want? What did Iraq *have* which prompted invasion? What did Obama *have* which impelled Republican "attack teams," "tea baggers," stacked "town hall meetings," right wing attacks, hypocritical brandishments and stealth bombs from insurance companies? What do the rich *have* to curry continual and massive support from the Republican Party? What do particular congressmen *have* which demands that they attack Health Reform? Krugman: "They're against reform because it would cover the uninsured—and that's something they just don't want to do."[37] The good of species is on their agenda?

Need propels act and only need. No ID need, no act. So, if the reader is in tune, further conclusions can be met, namely,

RULE: One doesn't have to "talk" to initiate a conversation.

Does the reader recognize the fact that every suicide bombing, every "terrorist" act, every display of anti-species behavior within our own congress is an attempt at "communication"? Need propels act, so, with an understanding of the above rule, do we find politicians schooled in human behavior asking, "What is their need"…to delay votes, filibuster, say No, restrict voting rights, delay funding for rebuilding infrastructure, or to bomb hotels, blow up restaurants, set off roadside devices, attack police stations, bomb hospitals, etc.?

Every instance of terrorism, in house or out, is an attempt at communication, but *is anyone listening?* If a schooled diplomat, national leader, or anyone with public voice asked, "What is your need Cantor, McConnell, Taliban, Al Qaeda, Assad, Kim Jong Un…?" after every instance of terrorism (threats or refusals to act in times of emergency, realized or not, are acts of terrorism preventing species advance) and such question was publicly proclaimed across political boundaries, do you think that someone might take the trouble to reverse engineer the act to discern the need and figure out a way to fill the gap? From the attention-getting refusal to pass a Jobs Bill or to raise a debt ceiling or…(remember what vultures feed on) "What is their need?"

Hawks and toggle-switch politicians chafe at possibilities for communication which would open doors to answers. *Questions can't be asked because they don't want to hear answers* (which would involve listening!). To listen to answers, politicians would be under natural obligation to process response, even if covert and unsaid. So, no one listens. *No one wants to listen.* What we hear is dead silence among politicians purposely oblivious to shovels swishing through air piling mounds of compost higher and higher, heads purposely as vacuous as ping pong balls…out-of-*time*, out of touch, politicians so afraid of revealing *their own needs* and of questioners asking them…of *their needs!*

So don't listen, politicians. Don't open any doors to a game you'd be embarrassed to play. Don't respond even if you hear distant whimpers urging surcease. Just countenance a depleted treasury while reading of casualties, families torn asunder, the starving starving, the disenfranchised disenfranchised, families of dead overseas you'll never be called upon to see and the maimed at home and brought home, travel paid for. But you're covered with health care, tenured via *fiat*, and never tested for competence. Infrastructure.

Chapter 12

TARGETS AND TOOLS

We discussed classes above. We understand that a disjunctive class is indefinable absent another disjunctive class. The class of citrus fruit cannot be disjunctive with the class of hummingbirds. There must be a bond, a potential for a merging of attribute. So is it with the human mind. (NOTE: The Japanese word for *mind* is "kokoro," similar to "mind" but with greater emphasis on interpersonality and empathy. Let's equate *kokoru* with our use.)

There is no class which can be disjunctive with mind except another class...of mind. Meaning, if our target is a human mind which we wish to change, we cannot use attributes of a class different in kind to do it. The mind is not physical. The mind is a compilation of ages past with all accompanying accouterments stashed in a conscious, aware, eyeball-looking locus. It cannot be burned, pressed, starved, or swayed via anything of a physical nature...actual or via intent. Our goal: to change minds controlling behavior.

Two behavioral attributes are *required* prior to slipping any trap to instigate behavior change: *transference* and *language*. First, there must be established the presence of a disjunctive bond—two + minds in tune (to whatever degree) relative to an issue, a goal, a purpose. However, without language (#2) there would simply be two sets of eyeballs looking at each other incapable of communication. (Language, we understand, is that vehicle through which neurons in one brain can manipulate neurons in another.) We then hit the possible types of "traps" through which minds can be changed...

Tools

The Challenge

"I dare you to lift that 50 lb. rock." "I challenge you to a 100 meter race." "I challenge you, Kim Jong Un, to restore equitable relations with the South." Naked challenges don't work *isolated from an initial common bond between players*. Why?

A challenge will work only within a conjunctive bond, transference engaged. Examples: *Conjunctive* bond—two friends playing chess. X says to Y, "I challenge you to checkmate me in ten moves." Y answers, "Challenge accepted." Then the disjoint *disjunctive*: Two neighbors, Y with a dog that dumps on X's lawn. They don't like each other. X says, "I challenge you to keep that dog from dumping on my lawn." Y doesn't like X so he says, "I don't accept. He can dump wherever he wants." We use a challenge then only between two conjunctive players, both in bond. If not in bond, the challenge is not effectivex.

Res, in Latin, means *thing*. When we *reify* something, we "thing" it. To reify the beauty of a Mona Lisa, we tap onto it a term, "beautiful," and reify the term to epitomize "beauty." We reify words in the Bible, the Bible itself, and the pedestal upon which my wife stands. *Things*…which they aren't. If something, anything, can be reified, it won't commerce with mind. To wit…

An i/e challenge is a bumper sticker, a sentence/proposition which can be inked onto a banner and held aloft, stuck on a wall, or trashed…a Post-it note to be examined, then treated in accordance with *the needs of the challenger*. Any challenge is first directed, *in time*, *from* an A. The A prime receives the challenge, *in time,* subsequent. The order of sequence leaves the receiver (Catch the ball!) either willing to accept the challenge (the ball) or to drop it. Two, every challenge carries a *reified substance*—a rock, a race, international probity… The mind assumes second place, affording first place to the nature of the challenge's substance. So, with dependence upon the needs of the one challenged, the challenge may be either accepted (giving thereby virtual precedence to the A-challenger, the A primer assuming vassal-status to that of the challenger), or denied, he who was challenged maintaining ID status quo, dismissing the status of the A challenger and giving height to his A prime ability to do so.

No change of mind, only enforced petrifaction of A prime's ID. Challenges between i/e combatants don't work.

The Positive Injunction

A positive injunction, like the challenge, works only with two disjunctives with a conjunctive meld possible.

"You *can* lift that rock!" "You *can* win that race!" "Kim Jong, you *can* open equitable relations with South Korea." "Johnny, I know that you *can* get an A in algebra. Just do it!" But Johnny hates algebra. He loves history and sees no need for algebra and doesn't appreciate parents who can't recognize his needs, wants, or inclinations. To get even, what does he do? Right.

If someone tells me that I can lift that rock, I can do one of two things: either lift the rock and grant affirmation of ID precedence to the positive injunctor, or refuse to lift the rock and maintain ID independence and homeostatic autonomy. If I lift the rock, I give the injunctor reason to crow but must assume thereby the role of supporter…for him! If I wish not to be a supporter (in whatever context) but to be independent (in accordance with my brain's desires) I will refuse. I could, however, attempt to lift the rock and fail, proving that the A-injunctor didn't know either "me" or my capabilities, thereby proving him ignorant (of whatever). In any case, no one can tell me what I can or can't do. Try telling any tyrant or House Speaker that "he can" (a positive injunction leveled at a disjunctive counter) and watch the reaction (see below). (Depending on usage, possible synonyms: *urge, encourage, insist, spur, goad, prod, entreat, be able to, make it, take care of…*)

The Negative Injunction

…initiated between two or more i/e sets, *the only injunction that attacks the ID-mind.* "You *can't* lift that rock!" "You *can't* win that race." "You *can't* normalize relations with South Korea." Here the focal point is the *ID capabilities* of the A prime. With the negative injunction, it is not the "substance" of the injunction but the capabilities of the A prime ID to execute. We shift the "challenge" not to the substance of act but to the worth, the value, the ability of the A prime ID to *behaviorally relate* to an injuncted act *which he can perform* (*he can*, otherwise the negative injunction is useless). The A primer *must* assume the negative injunction to be a direct, *time-less* assault upon his ID.

Can he lift the rock even though A-ID said he couldn't? If he does lift the rock, he elevates his ID "above" that of the A-ID injunctor. He won (or did he?). (If he can't lift the rock, the negative injunction should not have been initiated in the first place. Reason: We *want* the A prime-ID to counter the negative injunction—to change ID to a chosen course). However, if the A prime leaves the scene, he admits weakness, an "inability" to perform the act and must suffer the ignominy. So, we understand that the negative injunction must be applied with circumspection.

The Double Binder

And finally, the **Double Binder**, an attack strategy which hits an A prime target right between the eyes, a strategy which can't be avoided once stated—a direct assault upon that most precious commodity of any one of us: the ID, public and private. A little history...

The Double Bind originated with Gregory Bateson and his colleagues at Stanford (We are not discounting Leon Festinger). Particularly, the DB was formulated to describe the often used language of "crazy" parents with schizophrenic ID's. The DB was, by them, applied like a double-edged sword: "The more you do exactly what I ask, the more I'll love you," (but Charlene wants to go to the movies and not stay home) or, "Eat everything I lovingly cook for you to show that you love me," (So Charlene eats, stays fat, no boy gets interested and Charlene stays home to keep Mommy company), etc.

Bateson defined the double bind this way: Ingredients include "...two or more persons [parties, factions, governments...], repeated experience, a primary negative injunction, a secondary injunction conflicting with the first at a more abstract level, and like the first, enforced by punishments or signals which threaten survival; a tertiary negative injunction prohibiting the victim from escaping from the field..." and, to close, the acceptance that all of the above ingredients are "no longer necessary when the victim has learned to perceive his universe in double bind patterns."[38] These injunctions are more precise than they need be. Let's simplify...

Our DB (Double Binder) consists of one negative injunction (NI) followed by supporting **tiers**. Example: "You can't ___ (NI) because of A___, B___, C___, D___, etc." Simple. Let's put our tools to work...

At a December, 2011 Press conference, Obama's Press Secretary, Jay Carney, said something like, "They (House Republicans) *have the ability* [can] to pass the Payroll Tax Extension." If Obama and Carney *wanted* the House Republicans to derail the bill, Carney gave them all the ammunition they could ever want to mount an offensive. Why?

House Republicans are the A primes to Obama's A, and vice versa. The HR's knew that they had the "ability" but, since proffered *as fact* by Obama (Carney), and to preserve "Republican ID's," they really had no choice but to go A prime, which they did by proving *an inability* to pass the bill.

If you want a child to drink a glass of milk, tell him that he can't because it would make him strong. Will he then drink it? If you want HR's to do something, tell them that *they can't* because of x...y...and z (with an honest layout of reasons...tiers, examined fully below). To preserve their A prime ID's, what choice could they have? Either submit to A's categorization and become emerged within Obama's A ID (and lose their own to that extent), or go counter *and further strengthen an ID as independent and protected unto group womb*. The real choice then becomes evident: either perform for species benefit and "man up" to species affiliation and concern, *or* reveal the weakness of ID's totally dependent upon a leader's linear platform coupled with abject fear of group exclusion if votes vary from the theme. Dissonance. The weak retreat unto i/e groupings; the strong put family and species first, sacrificing infantile, immature ID needs. Then consider Pakistan...

Zakaria reported on a piece by Stephen Krasner, Stanford Professor who worked in the State Department under G. W. Bush, who "makes the important point that Pakistan's *behavior*...is part of a deliberate strategy to keep Afghanistan weak and India off balance. Krasner advocates cutting off all aid to the military until it changes course..."[39] Do we recognize the problem when Pakistan's military "sucks up almost a quarter of the (its) federal budget"? Set 1: the Military. Set 2: the "civilian" government. Set 3: Afghanistan. Set 4: India.

Now add Set 5: U.S. aid in the billions. A statistician could quickly tally the interrelationships among these sets (1 x 2 x 3 x 4 x 5 = ?)? Dissonance added to dissonance adds dissonance in exponential order making a targeted resolution nearly impossible. If a "regime change" is wanted, the sets must be reduced to those capable of revealing a hunger with ID dependence. You can't get a child to drink Nestle's cocoa when sitting among 30 classmates who don't like chocolate. Remove the classmates and perhaps he'll drink. Reduce to manageable sets or don't get involved. The issue becomes one of starvation, a reduction to life-and-death thirst. If this can't be achieved, take a seat and either let the sauce reduce to basics or implement strategies that will accomplish the reduction. Behavioral communication might then become an option and not before. Politics is behavior. Personal interactions are behaviors. Regime change involves behaviors. Where is behavioral expertise demonstrated in foreign policy? Our foreign policy is ripe for the implementation of Double Binders. [We close with a few, just before the Epilogue.]

To change a mind is to invoke dissonance. We understand the hierarchy of relational operations, from the elemental and immature to the developmentally mature. We understand the A-A prime split—the most basic operation within any act of cognition. We understand that the underlying principle for every human act within a culture crowd is the acquisition, protection, preservation, and maintenance of the individual ID. We understand language whereby we can bounce operational relations from skull to skull, never leaving home. We understand belief, that concatenation of operations stolen from structural operations and stuck with ink, like a tail on a donkey, on phantasms and holy ducks in the hopes of permanence beyond the now of time and for explanations of thunder in the night, but never discussed in schools. We understand enough.

To change a mind is to understand the pinions and fears which stick ID's flat against walls, making immobile minds petrified through habitual act, never on their own capable of changing course. But we know what the petrified-in-station don't, otherwise change would be so much harder. Change an al Quaedan, a Taliban, a congressional zombie tied to a maypole, a Tea Partier, a Beck or Limbaugh… ("Go ahead, change me!") Well, if we can't, we lose.

Beliefs are story lines which hold groups together, every out-of-time belief built on artificial constructs—alphabets, words, language, and ink from a stylus. Structured within a medium, honored as creations from sources unknown, beliefs decry time, but the *now* of time must be dealt with.

Dependency is a primary issue…dependence upon belief, dependence upon Johnny at the other end of the phone line, dependence that *green* to me means *green* to you, dependence that the byline of the crowd I belong to has a foothold in reality, dependence that the paper bills in my hand are equal to a loaf of bread, dependence that Allah is God and that my ID is correct and stable for believing it, dependence that words written eons ago represent operations of mind permanent unto today; dependence that my identity, as correctly founded, is capable of directing others along whichever paths I may choose. But, if any case of dependency is proven false?

For this is the case with every extremist. Every extremist is fearful unto death of a false ID…the exposure of an ID based on deceit, on ineffectual belief based on what the crowd "thinks" or the "Party" thinks or the "leader" thinks or what his religion provides. For the extremist, there is no choice…commit or drop out, and singular isolation is what everyone fears above all else…loneliness, extrusion, dismissed unto hell.

So "signed-in" congressmen agree to the commonality of a group belief that taxes should not be raised, that government spending in a time of crisis is anathema, or that a Norquist holds power as a Robespierre with a guillotine because he says so and congressmen "believe." Each wraps himself within the heavy cloak of party with a surrendered ID when the natural ID of a maturely developed species-man goes wanting. "Republican," "Democrat," proxy ID's unidentifiable by suckling babes. Who will verify, who will validate the correctness of ID?

The answer to all of this is, of course, education…education into the workings of the mind, the brain, and the functions of every itty-bitty item within, beginning from *within* the child, not imported from a Texas school board or from a federally mandated Every Child Left Behind pogrom, but such exposure, in turn, is frightening to those who mutually cling to foster groups for salvation.

We, in turn, are ignorant of social anthropology…that an invasion of a nation/organism would cause an increase in macrophages, IED's at roadside. Yale law school doesn't teach this nor need it when nepotism becomes the password to the buffet table.

No mind can be changed if reference is given to tokens of time past, of reference to crowds clinging in incestuous bond for ID protection while the world flitters past. To change a mind is to strip it bare, to prop it naked against a non-sensual wall and pin it there. Beliefs, with roots planted in printed past, are out. Groups however are *in*… groups breathing in unison with leader's lungs, in time, now, with dependencies hanging like remoras on the undersides of sharks.

To change a mind is to force its submission to a recognition of potential fallacy, that what that mind thinks it is, is subject to revision. Each mind considers itself stable, adequate, full and developed to the moment, wrapped up in the nomenclature of name…John, Michelle, Achmed, or House Speaker, Minority Whip… Strip the artificials and make-ups of name and bare the breast. We must first do two things: *remove A primes and crack open ID's.*

1. Remove A Primes

This is simple but requires a bit of pre- post-analysis. Example: with the Jobs Act in focus (Obama touring Ohio, Boehner's home state, 2011) touting the need for the bill, aren't the negative rejoinders by the Republicans *anticipated in advance?* "We've got to see the plan [the details]," says Boehner. Of course. Step One for Boehner. Step two will be to deny the plans once offered. Step three, four, etc., will be to itemize details, then to reject each one in sequence. This is not anticipated?

The problem with "politics" is that it's far too often performed on a one-man stage. Obama in Ohio, Boehner in Washington D.C., or one in this house, the other in another—but never face to face, in time, with evidentiary documentation in hand by either party to substantiate position (solidly based tiers). Avoidance of confrontation is the key…hurling rocks while behind a distant wall. The "tiers" upon which the naysayers are dependent are source of funds, throwback to TARP and stimulus funds saying that "not one job was created" (evidentiary, authoritative, solid proof to the contrary not available?), and whatever else they might come up with "substantiating" a rationale for not passing the Jobs bill. We are not politicians, but what might they come up with? So... *Disarm by publicly stating each objection possible, exactly as might be formulated, in advance.* Purpose? To purloin each and every A prime argument opponents to a Jobs Bill (e.g.) might use—each possible reason for objecting (If, in a chess game, each move by the opponent has been anticipated by positive defense, who wins the game?). *Removing A prime arguments isn't done.* Instead, the game is begun, each player then running to his sidelines to mull over what *he* will do, not what the other guy is planning. If the A primes are removed, adequately and exhaustively, what stanchions are then left for naysayers to lean on? Nakedness has been achieved but if "politeness" to congressional peers takes precedence over the creation of jobs and a total uplifting of this nation's character and productiveness, then we're really in the Little Leagues, sweetness and conviviality reigning supreme while 46 million in this country remain below the poverty line.

Obama (or anyone in similar position) must identify *each and every possible obstacle* which might be forthcoming to a proposed act, state each possible objection to the obstacle openly in public forum, and leave naysayers naked. The only recourse then left for naysayers will be to vote No with no substantiation whatsoever, true colors then evident. This they don't want. Conclusion: Either allow the game to be played on their turf, according to their rules, or win. This is an either-or.

2. Crack Open ID's.

The easiest and most direct way to crack open an ID is to attack the illusion of competence...that *what* Andy wants is what he *really* wants, that Andy is *who* he thinks he is, that Andy is *what* he thinks he is. As an A prime, *publicize broadly* the "fact" that Andy *can't* (do this or that)...*because of* who or what he thinks he is (But he *potentially* can; otherwise we're wasting our time). Examples...

Dick *can't* switch sides (**NI**) *because* then he would have to admit to years upon years of a falsely developed and wasted ID (**T1**). If true, Dick is lost, indoctrinated in false cause without inner resource to escape. If Dick does realize a false ID, he then *can* switch sides indicating independence from forces which would bend him as wished, but will he? By choice, he will either act with fortitude or suffer ID schizophrenia.

Anne *can't* admit to prejudice and bias (**NI**) since that would expose an ID structured on skewed data (such data having been proven false, **Tier 1**). If true, Anne *is* biased and must then attract like followers in prejudice to form a mutually protective womb.

NOTE 1: The reader has noticed the sequence in a Double Binder: a Negative Injunction (NI) states what *can't* be changed followed by supporting Tiers One, Two, Three, Four... *If no supports, there can be no Negative Injunction.* Any isolated negative injunction foisted by any claimant, politician or otherwise, lacking supporting tiers is nothing other than a dash of war paint without substance, a smokescreen hiding fear. "Spin" in other words.

NOTE 2: Double Binders can be disguised, but won't carry the same effect as with the outright "can't." Examples: "You're too short to play basketball," or "This curry is too spicy for you." Simple declarative sentences. As to basketball? "OK, if you say so, but I've got a game scheduled at 4:00." Parent-child bond, no threat to ID, no assault. Another: "The controllers in Afghanistan are really too embedded in the Quran to lead a truly democratic society." Or, "Karzai, as titular head of a tribally fractured Afghanistan, will be proven unable to coalesce the country." "OK, your opinion." Deal done and nothing changes. No threats to ID, no assaults on ID abilities or construction.

The word "can't" carries a distinct connotation. It means *can't.* Applied to an ID, the confrontation is direct, inescapable, and wrapped in time. The imputation of "You're too short to play basketball" is, "You *can't* play basketball because you're too short." The former can be rather easily dismissed as a slight slight. The latter hits the ID. "Oh, yeah! Watch me!" The words used then, can indicate the degree of ID attack one wishes. Subtlety sometimes wins but oftentimes gets shuttled aside with but a few feathers ruffled. Therefore, the degree of DB emphasis must be outlined before use and carefully thought through.

Another switch to DBer presentation is to present tiers first. Most parents have used this approach at one time or another. "Johnny, you're only 16 (T1). You've only driven the car around the block (T2). Our insurance doesn't cover you (T3)." And on and on. NI? "Therefore, you *can't* take the car to the prom." The effect of the NI has been mitigated. Johnny reacts with aplomb, but realizes the truth. This approach is certainly different from those responses studied extensively by psychologists in England who ascertained the responses of low-econ parents when asked by their children for something, or to explain something, or to do something... The parental responses were curt, sharp, and cut-offs. "Don't ask." "Shut up." "I don't know." In short...no tiers. If such an approach were entertained by national leaders, the impact would be insulting, negative, and probably promote hostile reactions. Certainly a He-thinks-he's-boss response would float to the surface. Here we stick to the *can't* of the NI as a direct, frontal, ID assault. We now hit some specific applications, full frontal approach ...

Using DBers Against Groups

For this is the crux of the matter. To which groups should, could we apply DBers? When? Why? We need not DB a wife who says, "More cream pie?" when calories can simply be dismissed with a No. We need not DB a Boy Scout asking, "May I help you across the street?" There are boundaries, limits to behavior which cancel out interference, and other behaviors which demand it. Where's the distinguishing line?

There's a common reference in ethics to a man swinging his arms up and down at the sides of his body. "No problem," we say, as long as his swinging arms don't interfere with "my space." This is conservatism, conservatives not understanding the operative (cognitive) basis for their positions. It's also a problem of logical ignorance, and we touched this above. The issue is one of *illegitimate extension*, simplified in this sentence/proposition: *The military consists of hard materiel, personnel, supply chains, and servicemen.* We see the problem: *personnel* consists also of *servicemen* (and women). *Illegitimate extension.* Relevance? In early 2012 we've witnessed the brouhaha concerning women's rights—contraception, abortion, Planned Parenthood, etc.

The question must be asked: What right does the federal government have to impose its wishes upon the individual rights of women? Let's try an analogy…

A student is accepted into a college as an official student member (official citizen) pays his tuition (taxes), takes the class (contributes to the economy) and is given a grade (salary). This student, as official, is required to wear clothes to class, not disrupt proceedings, and do the work required to get a grade. There are protocols relative to behavior associated with student life in school and on campus. However, no teacher can require a student to eat breakfast, to wear blue and white socks, or if a female, to wear a tampon. There are limits to what can be demanded of an official student, a limit to which the arms of the institution can swing without interfering with student rights.

A citizen of this country is, ipso facto, a defined citizen with all rights and obligations attached thereto. The dispenser of such authority is the federal government, authority given, surrendered, by said citizenry. The obligations and rights of each citizen are then defined within the rubric—citizen. Such rights and obligations go no further. The government cannot demand that I go to church on Sunday, eat spinach, or not use a condom. As a citizen, in turn, I fulfill my rights and obligations and *need do no more*. If a government (ours) then demands that I (we, women) do other than demanded within the basic rubric of *citizen*, it has defined each citizen in terms of an *illegitimate extension* and has overstepped its bounds. Therefore, our federal government has *not* the right to interfere with a woman's bodily health concerns since such concerns do not fall within the legalized definition of *citizen*—a term delimiting the reach of federal authority. The government does have a right, however, to protect its citizens and to care for their welfare as those legal commodities upon which the government itself depends for its own existence. The promotion of the health of its citizens is, therefore, *obligatory upon government*, for its own "health." This means that "universal" health care is obligatory upon government and we, as citizens, have the right—under the rubric citizen, to have it, including support for Planned Parenthood which devotes 80-90 percent of its work for women's health care. (Note that of the top 23 "civilized" nations, the U.S. ranks 23rd in infant mortality. Reason? Women about to deliver arriving at medical emergency not having seen a doctor prior, uninsured as they were.) Contraception? This does not fall within the extension *citizen* but does fall within the inherent rights of the individual as *person*. Person rights, per se, do not equate with governmental rights. For government to extend its interference into rights within another domain is again, an exercise of illegitimate extension. So…

Double Binders…when, where and why? We use them when individuals, governments, or any compilation of groups extend themselves into domains in which they have either no legal or natural rights. DBers then involve ethical transactions…species rights as opposed to decrees of groups which would disregard, dismantle, or eliminate such rights. And so we proceed…

Targets

Identity Based Groups

No act need be involved in the establishment of identity other than that of, in some manner, sticking a tail on the donkey—wearing a Green Bay cheese head hat, a logoed T shirt, a lapel pin, or sitting in your team's cheering section at a college football game. Example:

The image of a woman wearing a brimmed hat with tea bags hanging from its edges. Purpose: to identify the wearer as a Tea Bagger. Maxim: *The need for acceptance of an ID is directly proportionate to the extremes of behaviors displayed.* (If true, this woman tea bagger had extensive needs for ID acquisition beyond her ID developed at that point in time. If false, wearing the tea-bagged hat was nothing other than a frivolous attempt to curry attention.) Behavior. Let's pluck the chickens…

DB: (NI) Republicans *can't* allow unemployment figures to decrease and employment to rise for fear of losing the '12 election. Since the war cry of Republican extremists is One Term Only, *it matters not* as consequence that families will face severe hardships, businesses will fail, governmental revenues will continue to decrease…all the sidebars to intractable group (operationally immature) ID-protective dictate (T1 True?). Among adversarial lawyers, the "judge in absentia" deciding any case in both House and Senate will be the outcome of their case as determined by party vote, the public banned from the courtroom. If unemployment increases, the adversarial extremists win and their ID's remain intact (T2). If unemployment decreases, the "judge" overseeing the case will vote for the prosecution and the defendants lose (T3). Lawyers are lawyers, after all.

DB: (NI)Congressional members, divided by political party, *cannot* by definition have as a performance goal the establishment of a "more perfect union" as stipulated in the Preamble to the U.S. Constitution.

While The Preamble to the U.S. Constitution states, *We the People of the United States, in Order to form a more perfect Union, establish Justice, insure domestic Tranquility, provide for the common defense, promote the general Welfare,* etc., Congressional members, meeting in joint session in the Capitol Building, display *explicit i/e conformity to party platform and its leaders directives, suborning secondary fealty to elected positions as governors, representatives of electors* (anti-conjunctive ID's), Democrats sitting in one section, Republicans in another resulting in (T1) a blatant disregard for the intent of the U.S. Constitution *to secure a more perfect union through Unity of Purpose* (inclusive-nominally disjunctive sets antithetical to cohesive union), and (T2) obeisance to *anti-union postures, party controlled, overtly contrary* to the intent of that Constitution each congressman swore to uphold, protect, and defend. (T3) The two-party system therefore is un-Constitutional, anti-Constitutional, and perforce disruptive to the very intent of the Constitution and such should be evident to any citizen who so considers. Or…

DB: (NI) To secure a more perfect union *through Unity of Purpose* as stipulated in the Preamble to the U.S Constitution, *is impossible* for the U.S. Congress (T1) as is evident by the *in-situ*, in-time requirement that members of the two political parties sit in opposing, disjunctive, *anti-union, de facto* opposing sections when in joint session, each to maintain *Party identity*. (If true, sitting posture admits to anti-union inclination, disinclination to bond, and to an agenda other than that of striving for a more perfect union *through unity of purpose* as addressed in the Constitution. If false, the *a priori* two-party regimentation of congressional divisions *can* be terminated in witness of a quest for a unification of goals and purpose.)

The NI propositions remain true as long as the supporting tiers cannot be proven false. If the supporting tiers are true, the two-Party Congress may be categorized as un-American and contrary to the U.S. Constitution. And so is it with any extremist group. Posit the either-or contraries in terms of DBers supported by solid tiers and apply. Species beneficence is dominant. Other than species benefit as a goal, every platform upon which an extremist group bases its support is subject to Double Binder attack.

Inclusion Based Groups

In a sense, every group is an inclusion-based group. The concern we have is upon emphasis, in the political sphere particularly. Let's form an inclusion-based group from the beginning…

If I drop a speck of honey on the kitchen counter, a group of ants will coalesce and bond. Natural. Ant communication, not the vehicle we use. However, to form an inclusion group (political) someone has to use language to proclaim a position, whatever it is. Others will listen and agree or not, but whether they agree or not, groups are formed. The issue becomes…why did the initiator (and there was one) open his mouth in the first place?

We understand the Epididymis Constant—that every man, without exception, is born and bred to assume dominance in as many areas of his life as is possible. But with language—our tool for interspecies communication, we can wrap and warp any existential, environmental, political, or lamb shank recipe into a formula, a program delineating response as to a stimulus, and for others within earshot, a chance to join in with support. And they do. It's time filling, after all. But a politician, or prospective candidate for ___, why does he open his mouth? No one drops a baited hook into the water unless he thinks there's fish there, and no one goes fishing unless there's an opportunity to do so. So what does an ID needy, vocal, language proficient, effluent product of the Epididymis, observing a mass of potential human bait balls (food to requite an un-sated ID) do? He picks his pond, employs an A-A prime hook with bait compatible with the needs of the targeted fish, and drops it in. Success! Fish are caught, a crowd gathers, and he's in the running. The question is… what are the needs to people-fish in the first place?

First, the Epididymis Constant is…constant. We each strive to be number one, at something. So who's not gathered around someone else's fishing line? People walking all over the place. Free for grabs. Throw out a line. Politics…free for anyone without lockjaw. No restrictions (other than age). No licensure, no requirements, no review boards, no assessment protocols…just bait the line. And who comes to view the sport? Bait balls, humans with time to kill, swords to swing, un-sated ID's reeking of intent to seek revenge for boredom in a world empty of self-knowledge, empty of an understanding of neuroanatomy or brain functioning, empty of the operational nature of species, empty of a brain equipped to recognize the ID needs of man, empty of the meaning of life and its purpose. The fisherman is out to include…fish in his bucket. And what he won't do to catch them…

Second? The lure…the lure he likes, the lure most compatible with his needs. Shall he go for the Christian-right-evangelical-wing fish or for the no-Obamacare fish or the don't-tax-me fish or… He gets the correct lure to match, drops it in the water and reels in. Compatible fish—*included*. Those unpalatable? *Excluded*. Now…observe ten little Indians, all in a row, each with a fishing pole, line, bait, and the kinds of fish caught. The extremist politician…not for species good, but for his own…sheltered in ignorance of you, me, and the natural bond between us all. To expand a bit…

In general, the greater the number of prophylactic glyphs (2D) supporting a group's platform, the greater the extremism. Following this rule, religions assume first place. Consider the Bible, the Quran, the Talmud, etc., glyphs accumulated over time, each in succession, accumulating equally the need for groups to justify ID's built on past act justified by platform: Christians, Jews, Muslims, Jehovah's Witnesses, etc. In general, groups with fewer linear glyphs are the less extreme: Doctors Without Borders, Boy Scouts of America, Paralyzed Veterans, etc. Revolutionary groups ("Out with Mubarak!") are not inclusive but *exclusive*. Inclusion, carried to the extreme, is similar to the acquisition of money by banks. The greater the amount of money accumulated, the "greater" the ID; the greater the ID, the more likely it is that more money must be accumulated for ID fortification given the status of acquired ID established on a 2D base. Inclusion, as an extreme operational relation, then equates with a Ponzi scheme (as Rick Perry categorized Bain Capital).

Group Inclusion should be considered simply as that relational operation which requires input in the form of converts, acolytes, followers whereby the custodians of the mother glyphs become validated. Think birthday party: if everyone comes, included, the birthday boy's/girl's ID becomes validated. (Note that negation is not a primary but a secondary attribute of inclusive groups. Negation becomes a by-product when opposing groups find the intent of the inclusive groups inimical and so negate the inclusive group as hostile through reciprocity.)

Inclusive extremism requires excessive validation. As group sponsored, the intent is anti-species—group centered only. As anti-species, the platform must be maintained at all costs, otherwise, exposure to *natural* cause. If the intent of the platform *is* STEM directed however, the platform *can be changed* with positive effect. Consider evolution…species changing for species benefit, or professional football player-protective pads improved to prevent concussions, or the yard line for kickoff changed to the 30 to reduce injuries on a run-back. We run across these changes to rules beneficial to species all the time. However, when gerrymandering to preserve ID's in office, such acts become *exclusionary*-protective (i/e) to preserve *inclusionary* status already achieved. Changes to STEM based platforms (species beneficial) routinely occur within school boards, city governments…those with close ties to populations served. The further removed from tangible touch with populations served (*e.g.*, state governors, the House of Representatives or Senate, etc.) the greater the opportunity for legislatures to run amok for personal ID gain through the execution of biased act, no weight on the end of the fishing line…inclusion again carried to extreme for personal gain.

Inclusion can be achieved through *force,* either physically or through the imputation of group exclusion. Consider Genghis Khan, Bush 43's "You're either with us or against us;" Hitler's invasions of

Poland, France, etc., Khrushchev's Berlin Wall ("You're included!"), or the Tea Party's "My way or the highway!" and "Stand firm!"

Extreme inclusion can also be achieved through *idolatry*, and here we focus on politicians, "podium pols" who curry acolytes anxious for leadership of any type to direct transit through life, here or later, "followers" outside STEM directives or understanding of species' intent. Here we find the Jesus imitators who gather throngs at their feet to spiel forth dogma, directions, do's and don'ts and the why's needed to overcome what the Jesus imitators say threaten but which can be overcome with counters only they possess. The need of each? Validation, verification of transient, prone-to-termination, fractious, two-way-Paul-Revere ID's.

Any politician running for national office greets, meats, and speaks with potential voters. It doesn't matter who...Perry, Palin, or Paul, Gingrich, Romney, but let's take Mitt Romney, MR for short (Republican nominee, 2012). Question: As MR speaks to his crowd, who does the "including," MR or the potential voters? In other words, does MR include each and all potential voters in his inclusive data-bank during visits, or does each potential voter include MR is his/her input data-bank? Essential question. Hint: MR spiels at one stop, then moves on, so obviously MR can't retain each and every potential at every stop. MR gets an ID pump, then shifts scene. The potential voters retain details of the visits as they must to fortify vote decision when the time comes. So, it is the potential voters who do the including, MR who does the dropping off. MR does not include, save for the slavering which hand-slapping provides.

We understand that one standard requirement for any candidate running for national office is that he/she be free of any certification requirements relative to intelligence, behavioral aptitude, experience, honesty, social aptitude, bias, any area of academia, or empirically proven competency for any political position—a condition extant for some 270 years, political positions all absent job descriptions. Therefore, a given. We are left then with the inclusive notch relative to MR, or any candidate, registered in any potential voter's "political" repertoire. MR didn't give anything while campaigning but dots which a kid could connect to line out a rabbit. In any vote it is the potential, now voter, who gives from a personal database, however constructed. But let's get to the core…

Why did a Mitt Romney run for office? With 249 current millionaires in Congress, might we use him as but one example of ID need and ask…

Why would MR or anyone run for the office of President? With MR's money (@1/4 billion dollars) he could start his own country. Benefits are in tune with need; food for the sated—no benefit. Food for the hungry—benefit. The benefits for MR running for office? Let's note…

1) Famous father, George, Michigan governor for three terms. Wealthy. Any need to carry name onward, to "man up" to father's expectations (e.g., Bush 43) to proclaim, through act, independence? Or 2) since digitized "money" is outside the purview of STEM validation, "money" often diminishing the patina of ID's (i.e., Khadafy, Hussein, tyrants…), how can a "wealthy" man acquire ID validation independently of dead, digitized, "stockpiles," many off shore?

The need for validation is in tune with ID deficiencies…the fewer people needed for validation, the more secure the ID. If millions are needed for validation, *the ID need is proportionate*. Does MR have a "large need" to validate his ID "submerged" as it may be beneath a father's name and proxied within a ballooned bank account? Don't the wealthiest often seek multiples of human validators to compensate for holdings of non-human commodities (e.g., tyrants)? Does this then mean that 3) MR's primary motivation in running for the office of President was a quest for *independence* from his *dependence* upon bankroll, son-to-father lock-in? Or 4) that acquiring the *office* of President would be but a means to sate need for ID validation? Or 5) that the *duties* of such office would be but further means to both ensure continued ID validation? And lastly, would the ID of a Mormon having assumed the office of President validate the ID of the LDS as a nationally accepted "religion"? Would it matter that each pro-MR voting citizen would be complicit in helping to satisfy MR's needs, or that the consequences of MR's actions as President would fall upon 300 million citizens, locally, unknown numbers worldwide…*solely* due to one man's need for singular, independent, ID validation?

If any of the above tiers are correct, does that mean that those who would vote for MR also had *as a primary need* the validation of *their own ID's* regardless of the nature of government, national needs, or the qualifications of candidate involved? (But isn't this the case with all extremists?)

But there's another issue…Mormonism as an inclusive group. Consider the three major religions: did not Islam need to proclaim "dominance" if it wanted a seat in the world's religions following upon Judaism and Christianity? If the same two, Judaism and Christianity, were the main religions in the U.S., would not the entrance of Mormonism need to proclaim "dominance" if It wanted a seat at the religion table? Consider also the epididymis constant—that each of us has an in-built drive to achieve dominance. Could this drive be ignored by a man (a one time Mormon Bishop), backed by the solidity of LDS and a Tabernacle Choir? The LDS is the fluid which carries MR through the *vas deferens*, urged on with the power of money, hopefully to represent both himself and the LDS at a merging with the Ova-l Office. Mormonism uses MR, and MR uses Mormonism. Inseparable. Dominance. "I like to be able to fire those who service me." With money as the lubricator, is there any difference between Islam and Mormonism, between an Imam and a Mormon Bishop? And isn't all of it but masks hiding the true STEM nature of man, that while Islam changes a bit here and there, can't a Mormon also be allowed to "flip-flop" endlessly without a GPS trying to find a "core" (other than money) to which he could glue his ID? (And what better argument for a separation of church and state?)

MR got elected. The income gap between the 1% and the 99% *grew larger*, derailing a promise made by MR to close the gap. In Facebook, a friend can be un-friended. However, when a human commits to a promise, when a human submits purpose and life intent to a poseur, how can the vote be un-voted?

In short, the vote for MR was hijacked. No penalties involved, no preventive restrictions placed on the honesty or dishonesty of platform posed. But to prevent disclosure of the ineptitude of process, tenure for hijackers was assured by a Constitution lest all who were so elected be subject to immediate dismissal, leaving the cupboard bare. And all of this simply due to the inadequacy of understanding the inclusive operation, the needs of ID deficient men, and resultant commitments to action that concluded, included in-time events may require. It is not you or me who ranks in these electoral proceedings but rather the stipulations of a constitutional spreadsheet which diminishes each of us to 10 pt. Helvetica, protected by lawyers who acquire income by sanctifying the font. And so to two Double Binders…

DB 1: (NI) It is impossible to modernize an antiquated voting system in this electronic age through computerized voting (such as used on *America's Got Talent or PayPal,* or in Canadian cities or occasional U.S. military posts since (T1) entrenched political machines, inclusive, control mechanics, logistics, and platforms, and since (T2) such modernization would provide undue power to the voter and (T3) would lead, no doubt, to adaptation of in-put votes to out-put recalls with equal ease. Are any or all of the supporting tiers false? If not, the DB is true. Conclusion: this "democracy" cannot modernize itself to live up to its name—Democracy.

DB 2: (NI) It is impossible for any leader of any extremist/inclusive group to take responsibility (T1) for the gamble presented to electors, that the time and effort extracted from their terminal lives in the support of a proselytizing leader will not be wasted through the candidate's defeat at the polls with the verification of followers' ID's dashed, or (T2) to admit to a need for ID food through support cultivated from the ID needy, or (T3) to admit to not being assessed by an independent evaluation board as to fitness for office, or (T4) to admit to the natural "correctness" of any opponent's platform or to any ability/capacity to meld in conjunctive bond with any A prime platform for species' benefit, or (T5) to admit to *any* degree of independence from party platform, or (T6) to the usurpation of funds (Citizens United +) which could have been used for education, student loans, Medicare, Social Security, the rebuilding of infrastructure, etc. (NI + tiers: True or False?)

Inclusion based groups, as such, are exclusive to either disjunctive or conjunctive potential.

Disjunction Based Groups

Our linguistic data bank consists of classes. Samples are countries, schools, teams, tribes, investment groups, apples, political parties, boats, cheeses, airlines, Greek gods, mythical animals, comic book superheroes, and types of government. It is a violation of class to put into disjunctive mode sets from disparate classes.

The disjunctive mode consists of two or more classes related via a common bond—an issue, a goal, a whatever. Two football teams are disjoined yet related to a common goal: victory. The teams are equal in number, joined in rules of game and field of play. Two school board members are disjoined yet related to a common goal: where a new elementary school should be built. The following demonstrate violations of class: Amnesty International vs. an apple, Navajo Indians vs. The Statue of Liberty; Syria vs. Assad; Dole Pineapple Corp. vs. Terry Bradshaw; Republican Party vs. U.S. Government. From the latter can be seen the flaw: The Republican Party, as party and as class is not *government* and can only be disjoined *from another political party*. Here, the Democratic Party. To say that either party equals the U.S. government is to commit a *violation of class*. Not understanding this violation makes commonplace the statement by Eric Cantor immediately prior to the onset of hurricane Irene, to the effect that the House would OK funds for hurricane relief only if the administration engaged in spending cuts. The violation of class—hurricane relief for millions of breathing STEM citizens vs. federal reduction in 2D spending is so overt as to raise few surprised eyebrows. Cantor's occupation: lawyer, adversarial.

So we, our government, are hit from within by a triple whammy: One, the majority of congressional members are lawyers each of whom, by professional inclination, is adversarial. Two, as party members, ID is acquired *primarily* by membership within their initial, ID-enforcing groups (i/e Republicans or Democrats) to which fealty must be paid for ID sustenance, and three, no reference whatsoever in a congressman's oath of office requires that party affiliation be made subservient to position as representative governor or that the ID of congressmen be as *independent* adjudicators of Constitutional act, or that the national ID of country supersede any trans-national bond as party members.

Since party affiliation crosses state boundaries and is therefore national in scope, ID allegiance to party may well be at cross-purposes to interests of country—nation not aligned to political party. Imagine the consternation among party members then if, in the oath of office, each member—House or Senate, were to swear to a subjugation of party affiliation to that of nation! The current, most banal "Constitutional" oath opens wide the door to hypocrisy by all who align themselves first with party, subscribing to second place contributions to national governance. Taking this current oath of office, each member need hold a hand behind his back with fingers crossed. There are no alternatives unless, of course, the oath is changed [see Confluence Found, below].

Unless i/e party priorities are subsumed beneath allegiance to nation and to the construction of disjunctive sets with the purpose of conjunctive alliance, anti-Constitutional, anti-species party affiliations and obeisances to party dicta will assume dominant, divisive, disruptive position within our government, and (DB) will never be changed....never, all logic and species beneficence foresworn (and we will be proven correct).

Generic DBer applied to Disjunctive Groups...

(Substitute for X and Y groups of your choice, and for Y, the issue of your choice. Rephrase as necessary to fit the situation).

DB: (NI) It is impossible for Group Y to enter into dialogue with Group X concerning issue Z since (T1) a conversion of group sponsored ID's would be required (constituents opposed), and (T2) a conversion of in-place ID's of individual members would be required, remanding said members to the insecurity of ID doubt and forced alteration. (T3) Transference would be required to enter into communal dialogue—transference requiring, by definition, two or more groups in acquiescence to *mutual* consort on a plane outside the ID rubrics of either disjunctive group. (T4) The merging of two aspects from two disjunctive groups requires the creation of a third relational operation, conjunction, forcing either disjunctive group to foreswear its disjunctive status and ID group support. (T5) The alteration of any disjunctive group into a conjunctive orbit makes vulnerable the i/e stanchions upon which either group rests—a vulnerability conducive to either group dissolution or ID alteration. (T5) As the ID's of both Group X and Y are totally dependent upon their possession and control of... (a boundary line, lake, river, city, hot dog stand, mountain, tribe, state, region, rights to…, etc.), to relinquish such possessive control will be to shatter the ID's (of either group), neither possessing the mature capability of foregoing such control to yet maintain ID stability. (T6) Conjunctivity is a pro-species attribute of group behavior, naturally antagonistic to the safety of a homeostatic disjunctive group with in-built recourse to i/e ID security, conjunctivity beyond the operative reach of either i/e embedded group.

Apply this DB to any two disjunctive groups of your choice. Did conjunctivity occur? If *not*, supporting tiers are proven correct and the ID's of both groups have been recognized, each and all suffering the ignominy of public and private exposure. Dissonance *en masse*.

If conjunctivity *did occur*, group participants proved the DB wrong, the ID's of both groups and their members to be publicly recognized as pro-species with ID's firmly grounded in propensities for species good, and should be proportionately rewarded with individual ID's publicized.

Who is so capable?

Double Binders and Foreign Policy

Russia, China, Iran, Afghanistan, Syria, and Pakistan

Sometimes the need for a DB is obvious (its nature and purpose understood). Such was the case in February, '12 when **Russia and China** vetoed a UN resolution condemning the atrocities in Syria. The U.S. ambassador called the action "despicable" and "disgusting." She lacked understanding of the nature of what she said, the effect, and the nature of a negative injunction. Let's set it…

Saying "disgusting" and "despicable" did nothing but drive the motivating forces behind Russia's/China's positioning further into shell. Obviously also, were the motivations behind the vetoes: both Russia and China fearful (fear is always the cause of trenchant negativism) of proletariat uprisings as well as a loss of vested economic and political interests. So to transference once again…

If a negative injunction is initiated, the ID is attacked immediately. Transference is initiated immediately. Any ID attacked as to competence reacts immediately. Tell anyone that he can't_____ and you've got his attention. That's transference—his ID attached to your ID awaiting development. The proper response from the U.S. delegate, to both Russia and China, should have been: "It is understood that humanitarian concerns are of lesser interest to either of you—no matter the number of deaths, than the retention of political power and economic gain. For those reasons we understand that neither of you could have passed the resolution." The negative injunction is understood: "You couldn't pass the resolution because of self-interest and your capacity for conjunctive act was revealed as nil." Impotence admitted, and people die. Effect of the DB? Guess the effect upon millions of people, particularly Russian and Chinese upon hearing the DB rejoinders, *widely publicized*: *"They couldn't because they cared about retention of their power and influence more than the deaths of thousands."* ('Could that be us some time?') Following the injunction, could it be said that either Russia or China turned a profit (and would not each be wary of such i/e negativism in the future)?

The negative injunction enjoining a DB can take a different twist, transference enjoined in a different manner. If I praise you, I've got your attention. You'll be waiting for more (Everyone wants their ID "pumped up" and verified as to competence). Of current concern is **Iran**. Will Israel attack the nuclear development sites in Iran? If attacked, would Turkey, China, etc., come to Iran's defense? Would Iran, in retribution, attack U.S. bases whenever, wherever feasible? The problems stack up. Goal: to bring Iran "into the fold" and "force" them to either desist development of enriched plutonium or to make transparent to the world each stage of their processing, and purpose. The first step: engage transference. How?

To "defeat" an "enemy" using DB's is to put him on the hook leaving him strung open against a wall with no alternative but to respond. So let's attack Iran using DBers (but so veiled! Note that the two approaches following are riddled with DB's).

Iran

Approach 1: Establish Transference

We assume that the President of the U.S. would like the problem solved and that he would do anything reasonable to do it. The Secretary of State likewise. We'll work with the President here, or POTUS. Scenario...

POTUS stands behind a rostrum and *addresses the American people*. First, he discusses the problems with Iran and their nuclear program in detail, using specifics as necessary. Second, he enters into a discussion of both Iran's (Persia's) *history and accomplishments*, perhaps in this order (reduced)...

Persia (Iran was officially recognized as an Islamic Republic in 1979) contributed to our lexicon such words as *bank, check, pajamas, orange, spinach, lemon, saffron, sugar, eyebrows, daughter, peaches, tulips* and about 300 words additional; they were also the originators of Sanskrit and cuneiform...

Historical contributions: the first human civilization, the first empire, the first passport system and postal service; first to standardize weights and measurements; King Xerxes planned and worked on the Suez Canal; Darius the Great instituted the first tax system initiated customs duties and a legal code; King Darius devised the first human rights charter guaranteeing freedom of religion and equality for all; Cyrus the Great under whom, for the first and last time, all governments in the world were under one ruler, also noted for the Cyrus Cylinder providing the first human rights charter; and the silk road...

Medicine/contributions: the first caesarean, the first use of anesthesia; the great Avicenna (Ibn Sina) who wrote *The Canon of Medicine* and *The Book of Healing* along with treatises on philosophy, logic, physics, geometry...; Persia had the first contemporary medical college; today Iran has over 400 medical research facilities with units specializing in kidney, liver, heart, lung, and cornea transplants and has specified over $2.5B in stem cell research; discovered the speech gene (SPCH1), spermatogonial stem cells, and is heavily involved in the development of biomaterials...

Science/contributions: Alhazen (985-1040 AD), the father of optics, surmised that the speed of light was finite. To date, Iran developed a solenoid detector used in the Large Hadron Collider (CERN), is deeply involved in nanotechnology and super computers; developed shearface microscopy; is ranked worldwide in all scientific branches; produces journals in all major scientific fields; in 2008 had 9570 natural inventions registered…

Physics/contributions: first to develop rudimentary batteries, subterranean aqueducts, built gas turbines and power plants, invented the cable modem, built advanced radar for use outside earth; some say founded practical physics; heavily into aerospace programs… 70% of students in engineering and science are women.

Mathematics/contributions: algebra, trigonometry, and the logarithm table originated in ancient Iran.

Ever buy anything on eBay? Credit Pierre Omidyar, a French-Iranian, Tufts graduate and co-founder.

But there's a bit more.

How many citizens of any nation are given the opportunity, *en masse*, to enter into an international problem as presented to them by their national leader? The problem is caste. The further isolated the governmental ("ruling") caste from all other castes comprising that nation, the greater the tyrannical structure and *less secure* is the ID of that government. The greater the homogenous meld of government (societal decision makers) with all other castes within that nation, the greater its democratic nature and the *more secure* is that government as to status and STEM ID. Problem: Traffic flow…

Consider a train track operator sitting in a central signal box. He can switch an incoming train to this track, or that, or signal Stop to a train either unwelcome or for security of ID. Traffic control. It's exactly the same within neuronal execution, beliefs the operator. Is Judaism, and its seat in Israel, a threat to Mahmoud and Shia Islam? If so, signal a Stop and close the track. However, is Judaism (and Israel) welcome as an A prime so as to erect an "enemy" to which Mahmoud might direct a "defense" and elevate thereby an ID otherwise bankrupt of conjunctive STEM incentive, absent such within i/e Shia Islam? (The more impressive the A prime, the more impressive, as subsequent, the A. *If the A prime is insufficiently impressive, powerful, or threatening, make it so* by any means available (Consider "yellow cake," Hussein, WMD's, etc .) So diminutive Mahmoud, dressed from poverty and outfitted through a familial name change, becomes the more powerful in proportion to the depth he (and nuclear cohorts) can order the construction of a uranium enriching site, centrifuges built 260 feet below a shelf of rock for protection against possible bombardment (at the Fordow facility outside Qum).[40] Is there a direct correlation between the depth of a fortified site and the fear of exposure of falsely structured beliefs? Is fear of exposure the cause of it all? So, POTUS might delve under the covers, and pick and choose from the above and the following…

NOTE 1: People in nations across the globe would sit in wonder at a POTUS outlining, describing, and discussing among the *entire citizenry of his nation* an issue addressed by circumstance to that nation's government. People within dictatorships and tyrannies could then only look with envy at the possible cohesiveness of other peoples—castes cast aside, and wonder at their own.

NOTE 3: Do we also realize that the detailing of Persia's/Iran's magnificent history to American citizens does nothing other than cause schizophrenic dissonance—among Iranians? If we know what they know—the underpinnings of the data-banks of *their* global ID's, how are we different? Then, *who* would make us different?

Approach 2: Iran and Tom Brady

Tom Brady, Patriots QB, standing behind the center looking over the defense: 'One-on-one in the left flat looks good; Tony, our wide right receiver can outrun Chester—looks good; their safety has a bum ankle; the wind's at our backs,' etc…Brady looking for weaknesses he can exploit, and finds them. We do it backwards. We look for the opponent's *strengths* and tie into those—control of Hormuz, nuclear development, petrified Islamic theocracy, oil, threats to Israel, threats to arm Lebanon, Hamas, Afghanistan…Revolutionary Guards, minerals or threats to do this or that. Khamenei and Ahmad both need A prime sustenance as does Netanyahu and Obama. They complement each other, as they must to appear gainfully employed, war hawks in particular thirsting for A prime opposites. Let's look for *weaknesses* in our relationships with Iran. Let's open another book…

Major newspapers, such as *The Boston Globe*, have special ad sections addressing open positions in the executive, scientific, biotech, technology, CEO, and teacher ranks across the globe, ads detailing qualifications—aptitudes, interpersonal skills, academic background, publications, etc., with full disclosure of job description. We find no job description for the position of President of the United States in newspapers or elsewhere. To a couple of Aristotelian sorites (a syllogistic form)…

First, since there is no job description available, anyone can apply. Since anyone (usually with enough money) can apply, anyone does. Since anyone does, we find anyone scrambling for the ID food the position might offer. Second, since no job description is available for the position, there are no stipulated qualifications required. Since no stipulated qualifications are required, we find candidates with all sorts of aptitudes (and not), all sorts of eccentricities (and not), all sorts of backgrounds (and not), all sorts of intellectual, personal, behavioral, religious, prejudicial, bigoted, and academic (and not) positions in the mix with no Review Board. Joe the Plumber is currently in the race for Congress in Ohio's 9th congressional district. Then again, how many oddballs does the reader recall running for political office? So where are we going?

Mitt Romney said in early March, '12, that he would put "aircraft carriers and warships" outside Iran's front door. Should we elect a Romney if he would hold true to his word? Michael Oren, Israeli Ambassador to the U.S., and Netanyahu each played chorus to the other saying that "we have tried diplomacy. We have tried sanctions. Neither work." Did anyone expect anything other? Interesting it is that the most necessary approach, the primal approach, the most overlooked approach is nowhere in the mix. Behavior.

Richard Holbrooke, envoy to Afghanistan, Pakistan, and Ambassador to the UN, could not have been as effective as he was if he had not initiated transference before negotiations. There must exist *some degree* of potential disjunctivity for transference to arise. Between Israel and Iran? Doubtful. Sanctions? We understand that sanctions can't work. Sanctions are applied by a more powerful country to a lesser, are initiated by a disjunctive power to a lesser, in effect driving the "sanctioned" nation into an i/e (inclusive/exclusive) shell. Sanctions do nothing but cataclysmically split behavioral classes of nations into petrifaction making it impossible for the "lesser" state to behaviorally activate itself without breaking its shell like a newly emerging chick (and if it does break its shell, it doesn't forget who forced it to do so). Can we see a Khamenei or Ahmadinejad (soon, it seems, to be excised) taking on a hair shirt for either the U.S. or Israel? Behavior, Tom Brady and Mitt Romney...

Mitt Romney, Mormon, member of an i/e religion (You're either in or you're out), "air craft carriers and warships"...straight I/e behavior. If elected President will peace will suddenly rise from the doldrums of ineffective negotiations, or will arise the possibility of a pandemonium of deaths because of a "leader" empty of behavioral verse?

Babak Dehghanpisher writes in *Time*, March 2012, "The regime (Iran's) has maintained a united front against the bellicose threats of Benjamin Netanyahu and the White House's refrain of 'all options are on the table.' A strike (by Israel or the U.S.) would resurrect the regime from the dead."[40] Romney, Commander in Chief. The Office of President has no job description. Anyone can apply, and does.

Tom Brady's approach, on the other hand, would note that (from the same *Time* article), *"74% of (Iranian) respondents said they were in favor of normalizing relations...Khamenei has long blocked any attempt by Ahmadinejad to reach out to the West because that breakthrough would give the President (Ahmadinejad) enormous political capital... Ahmadinejad mentioned that Iran was ready for talks with the U.S. in nearly every interview he gave (in) New York City for the U.N. General Assembly...Khamenei realizes that any rapprochement with Washington on his (Ahmad's) part would diminish their support for him (Khamenei)...the beleaguered President could try to chip away at Khamenei's authority, perhaps even advocating radical policy goals like dialogue with the U.S. or more transparent nuclear negotiations...."* The Tom Brady approach. Can a football QB see weaknesses in an autocratic system that "professional" politicians can't, or won't?

Which politicians understand the nature of operational development, the levels of behavioral maturity, and if so, do they understand that no commerce can exist between different classes of behavioral maturity—between disjunctive and i/e, between conjunctive and disjunctive, between conjunctive and i/e? Well, it's unnecessary to take a guess. The answer is None. So how to stifle intransigence among the U.S., Israel, and Iran? *There is only one way* and we know what it is:

establish transference which can only be achieved by moving involved parties to disjunctive status, and this can only be achieved through talk, and then only if the parties involved recognize and accept an equality of presence. That means for both the U.S. and Israel to "back off" and *talk with Ahmadinejad!!!!* That's all. Do we think that Iran will nuclear strike anyone with Ahmad or ambassadors in the White House like Japan did, 1941, with its ambassadors sipping tea at 1600? Want Khamenei out? Talk with Ahmad. Want to be fiends with Iran? Talk with Ahmad. Want Ahmad to exercise responsible, behavioral maturity? Talk with Ahmad. Want to see Khamenei drop three points in Iran's Popularity Poll? Talk with Ahmad before he is forced to leave office and give both him and Iran something…something…anything! But, if war is wanted with Iran, impose silent sanctions and allow war hawks to direct the actions of both Israel and the U.S. If peace is wanted…if peace is wanted… (God, it's hard to be men, isn't it, stuck within political parties, SuperPacs, lobbyists, right-wingers, evangelicals, birth control, elections, the price of oil, Planned Parenthood, religion…? Just to be a man is so hard.) But if peace is wanted…*find a man.*

(Oh, you *can't?*)

Afghanistan—Stay or Leave?

Why aren't 14 year olds allowed to drive? Is this to say that there are maturity levels obvious among the behaviors of individuals? Is this to say that some 15 year olds are more operationally mature than a 91-year-old mother-in-law? Could this possibly mean that even nations might be disparate in operational maturity? Are indeed, some nations, collectively, more "conjunctive" than nations stuck in i/e, glue-tied bonds to tribes, religions, theocratic autocracies? Well, yes. What is the level of "communication" which must then exist between any two such nations—one disjunctive and the other i/e (inclusive/exclusive)? The upper can reach lower, but the lower can't reach the upper—no experience, anchored in past debris and hanging on for dear life to sources of ID food—tribes, etc. So, what to do…attempt to "mature" a lower nation to upper level dialogue (through patient, painful education), or, allow the lower level to mature on its own, discover on its own, experience on its own, model itself on behaviors visible from upper level echelons and thereby acquire an ID independent but anchored in self-earned experience, earned "my way" with experiential behaviors thereby becoming an integral part of national esteem and Identity? Plato wrote in *The Republic* that "education" can't be forced on anyone. Force Afghanistan to mature, to play on someone else's terms? That won't work folks, and if attempted, will come back to bite.

What do we do with kids who must go off on their own to learn, to experience life, to find out who and what they really are? Do we force them to stay home, to go to this school, to study this major, to not date Matilda? If we do, we can say good-bye to our kids and we lose. We let them go if valued at all and hope for a 50-50 optimal result. Same with Afghanistan. If we want them all (governors included) as friends, we had better let them go on their own terms, and depart. It's not our campground. It's theirs. Just keep an ADT Pulse system fully operational.

Syria

The recent events in Syria have conclusively proven that…

First…the maintenance and protection of the individual ID supersedes all other human drives including that of survival for a true leader would sacrifice his life to save the lives of thousands of his subjects. A true tyrant however, absent species concerns (the welfare of his people) would kill his subjects with no tremor of conscience. The latter Bashir al-Assad could do and does.

Second…the position of any national leader (President, King, Queen, Prime Minister, etc.) is always based on 2D script which, as timeless, is used as the proxy platform upon which the position of the leader's ID (party's, etc.) is based. As all 2D script of whatever nature is based on artificial lettering, etymology, linear histories, and the need to create such for the creation of platforms for group cohesion, the 4D STEM nature of man an incidental in the upkeep of ID maintenance.

Third…no religion is or can be universal in nature (Islam, Catholicism, Judaism, Buddhism, etc.) since each group, based in linear platform, determines the use to which the tenets of the respective religion are used. Islam, therefore, if universal in nature and if absolutely intrinsic to the nature of man, would have demanded that neighboring nations, also "based" in Islam, intervene to remove Assad from office and to save the lives of adherents to the "mother" religion since intrinsic to the nature of man. No intercession by any neighboring nation occurred. Therefore, the "natural" identity of Islam is provincial as determined by those groups which assume ID's under its mantle.

Fourth…the inability of non-Islamic nations to coalesce in common cause to prevent the slaughtering of Syrian innocents validates equally the provincial nature of all non-acting governments as based in script, not *de facto* intrinsic to species nature or well-being.

Fifth…the inability of Islamic leaders to act of the behalf of Muslim brothers, sisters, mothers, and children slaughtered by Assad's forces validates the propositions offered above.

(The above proofs *can't* be proven incorrect, a Double Binder each when embedded within NI propositions.)

Pakistan…

Compiling all acquired to this point, what might be the results if a POTUS or a Secretary of State assumed station behind a most public rostrum and stated the following, again to a world-wide audience:

> "There is no individual or group within Pakistan—civilian, military, or religious, capable of structuring and effecting a long-term, stable, civilian government…one which would guarantee its citizens the full spectrum of human rights including the rights of religious choice and open and free voting, or a government capable of reaching rapprochement with either India or Afghanistan, or capable of identifying and eliminating terrorist threats to the innocent everywhere. Within Pakistan, excuses will abound, proving that such an expectation is beyond any possibility of realization, as is a Pakistan successfully evolved into the 21st century."

It is impossible that one of this nation's top leaders would take such a public stance, execute a Double Binder, stick a virulent worm in multiple ID's, and then go to lunch…having just changed the world.

Epilogue

CONFLUENCE FOUND

And so we find...

...that we live in a universal society in which the welfare or deprivation of man's well being is based on systems of artificially constructed numerology, not a one of which contacts the essence of this species core...

...that we survive in a three-branch system of government in which wanton sedition is practiced by non-governmental political parties for the exclusive purpose of in-time ID gain, mindless of the welfare of families of citizens.

...that our three-branch form of decreed government and the millions of citizens it was intended to serve can at any time be held hostage for ID gain by a single deficient ID-deprived Senate majority head, or Minority whip, or whomsoever through filibusters, No's, or other stratagems designed to thwart civil progress solely for the purpose of ID acquisition.

...that executive, congressional, and judicial tenures are guaranteed by a Constitution which serves with the same force as a union contract, disallowing collective bargaining from any oppositional group, allowing personnel ill of character, morals, and species concern free reign to jeopardize society through any means to them available.

...that one man in judicial robe can effect the diversion and dissolution of billions of dollars into campaign allotments, money otherwise better spent for human welfare, or cause thousands of lives lost through denials of health care, or allow indirect elections of morally, ethically, intellectually deficient governors who would sacrifice thousands upon thousands of lives in capricious cause.

...that the Epididyan ID (if ignorant of species' nature) trumps species consort...that the preservation of group ID's trumps species' consort...that the preservation of any caste's ID trumps species consort, and that this U.S. government consisting of three disjunctive castes (the executive, judicial, and congressional), each, by definition striving by inherent structure to retain and preserve ID status, is, by nature, anti-conjunctive. The singular identifiable bond among three disjunctive "governmental" sets is the nature of this human species, an understanding of which is *purposely* shunted aside through restrictive educational services by minds *purposely* closed to avenues for species advance, this to preserve empty, understanding-bereft, locked-in, i/e, immature operative minds each fearful unto death of exposure to righteous cause based in species' needs. An operationally mature government? In these conditions? Impossible. Disjunctive governmental bodies are antithetical to conjunctive species.

To each and all is a solution. The means are at hand, the common will in absentia. Until found, we, as devoted fathers, can solidify our IDs within family and touch nature to serve as species calls, as I with my children, and so to my son...

Andrew, my son, was 23 years old when he died. Andrew suffered from encephalopathy, static quadriplegia, epilepsy and who knows what else. He couldn't talk. Grunts and vocalizations indicated his moods and wants. The only word I ever heard from him was *apple* when he was about a year old. Nothing else.

Andrew changed the lives of so many of the aides who cared for him at those few special facilities who cared for the severely disabled. Andrew could tell in an instant which aide he liked and with whom he would be comfortable, always correct. He would take someone's hand, if trusted, and direct movement. He would look into eyeballs and spill either a No or a current of pure love. He couldn't take care of himself hygienically nor could he dress himself nor feed himself. He could, with shaking hand, fork various foods into his mouth or drink from a glass.

In order to get a legal death certificate for a client under special care, an autopsy must be performed to determine cause of death. After burial proceedings, we received the results. I opened the letter detailing the autopsy results and read...that the heart was unavailable for examination, so too the kidneys, the liver, veins and arteries, lungs... and stopped. Further pages remained unread, still and forever. And I cried. My son. People today walking, living because of his donated heart, liver, organs of what number. People living because of Andrew, thankful to someone, someone unknown, for pure gifts of life. Andrew's.

And then we elect politicians who, with but an inclination of head or word of mouth send thousands to their deaths, cause hundreds of thousands of families discord and poverty through dislocation and who become honored through title bestowed by those equally ignorant, equally un-tested as to the nature of us who weep and gnash at the inequities of a dysfunctional order, who think of politics as a game and track movements of candidates as one would track totems on a Monopoly board.

Politics is not a game. Politics is the behaviors of men and women, politicians, who, ignorant as to nature seize opportunities as predators to herd sardines, herring, and assorted varieties into cantons, electoral and gerrymandered districts, parishes, wards...each and all bait balls from which to cannibalize and grow in illusory size, taking... taking...taking. The Palins, Bachmanns, Limbaughs, Gingriches, Romneys, Santorums...name them...mouths agape, eating with every breadth and chomp of jaws...gathering the souls of men and women who ask fervently to be eaten by some leader, any leader, who could direct them to fertile ground, this society offering no base and depriving schools the possibilities of discerning such.

The traumatic legacy left by Bush-Cheney has left men uncertain, in doubt, absent trust in government and in those of leadership positions. As parents, for nine months they surrender ultimate trust to nature for a child healthy and whole, then among peers lose all trust to waver and quake...a black President, a white wisp of Senate leader fearful unto death of a counter who might, could, would do an act beneficial to man of which he, Senate leader, is incapable and resentful to core, antagonistic to any possibility of Presidential success. Then a House leader, ambitious from Mother's lap, socially apposite and self-pocketed into positions of defense through deep and absolute need to retain an ID posture in the face of a President's natural disposition to benefit the universal.

Men, women, and perhaps children walk this earth with Andrew's parts pumping their lives, while politicians pour these same lives into unemployment, hunger, dysfunction, poverty, dismay and forced ignorance by restricting national advance through education, opportunities for employment, universal voting and civil rights through equity, all for the establishment of ID's which are as fleeting as the suits they wear.

Every nation on earth has had, on its soil, mass graves, inhabitants merging through decomposition, one into the other into the other, any individuality identifiable only by DNA variances or dental examination, the merging of species…black, white, yellow, brown, each then having no capability to exude an in-life, living choice of religion or political party, of social status or of profession, pocket constitutions and guides for the holy dissolved within acidic, viscous fluids. Just remnants. No names…no markers, no headstones, no titles, no indicators as to services rendered or prevented, the cloth of identity under which each sailed, decomposed into common mesh.

We therefore propose a new universal Oath of Office to be taken by all politicians, state and federal…

Do you solemnly swear to function in this office solely for the welfare of the citizens of this nation and to place this nation and your obligations to it above any party affiliation, do research appropriate to the office and functions you will perform; be well informed as to the functions, ramifications, and effects of any and all decisions you will make relative to that office and to those committees upon which you will serve with no bias toward any section of this nation or body based on religion, gender, national origin, socio-economic status, ethnicity, or sexual orientation of its members, and that, with all other congressmen of whatever party or section of country represented, you will consent to be buried or ashes entombed within a common site, your name forgotten, identity unrevealed and unmarked?

Confluence found

REFERENCES

CHAPTER 1

1 Trisha Gura, "Reproduction," in *Body:* "The Complete Human," *National Geographic*, Washington D.C., 2007

CHAPTER 2

2 *Sun Sentinel*, 3-24-05, p. 21A
3 Alfred North Whitehead, *Science and the Modern World* (New York: Mentor, 1960) p. 135
4 Ed Wasserman, psychologist, University of Iowa, quoted in Jeffrey Dluger, "Inside the Minds of Animals," *Time*, August 16, 2010, pp. 34-43
5 Ernest Becker, *The Birth and Death of Meaning* (New York: The Free Press, 1971)

CHAPTER 3

6 Gerald M. Edelman and Guilio Tononi, *A Universe of Consciousness* (New York: Basic Books, 2000)
7 Romela Thasper, *Asoka and the Decline of the Mauryas* (London: Oxford University Press, 1960) p. 200. (quoted in Wikipedia)
8 "We are the 99.9%," *NY Times*, November 24, 2011

CHAPTER 4

9 Rita Carter, *Mapping the Mind* (Berkeley: The University of California Press, 1999) p. 147
10 *Ibid.*, p. 189
11 Gerd Sommerhoff, *Logic of the Living Brain* (London: John Wiley & Sons, 1974) pp. 41-46
12 Steven Hawking, *A Brief History of Time* (New York: Bantam Books,1988) pp.156-157.

REFERENCES

CHAPTER 5
13 Michael Grunwald, "Ben Bernanke," *Time*, December 28, 2009, p. 54

CHAPTER 6
14 Joe Keohane, "How Facts Backfire, Researchers discover a surprising threat to democracy: our brains," *Ideas*, *Boston Sunday Globe*, July 11, 2010, p. C1

CHAPTER 7
15 Carter, *op cit.*, pp. 128-130
16 H.A.R. Gibb, "Islam," in R.C.Zaehner, *ed.*, *Encyclopedia of the World's Religions* (New York: Barnes and Noble, 1997) p. 171
17 *Ibid.*, p. 183
18 *Ibid.*, p. 171
19 Ibid., (Quran 42:49-50) p. 173
20 Ernest Becker, *The Structure of Evil* (New York: The Free Press, 1968)

CHAPTER 8
21 Bob Woodward, *State of Denial* (New York: Simon & Schuster, 2006) as quoted in *Newsweek*, Oct. 9, 2006
22 Leslie Kaufman, "G.O.P. Push in States to Deregulate Environment," *New York Times,* April 15, 2011
   "Fallacies in Thinking" Resource: Celestine N. Bittle, O.F.M.Cap. *The Science of Correct Thinking* (Milwaukee: The Bruce Publishing Company, 1951)

CHAPTER 9
23 *Time*, May 2, 2011
24 Gibb, *op cit.*, p. 171
25 *Ibid.*, p. 174

CHAPTER 11
26 *The Structure of Evil*, p. 191
27 *The Denial of Death*, p. 143
28 *Ibid.*, p 143
29 *Ibid.*, p 143

30 *Ibid.,* p.144
31 *Ibid.,* p 146
32 *Ibid.,* p 147
33 *Ibid.,* p 147
34 Gregory Bateson, *Steps to an Ecology of Mind: Collected essays in Anthropology, Psychiatry, Evolution and Epistemology* (Chicago: University of Chicago Press, 1972) quoted in Wikipedia
35 Fareed Zakaria, "This Isn't the Return of History," *Newsweek,* September 8, 2008, p 63
36 Samantha Power, "A Question of Honor. How humiliation can shape national interest," *Time,* August 25, 2008, p. 22
37 Paul Krugman, "The War on Logic," *New York Times,* January 16, 2011

CHAPTER 12
38 Bateson, G., Jackson D.D., Haley, J, and Weakland, J.H., "Toward a Theory of Schizophrenia," *Behavioral Science,* Vol 1, 1956, pp. 253-254
39 Fareed Zakaria, "Friends Without Benefits," *Time,* December 12, 2011
40 Babak Dehghanpisher, "The Ayatullah vs. The President," *Time,* March 5, 2012, pp. 32-35

INDEX

www.ingramcontent.com/pod-product-compliance
Lightning Source LLC
Chambersburg PA
CBHW060238290526
45789CB00001B/95